SLOVAK ACADEMY OF SCIENCES
INSTITUTE OF HISTORICAL STUDIES

STUDIA HISTORICA SLOVACA

XX

A Guide to Historiography in Slovakia

Edited by Elena Mannová and David Paul Daniel

Bratislava 1995

The Open Society Fund, Bratislava, Slovakia provided the financial support which made possible the publication of this work.

STUDIA HISTORICA SLOVACA XX

A Guide to Historiography in Slovakia

Edited by Elena Mannová and David P. Daniel
Translation by Jasna Paličková and James R. Papp

Printed in the Slovak Republic by
Polygrafia vedeckej literatúry a časopisov SAV

ISBN 80–967150–8–9

CONTENTS

CONTENTS

PREFACE

Slovakia is a new country whose population has a long history. The Slovaks have lived for over a thousand years in the territory ranged between the northern arc of the Carpathian mountains and the central Danubian basin. But, they were not the only inhabitants of the region and, except for what are really brief moments in their history, the Slovaks did not govern themselves. Their history is closely intertwined with that of other national or ethnic groups in region. Thus, Slovak historiography is not to be limited to or identified solely with the "national state" aspirations of the Slovaks but with their complex cultural, social, economic and linguistic development. Like the history of the Slovaks themselves, Slovak historiography is practically an unknown territory for most historians. There are many reasons for this which need not be expounded here. Rather, this volume seeks to eliminate at least one reason for the lack of knowledge about the history of Slovakia and the Slovaks, that is, the unavailability of materials in a world language.

This volume of brief essays has as its modest goal, to provide to a broad, English reading public an introduction to historical work and publications in Slovakia with special emphasis upon works produced during the past half century. Because of the space available, the editors of this volume asked the contributors to focus on what they believed were the crucial issues of historiography in Slovakia and to present an indication of what they believed are major works of Slovak historical research. Therefore, the collection of essays is not comprehensive but indicative and personal. It does, however, provide an accurate, if selective, glimpse into the development and current state of historical scholarship, concerns and interests in Slovakia.

This volume is not the first to present material concerning Slovak historiography in English. In 1984 Studia historica Slovaca XIII presented Chapters from Slovak Historiography till 1918 which reflected the then current attitudes towards Slovak history and historical scholarships. Since then, the "gentle" or "velvet" revolution brought tremendous social, political, economic and even intellectual changes to Slovakia. This volume is, therefore, as much a manifestation of the current state of historical thinking or concerns in Slovakia as was its predecessor and reveals much about how Slovaks have attempted to understand not only the long and rich history but also the changing framework within which that history has and is taking place.

The organizers of this volume wish to thank each of the contributors and translators for their co-operation, patience and acceptance of the limitations of space and scope. We also extend our thanks to Dr. Pavol Petruf, CSc., Dr. Eva Kowalská, CSc., Dr. Eduard Krekovič, CSc., RNDr. Miroslav Morovics, CSc., Dr. Vojtech Dangl, CSc. and Dr. Michal Otčenáš, CSc. for their valuable assistance and special thanks to Mária Kubrická and Dagmar Pelčáková who prepared the typescript of this volume. Finally, we thank the Open Society Fund for its gracious financial assistance to the preparation and publication of this volume.

Editors

SLOVAKIA: HISTORY AND HISTORIOGRAPHY

As the following contributions indicate, Slovakia, a land of 5.3 million people, is well equipped with an extensive infrastructure for historical research, education and the cultivation of an historical consciousness. A certification in history is available from eleven faculties at five universities and colleges. At the research institution of the Slovak Academy of Sciences, history is investigated not only at the History and Archaeology Institutes but also in those for Oriental Studies, Ethnography, Linguistics, Literary History, Law and Political Science. The army in Slovakia also has an historical research and documentation unit. There is a rich network of general museums and specialized ones for mining, technology, agriculture, trade, transport, literature, education and many other topics. A hierarchy of archives, from the central state archives to district and smaller regional archives, has a well functioning infrastructure available to the researcher, catalogued collections, a modern information network and libraries. The national Slovak Historical Society has 520 members. There are a number of specialized and regional historical and museum societies as well. Our historical consciousness has helped to preserve many historical monuments. There is national inventory of major historical landmarks and a system of laws and institutions for their restoration and preservation. Even as a young state, the Slovak Republic is seeking to present itself as one anchored in a rich past. In the official calendar there are four state holidays and eleven days of observance connected with historical events and personalities. The preamble of the 1992 Constitution has an historical section, and Slovak coins and banknotes depict historical monuments, personalities and symbols from prehistoric times to the present. Further, the Slovak national anthem was written in the 1840s, and from 1918 to 1989, it formed part of the combined Czechoslovak anthem.

Most factors in the development of historiography and historical consciousness have their own past. University education in Slovakia has a tradition of several centuries, libraries and museums are mostly in historical buildings, and scholarly journals and annals have been published for decades without interruption. Despite this, Slovak historiography is often labeled and presents itself as "young". This always new and yet newly beginning syndrome –a sort of continual discontinuity– reflects some aspects of the development of historiography but even more the development of its object of interest: Slovakia and Slovak society.

The history of Slovakia shows an interesting cultural continuity. This is strongly reflected in settlements and landmarks. Often in a small area can be found and studied Romanesque relics, Gothic cathedrals and Renaissance fortresses and towns, Baroque ecclesiastical buildings and palaces, traces of Rococo and Classicism, and the revival styles of the nineteenth century. Centers of towns often are a confused composition: art nouveau and functionalism, Stalinist baroque of the 1960s and nascent attempts at post-modernism are juxtaposed. A second pole of the historical spectrum, visually less interesting than architecture but not less important, is education, represented, for example, in a number of secondary schools with centuries-long traditions. In the political sphere, the trends of modernization and secularization are anchored in the Enlightenment of the eighteenth century and survived a number of political changes and catastrophes. These crises were able to hold back but not halt modernization.

Discontinuity in Slovak history has been attributed above all to changes in the source of rule, political systems, and geopolitical factors. This is stressed more in recent history. After the disintegration of Great Moravia at the beginning of the tenth century, the territory of Slovakia was gradually absorbed into the Hungarian state, which survived independently for five hundred years. The Hungarian Kingdom, jolted by the penetration of the Ottoman Turks into the Danubian region, became part of the Habsburg monarchy in the sixteenth century.

Since the mid-nineteeth century, state and political changes have accelerated. After the failure of the Hungarian attempt to rid themselves of the Habsburgs in 1848-1849, and the failure of a Slovak attempt for a form of independence, there followed a period of Viennese centralism. The dualist monarchy, with centers in Vienna and Budapest, began in 1867.

Since 1918, the acceleration of changes created a kind of historical zone of continuous instability. The parliamentary democracy of a centralized Czechoslovakia was replaced in 1938 with an authoritarian regime of Czecho-Slovakia, again changed in 1939 for an independent Slovak Republic. In 1945, Czechoslovakia was renewed with limited "directed" democracy and in 1948 replaced with a communist dictatorship. The fairly broad self-administration of Slovakia in the post-war period was gradually restricted and in 1960 eliminated. The attempted reform of the system in 1968 resulted in the occupation of the country by the armies of the Warsaw Pact and the preservation of the Communist Party's monopoly of power, and the jettison of one of the products of the Prague Spring, the federalization of the Czech and Slovak Republics. The collapse of the power of the Communist Party in 1989 provided room for the renewal of parliamentary democracy, private ownership of property, citizens rights, the withdrawal of Soviet troops, and state reforms. On January 1, 1993, from a federalized Czecho-Slovakia, an independent Czech Republic and Slovak Republic were founded. The Slovak Republic had to address in parallel three very important challenges: the building of the structures of an independent state, the transition from a centralized to a market economy, and from dictatorship to a parliamentary democracy.

Rapid and substantial changes have taken place within the memory of one generation. Often dramatic, they concerned borders, language, ownership, as well as cultural and historical priorities. All changes, revolutions and counter-revolutions had their own cast of characters, bringing to the foreground different elites and social and ethnic groups, pushing others into the background or even liquidating them. The change in 1918 substituted Hungarian with the new, mostly Czech and Slovak administration. The new Czechoslovak Republic eliminated the privileges of the nobility and supported the municipal and village middle strata and intelligentsia. The system between the wars opened to allow the influence of the Protestant minority. The war regime of the Slovak Republic shifted into the foreground the Catholic majority and liquidated the economically and intellectually important Jewish minority. The war was followed by the post-war expulsion of the German population and an attempt at the quick assimilation of the Hungarian minority. The communist regime eliminated the bourgeoisie as a class, as well as other strata that had formed over the centuries: farmers, craftsmen, salesmen and free entrepreneurs. The social engineering of the communist regime even tried to transform the Ruthenian nationality into Ukrainian and the Uniate into an Orthodox church.

The common denominator in these radical changes of social structure, political system, state borders and foreign policy orientation was historical self-justification. Each political change was an attempt to change historical consciousness. This is particularly the case of changes in the twentieth century after 1918.

Political quarrels over the interpretation of history and historical argumentation in politics have, of course, an old tradition. Already by the eighteenth century there was a dispute about the autochthony of Slovaks on this territory, specifically their presence before the arrival of the Hungarians. This was useful for scholarship, for it led to greater interest in and research of the history of Great Moravia, the ninth-century state. Acceleration of Magyarization in the nineteenth century and, on the other hand, the growing demands of Slovaks for the recognition of their linguistic and national rights, influenced research on the trend of Slovak integration into the Hungarian state, but also the role of Slovaks and territory of Slovakia during the course of history. Slovaks did not have such clear and strong historical support as the majority of surrounding peoples. The centuries old, if only sometimes formal, existence of the Czech, Polish, Hungarian and Croatian kingdoms was the advantageous starting point for the forming of a new identity, the transition from feudal states to modern nations. In Slovak-Hungarian dialogue and dispute of those days, historiography–concentrating mostly on the history of the state and its representative–spoke Hungarian more strongly than Slovak. This is why the core of Slovak political argumentation was lodged not in historical right, but rather in natural right. These were the claims for recognition of a nation with its own language, territory, culture and national consciousness, for the legislative protection of schools, cultural institutions and public administration, and last but not least for a sort of territorial self-administration.

Our position–"we demand, because we are"–did not always sound convincing enough in the context of nations which were "sick of history". However, this was the principle that gradually became more common and more standard with modernization. Interestingly, from the turn of the century more historical features entered step by step Slovak thinking and argumentation. The state tradition of Great Moravia and the cultural traditions of the "Slavic missionaries" Cyril and Methodius, was a ready history consciously "created" by Slovaks as a nation. Included in this manifestation were the national revival, its personalities and cultural results, the years 1848-1849, and the activization of Slovak politics of the 1860s. It is characteristic, and also significant for the future, that already at that time there was excessive cultivation of historical traditions that were not positive, that is which did not concentrate on achievements and successes but rather on those things with a negative accent: injustices, persecution, and unfulfilled hopes, such as the constant refusal of all Slovak demands by Hungary and Vienna, the persecution of Slovak cultural institutions, the closing of schools, jailing and chicanery.

The paradox is that the historicized political argumentation and politicized history found its most fertile soil in Slovakia only in the twentieth century. History was used as an argument from Budapest against the disintegration of a "millennium-old" Hungary. From the Slovak side of the Danube, this was used as evidence of the Hungarian failure of historical self-examination. For justification of co-habitation with the Czechs in a single state, and an explanation of the concept of a "Czechoslovak nation", elements in politics and historiography were looking back to Great Moravia and the Middle Ages. On the other hand, those in favor of an independent Slovak nation and its self-administration in a new state, were also looking for their arguments in Great Moravia, and in the history of their language, literature, and interpretation of national revival. Disputes over the history of the settlement of Slovakia, its linguistic history, and the interpretation of such key personalities in Slovak history as Ján Kollár and Ľudovít Štúr, quite evidently had a political background. Fortunately for historiography, even if these disputes had pragmatic aims, they produced important monographs, articles and editions of documents.

This also applies to heated discussions such as concerning the role of Slovakia in the Czechoslovak Republic, which was the impulse for research into its foundation, the role of domestic and foreign factors, and so forth. The Slovak movement for autonomy was supported not only by natural arguments but by historical ones, for example the Pittsburgh Treaty of May 1918 concerning the interior administration of the future state of the Czechs and Slovaks. The regime of the Slovak Republic during the Second World War tried to reinterpret Slovak history in which independence was its destiny. After 1948 the communist regime tried to achieve historical identity by stressing the injustices of primal capitalism and the tragedies of economic crises, but also, for example, the failures of Czechoslovak political representation in Munich. This mostly negative arsenal was strengthened by positive historical arguments: for instance, the selective interpretation of the resistance during the Second World War and the role of the Soviet Union in the defeat of fascism.

In the 1960s, in an attempt for greater self-administration for Slovakia and reform of the regime–for "Socialism with a human face"–an interpretation of the Slovak National Uprising of 1944 which differed from the official one played an important role. Even towards the events of November 1989, historical arguments played a similar role, for example, the traditions of the democratic state in the period between the wars, and, on the contrary, emphasis upon the cruelties of the communist dictatorship, mostly in its first phases during the 1950s. Another historical tactic was to remind people of the occupation of the land by the armies of the Warsaw Pact in 1968.

A deeper analysis of the course of the great changes of the twentieth century shows that historical analysis always played only a supporting role. A reinvigorated, recalled history gave to movements, events and their representatives an ethical dimension and emotional charge, a higher and timeless legality, a consecration in antiquity and a kind of inevitability. On the other hand, opposition appears as treasonable and a useless effort to "stand against history".

The use of history in the preparation of future changes and for historical legitimization for already executed changes is not, of course, a uniquely Slovak characteristic. Neither are the impulses for so-called academic historiography coming from great social changes: wars won or lost, imperial expansion, or the feeling of being threatened. We know them from German, French and British historiography as well as that of the neighbors of Slovakia. It is difficult to say whether it is a Slovak or Central European characteristic that these non-scientific impulses and pressures are so numerous, frequent, and intense so that they make the creation of an integrated picture of history difficult. Even if historiography tries to create such a picture, and partially succeeds, its communication with its consumers–the public–is strongly disturbed and their historical memory and consciousness manipulated. Frequently changing and controversial official interpretations of history, personalities and events don't have the opportunity to be rooted and authorized and are constantly covered by new layers. The oscillation of historical personalities and events between heroization and canonization, tabooization and demonization in their official evaluation, has the result of shifting the social role of historiography from a national revivalistic one as the "consciousness of a nation" to that of a slave of changing politics. The close connection between politics and the interpretation of history in a land which has experienced democracy for only a quarter of the twentieth century leads, on the one hand, to a breakdown in the belief in the possibility of knowledge and, on the other hand, to a desire to penetrate beneath the surface of these manipulations. Distrust of the misuse of history supports the illusion that "true" history gives true answers to questions that are not in its competence. Historiography gives little and we demand too much of it.

The role of historiography in society led to a high level of risk in the profession of historian in Slovakia. Already before 1918 the important historian Július Botto was put on trial and his democratically-flavored book on the history of the Slovaks seized. In almost any period, there were pressures merely for existence, and after 1945, 1948 and 1968 there were purges, firings, and discrimination against individuals. Among the social sciences, history was the most afflicted by interference. Discontinuity of history itself, by too many changes, was reflected in the discontinuity of its future chroniclers, historians.

One of the results of the social fate of Slovakia and its historiography is that among the three roles of the study of the past–knowing "as it really was", education by history, and the consolation of history–political pressures led to concentration on the second function. In some phases, most definitely after 1948, this education was reduced to the mere rote learning of pre-fabricated and frozen formulas. Learning as an adventure of spirit, of ascending the peaks of the unknown only "because they are there", was never officially forbidden nor preferred. Because of unpredictable results, this was too risky. Last but not least, even the third, aesthetic framework of the knowledge and interpretation of history, that is, the pleasure of intellectual discourse and successful reproduction of knowledge, collided with official demands for purpose, transparency of the historical product, and the cult of the average. Although the government itself used historical arguments thoughtlessly, superficially, and disingenuously, they took them so seriously that authors could not cross the boundary of pedagogical tone and approved didactic stereotypes.

Slovak historiography has overcome its own long history. The databases of its knowledge are the work of several generations of historians. Incontrovertibly many of its institutions, schools, archives and museums were founded or expanded only after 1948, that is, while Marxism-Leninism was being proclaimed as official state ideology and these organizations had to acknowledge this ideology. Even today, active historians (apart from a few exceptions) were all educated and obtained their experience during this time and in this environment. Slovak historians were trying to balance this reality already in their congress of 1991*. Even some years of distance reveal that a great deal of the historiography of the "totalitarian" years is usable, that Slovak historical science along with all society was held outside of the mainstream of European history and historical science, but kept its contact with the world. It was outside, but at least within sight.

In Slovakia, "the land without kings," some insights of Marxist-Leninist historical theory have been shown to be useful. It oriented attention on social and economic history, on the history of culture, the national movement, towns, settlements, language, science and technology. These themes filled the gaps in "non-political" Slovak history, and also enabled at least a partial escape from its brutal manipulation. With the good research infrastructure of archives, libraries, schools and institutions, successful development of research is possible in the branches where it was interrupted after 1948, for example, in the history of the church and spiritual life, or where it was deformed, that is, in political history.

A greater problem is the development of research on the themes and branches and with the methods that have appeared only in the last decades. This is not because these would be completely unknown. Slovak historians took part in international meetings of historical scholarship after the Second World War in Czechoslovak delegations. The barriers of the Eastern Bloc only slowed down the development of people, books and ideas, never completely halted it. The reality is that the whole "restructuring" of historiography as well as the whole of Slovak society is taking place in an environment of intellectual free-

---

* HČ 39, 1991, 4-5, pp. 469-547.

dom but simultaneously in the environment of extended economic and material struggles. This common problem for post-communist countries could result in the social crisis and political pressures that previously resulted in the discontinuity and deformation of historiography - the historiography which genuinely learns, teaches, and even gives pleasure.

Basic Literature for the Study of Slovak History

SYNTHESIS

Slovak historiography, since the first manifestations of truly synthesizing works, has passed through a complicated development lasting several centuries. The development of ideas about history as a science was closely connected with the development of ideas concerning history as whole, which were not always understood as *magistra vitae.*

The beginnings of Slovak historiography go back to the seventeenth century. The first history of the Slovak people was written only in the eigthteenth century, during the period of the Enlightenment.[1] The growth of Slovak historical science in the second half of the nineteenth century joined pan-European trends, when the complicated process of forming a new nation culminated. The most important personalities of the Slovak life of the spirit[2] followed domestic traditions in accord with the ideas of Slavic mutuality trying, on the one hand, to impart European ideas to Slovak historical literature yet, on the other hand, retaining the national-defeating tendencies concerning the role of Slovakia in a common geopolitical unit with Hungary.[3] The result of this complicated development was the first synthesis of *Július Botto* at the beginning of this century, which strongly influenced the modern conception of Slovak history.[4]

A new stage in the development of Slovak historiography marked the founding of the Czechoslovak Republic in 1918. The widening of the institutional basis of historical work and the beginning of heuristic methods increased the amount of historical work done in the period between the wars. Among the main issues of interest were Slavic settlement and the Great Moravian Empire, the development of Czecho-Slovak relations from the remote past to the creation of the Czechoslovak Republic and questions connected to the role of a new

---

[1] PAPÁNEK, Juraj: Historia gentis Slavae. Pécs 1780.

[2] Pavel Jozef Šafárik, Ján Kollár, Ľudovít Štúr, Jozef Miloslav Hurban and others.

[3] For example: SASINEK, Franko Víťazoslav: Dějiny kráľovstva Uhorského. Volume I. Banská Bystrica 1869, Volume II. Turčiansky Sv. Martin 1871. This work was already considered superseded at the time of its writing.

[4] BOTTO, Július: Slováci. Vývin ich národného povedomia. Volume I. Turčiansky Sv. Martin, Kníhtlačiarsko-nakladateľský spolok 1906, Volume II. 1910. Third edition Bratislava, Tatran 1971.

state in Europe, as well as with its political development and national organization. The result of this organized scholarly research created the desire for new works of synthesis (*František Hrušovský, František Bokes, Anna Gašparíková-Horáková*). Though mostly published only after the Second World War, they were influenced not only by the accomplished level of Slovak historiography but also by the political situation in the period of its birth.[5]

Because Slovak historiography could not be supported after 1945 by works from the "Positivist" period of its development, it was forced to return to many basic questions. This was a period of very quick quantitative and qualitative development of research of national, regional and world history. New historical methods broadened the applicability of classical historical sources and evidence; works were written concerning content as well as methods that replaced earlier ones, and there was a need for a new synthetic view of Slovak history as a whole.[6]

Two volumes were published in the sixties, the pioneering *Academic Synthesis,* giving a concise explanation of the history of Slovakia from the earliest times to 1900.[7] This work remains unfinished; however, it did push Slovak historiography to new qualitative standards. The group of authors, doing extensive research, dealt with much material that had not been analyzed before and addressed complicated theoretical questions. In the later sixties, other works of synthesis were planned. In 1971, the first volume, *Slovakia: History,* of the ambitiously conceived *Synthesis of the Homeland,* appeared.[8] Using the newest Slovak re-

---

[5] HRUŠOVSKÝ, František: Slovenské dejiny. Martin, MS 1939; HRUŠOVSKÝ, František: Slovensko v dejinách strednej Európy. Martin, MS 1939. F. Hrušovský continued his historical production after emigrating in 1945, for example: This Is Slovakia. Scranton 1953 ; BOKES, František: Dejiny Slovenska a Slovákov od najstarších čias po oslobodenie. Bratislava, SAVU 1946; GAŠPARÍKOVÁ-HORÁKOVÁ, Anna: Tisícročné Slovensko. Bratislava, without publisher 1947.

[6] In 1955 the first version of "DEJINY Slovenska. Tézy" (The History of Slovakia. Thesis) was published as a supplement to HČ 3, 1955. This was a sort of preparation for a synthetic history of Slovakia, and became the starting point for the Slovak sections of an extensive Czechoslovak academic university textbook: PŘEHLED československých dějin - Maketa. I.-III. Praha, Nakladatelství ČSAV 1958-1960. The work, according to the authors, should serve as the basic for broad discussion of Czecho-Slovak history.

[7] DEJINY Slovenska I. Od najstarších čias do roku 1848. Compiled by HOLOTÍK, Ľudovít - TIBENSKÝ, Ján. Bratislava, SAV 1961; MÉSÁROŠ, Július and team: DEJINY Slovenska II. Od roku 1848 do roku 1900. Bratislava, SAV 1968.

[8] SLOVENSKO I.-IV. Compiled by TIBENSKÝ, Ján. Bratislava, Obzor 1971-1979. Volume I.: Dejiny. 1971, 1978. The second edition of this extensive historical synthesis of Slovak history was reworked and supplemented (added to the bibliography and index of names was a geografical index); Volume II.: Príroda. 1972; Volume III./1.-2. part: Ľud. 1974; Volume IV./1.-2. part: Kul-

search and (in recognition of their long mutual history) drawing upon Hungarian historical scholarship, the authors stressed the most important events and basic history of the national past. Compared with older works, which emphasized the development of expressions of national consciousness, these authors turned towards the social aspect, and combined the ethnic and geographic principles: the Slovak people in connection with the region of Slovakia. To create a complex picture of the development of Slovakia, the other volumes, devoted to nature, people and culture, were also essential.

Together with this project, the richly illustrated synthesis Slovak *History Through Word and Picture* (the first volume by Ján Tibenský[9] and the second by a consortium of authors[10]) was published for a popular audience.

In Academia in Prague, another extensive project was carried forth, *Overview of the History of Czechoslovakia,* investigating the past of the country from its pre-historic settlement to the present. A collective of important Czech and Slovak historians took part.[11] Organizing a great deal of data, this work allows quick orientation on issues. Contributing to this aim is a list of resources and recommended readings at the end of each chapter, giving an overview of historical works in the most extensive study of both basic and particular problems. However, only two volumes of the first part, studying events up to 1848, have been published.

As an integral part of both national and European history, Czech and Slovak authors produced a many-volumed *Military History of Czechoslovakia To 1918.*[12] Several other important works also widened the perspective and interests of Slovak historiography: for example, the popular-audience *History of Science and Technology in Slovakia,* the two-volume work *Pioneers of Science and Technology in Slovakia,*[13] and *A History of Slovak Literature.*[14]

túra. 1979-1980; In German was published: Die slowakische Volkskultur. Die materielle und geistige Kultur. Edited by HORVÁTHOVÁ, Emília - URBANCOVÁ, Viera. Bratislava, Veda 1972.

[9] TIBENSKÝ, Ján: Dejiny Slovenska slovom i obrazom I. (Do roku 1848). Martin, Osveta 1973.

[10] BUTVIN, Jozef - KOSTICKÝ, Bohumír - VARTÍKOVÁ, Marta: Dejiny Slovenska slovom a obrazom II. (Od roku 1848 do súčasnosti). Martin, Osveta 1981.

[11] PŘEHLED dějin Československa. Volume I./1 (till 1526); Volume I./2 (1526-1848). Edited by PURŠA, Jaroslav - KROPILÁK, Miroslav. Praha, Academia 1980 and 1982.

[12] VOJENSKÉ dějiny Československa I.-V. Praha, Naše vojsko 1985-1986.

[13] TIBENSKÝ, Ján: Dejiny vedy a techniky na Slovensku. Martin, Osveta 1979; PRIEKOPNÍCI vedy a techniky na Slovensku I.-II. Edited by TIBENSKÝ, Ján. Bratislava, Obzor 1986-1988.

[14] DEJINY slovenskej literatúry I.-V. Bratislava, Veda 1958-1984; DEJINY slovenskej literatúry I.-IV. Bratislava, SPN 1984-1987.

Added to these monothematic works was the university textbook *History of Government and Law in Czechoslovakia*,[15] which explains the development of governmental organization and administration in different stages up till 1918, knowledge of which allows us to discover those moments in history that determined our conditions of life.

Still missing, however, was a broad work analyzing the historical development of Slovakia from the earliest times to the present, and integrating this national history into the frame of European development. This gap was filled by a six-volume work resulting from thirty years of research in the post-War generation of Slovak historiography: *The History of Slovakia*, published by the Slovak Academy of Sciences, 1986-1992.[16] It gives an extensive and integrated view of the history of Slovakia from earliest times to 1960, with the goal of covering all essential parts of social, political, economic and cultural development. There are bibliographies, lists of literature and explanatory notes, but citations, consuming too much space, were not used.

The first synthetic even if not very extensive work since the changes of 1989 was *Slovak History*[17], from the faculty of the Institute of Historical Studies of the Slovak Academy of Sciences. It follows Slovak history from earliest times to the elections of June, 1990. It was published with the aim of helping those interested in Slovak history and culture to become quickly reoriented in complicated historical issues. Soon after came other works, though different in form and scope.[18]

---

[15] MALÝ, Karel - SIVÁK, Florián: Dejiny štátu a práva v Česko-Slovensku do roku 1918. Bratislava, Obzor 1992.

[16] DEJINY Slovenska I.-VI. Edited by CAMBEL, Samuel. Bratislava, Veda 1986-1992: Volume I. (Do roku 1526) Compiled by MARSINA, Richard. 1986; Volume II. (1526-1848) Compiled by MATULA, Vladimír - VOZÁR, Jozef. 1987; Volume III. (Od roku 1848 do konca 19. storočia) Compiled by PODRIMAVSKÝ, Milan. 1992; Volume IV. (Od konca 19. storočia do roku 1918) Compiled by HAPÁK, Pavol. 1986; Volume V. (1918-1945) Compiled by KROPILÁK, Miroslav. 1985; Volume VI. (1945-1960) Compiled by BARNOVSKÝ, Michal. 1988.

[17] MARSINA, Richard - ČIČAJ, Viliam - KOVÁČ, Dušan - LIPTÁK, Ľubomír: SLOVENSKÉ dejiny. Martin, MS 1992 (without notes, citation apparatus or bibliography, only an index of names and localities).

[18] For example ŠPIESZ, Anton: Dejiny Slovenska na ceste k sebauvedomeniu. Bratislava, Perfekt 1992; KUČERA, Matúš - KOSTICKÝ, Bohumír: Slovensko v obrazoch. História. Martin, Osveta 1990.

ENCYCLOPEDIAS

In Slovakia, there was a tradition of encyclopedias from the eighteenth[1] and nineteenth centuries. The first extensive geographical and historical encyclopedic description of Hungary was from Matej Bel, professor of the Bratislava Lycée, whose *Notitia Hungariae Novae*[2] with its structure and method of processing materials became the model for many other authors, though of less ambitious works.[3] The first national and linguistic Slovak efforts to create a scientific dictionary, in the early 1800s, were the only ones for a century.[4]

In the beginning of the twentieth century in Hungary several specific and also general comprehensive encyclopedias were created,[5] whose contributors included Slovaks. However, in the pan-Hungarian framework, they devoted little attention to Slovak issues and, at any rate, operated under the influence of the ruling ideology. Much more attention was devoted to Slovak developments by Czech encyclopedias, in whose creation Slovaks took part and which, until 1945, compensated for the lack of encyclopedias of the Slovaks.[6]

After the creation of the Czechoslovak Republic, as a result of the improved

---

[1] As the first encyclopedic work in Slovakia and Hungary, we can see it as a sort of instructive dictionary of ephemera by a professor of Trnava University SZENTIVÁNYI, Martin: Curiosiora et selectiora variarum scientiarum miscellanea. Tyrnaviae 1679-1709.

[2] BEL, Mathias: Notitia Hungariae novae historico-geographica, divisa in partes quatuor. Viennae Austriae 1735-1742.

[3] For example KORABINSKY, Johann Mathias: Geographisch-historisches und Produkten-Lexikon von Ungarn. Pressburg 1786; BARTHOLOMAEIDES, Ladislaus: Inclyti superioris Hungariae comitatus Gömöriensis notitia historico-geographica-statistica I.-III. Leutschoviae 1806-1808.

[4] Here we can mention TABLIC, Bohuslav: Slovenští veršovci I. Skalica 1805; KOLLÁR, Ján: Slovník slavianskych umelcov. Pešť 1843.

[5] PALLAS nagy lexikona I.-XVI. 2 Supl. Budapest 1893-1904; RÉVAI nagy lexikona I.-XX. Budapest, Révai testvérek irodalmi intézet 1911-1927, and others.

[6] SLOVNÍK náučný I.-XI. Edited by RIEGER, František Ladislav. Praha, Kober a Markgraf 1860-1874; OTTŮV slovník naučný I.-XXVIII. Praha, J. Otto 1888-1909; MASARYKŮV slovník naučný I.-VII. Praha, Československý kompas 1925-1933; KOMENSKÉHO slovník naučný I.-X. Praha 1937-1938.

condition of national and cultural development, new opportunities for the creation of an encyclopedia appeared. However, even though the schools had developed, and the activities of Matica slovenská had been renewed, the material conditions and authors for the creation of such works were still missing. Slovak scholarship was still immature and historical research was not sufficiently extensive. This was manifested in the first three volumes of *The Slovak Scientific Dictionary* (1932).[7]

After the Second World War, the first efforts to create a Slovak encyclopedia emerged in the fifties but they were suppressed and the editors sentenced to prison. Slovak scientists and scholars took part in the creation of Czechoslovak encyclopedias and dictionaries of different characters, from social sciences and the arts, as well as natural and technical sciences.[8] The preparation and publication of a broad, original Slovak project approached fruition in 1959 when an independent Institute of Encyclopedias was established in the Slovak Academy of Sciences. Since its creation, it has cooperated on the preparation of encyclopedias published in Bohemia and also drafted and begun to realize, in organization and scholarship, Slovak projects.

The first fruits of many years' preparation came with the 1977 publication of the first of three volumes of the *Homeland Dictionary of Communities in Slovakia*.[9] This was the first basic manual of the homeland capturing the changes undergone by Slovakia in its development. There are 3,155 Slovak towns and village organized in alphabetical order, with basic information, natural conditions, history (from the first archaeological or documented period to the present), and the development of culture, medicine, sport and literature. To allow the reader to integrate this information into the whole Slovak context, the preface contains studies from the basic branches covered in individual entries. Of great help as a starting point was the previously published survey of architectural treasures in Slovakia.[10] These are ordered according to historical importance and value in an architectural and urban context.

---

[7] SLOVENSKÝ náučný slovník I.-III. Compiled by BUJNÁK, Pavel. Bratislava-Praha, "Litevna" 1932.

[8] PŘÍRUČNÍ slovník naučný I.-IV. Compiled by PROCHÁZKA, Vladimír. Praha, ČSAV 1962-1967; PYRAMÍDA. Encyklopedický časopis moderného človeka. Bratislava since 1971 (softbound periodical); MALÝ encyklopedický slovník A-Ž. Praha, Academia 1972.

[9] VLASTIVEDNÝ slovník obcí na Slovensku I.-III. Edited by KROPILÁK, Miroslav. Bratislava, Veda 1977-1978.

[10] SÚPIS pamiatok na Slovensku I.-IV. Compiled by GÜNTHEROVÁ, Alžbeta. Bratislava, Obzor a Slovenský ústav pamiatkovej starostlivosti a ochrany prírody 1967-1969 and 1978: Volume

Experience from the preparation of the Homeland Dictionary of Communities, as well as different specialized encyclopedias,[11] was used in creating the *Encyclopedia of Slovakia,*[12] the first volume of which was also published in 1977. This was the first great project of its kind here, and was brought to completion by the publication of its sixth volume in 1982, so concluding the pioneering scholarly effort of these workers in basic research. To the hands of the general public came the most complex work at that time on the history and life of Slovakia. In its interdisciplinary approach and concentrated form, it mediates the most important information about the natural conditions, inhabitants, history, economy, social and political life, and cultural development in Slovakia from earliest times to the present. The great interest in all parts and periods of the history of Slovakia had finally brought about the publication of a Slovak encyclopedia as a separate work.[13]

On the accomplishments of previous encyclopedic work is based the first homeland encyclopedia of a smaller variety: *The Short Encyclopedia of Slovakia.*[14] It is not a reduced version of the six-volume work. Rather, its authors understood it as the first step in a continually updated series of one-volume encyclopedias which would give the public a constant picture of all aspects of life in Slovakia. On the long tradition of universal encyclopedic work Czech encyclopedic work was based, supplemented with Slovak cultural data.[15]

I. A-J. 1967; Volume II. K-P. 1968; Volume III. R-Ž. 1969; Volume IV. PAMIATKY na Slovensku. Súpis pamiatok. Compiled by LICHNER, Ján. 1978; PISOŇ, Štefan: Hrady, zámky a kaštiele na Slovensku. Martin, Osveta 1970.

[11] The lack of Slovak creativity in encyclopedia production, along with the effort to popularize scholarship, had by the 1970s led the publishing house Obzor to originate the important popular instructive edition *Malé encyklopédie* (Small Encyclopedias). In the framework of this project, works from the widest variety of natural and social sciencies have been published, always employing information from a Slovak context. These allow quick orientation in the given subject, providing basic information for practical needs. Published so far in this edition are the small encyclopedias of mathematics, chemistry, music, physics, health, film, researchers and inventors, biology, geography of the world, writers of the world, physical education and sport, the earth, astronomy, and journalism, and others have been prepared. Since 1980s, more ambitious encyclopedias have been published, without the "small" label.

[12] ENCYKLOPÉDIA Slovenska I.-VI. Prepared by Encyclopedic Institute of SAV. Bratislava, Veda 1977-1982.

[13] SLOVENSKÁ socialistická republika. Encyklopedický prehľad (Príroda, Dejiny, Hospodárstvo, Kultúra.) Edited by PLEVZA, Viliam - VLADÁR, Jozef. Bratislava, Veda 1984.

[14] MALÁ encyklopédia Slovenska A-Ž. Edited by HAJKO, Vladimír. Bratislava, Veda 1987.

[15] ILUSTROVANÝ encyklopedický slovník I.-III. Edited by KOŽEŠNÍK, Jaroslav. Praha, Academia 1980-1982; MALÁ československá encyklopedie I.-VI. Praha, Academia 1984-1987.

From our point of view, some specialized encyclopedias are significant, such as *The Dictionary of Ancient and Medieval Authors of Resources and Book Scribes with Slovak Connections,*[16] aimed towards all who research Slovakia history, especially its cultural and literary connections; *The Encyclopedia of Slovak Writers;*[17] *The Encyclopedia of Dramatic Art in Slovakia;*[18] *The Encyclopedia of Linguistics*[19] (Slovak); *The Encyclopedia of Archaeology,*[20] containing much cultural data; and *The Pedagogical Encyclopedia of Slovakia,*[21] which is the first complex work on education, teaching and enlightenment, from the Great Mo-ravian Empire to the 1980s.

Added to these many specialized encyclopedias is *The Historical Dictionary of the Slovak Language,*[22] which introduces the language of the period of the earliest times (as it is preserved in manuscripts and printed documents) before its codification by Bernolák at the end of the eighteenth century. It is also the concrete linguistic contribution to the solution of the formation and development of the Slovak national culture from the eleventh to the eigthteenth centuries.

On the same level of importance is *The Slovak Dictionary of Biography,*[23] a six-volume encyclopedia of the lives and works of personalities of significance to all of Slovakia from the Great Moravian Empire to the present, from all branches of material and spiritual culture, and political, social and economic

---

[16] KUZMÍK, Jozef: Slovník starovekých a stredovekých autorov prameňov a knižných skriptorov so slovenskými vzťahmi. Martin, MS 1983.

[17] ENCYKLOPÉDIA slovenských spisovateľov I.-II. Edited by ROSENBAUM, Karol and team. Bratislava, Obzor 1986. It is divided into three parts: first the foundation, which is the selected dictionary of Slovak writers; second, entries of background information on Slovak literary life (periodicals); and third, a brief synthesis of the history of Slovak literature.

[18] ENCYKLOPÉDIA dramatických umení Slovenska I.-II. Edited by MRLIAN, Rudolf and team. Bratislava, Veda 1989-1990.

[19] ENCYKLOPÉDIA jazykovedy. Compiled by MISTRÍK, Jozef and team. Bratislava, Obzor 1993.

[20] ENCYKLOPÉDIA archeológie. Compiled by NOVOTNÝ, Bohuslav and team. Bratislava, Obzor 1986.

[21] PEDAGOGICKÁ encyklopédia Slovenska I.-II. Edited by PAVLÍK, Ondrej and team. Bratislava, Veda 1984-1985. It also contains a general inventory of all educational establishments in Slovakia.

[22] HISTORICKÝ slovník slovenského jazyka I.-II. Compiled by MAJTÁN, Milan. Bratislava, Veda 1991-1992.

[23] SLOVENSKÝ biografický slovník. (Od roku 833 do roku 1990). I.-VI. Prepared by Biographical Department/Institute of MS. Volume I. A-D, Volume II. E-J, Volume III. K-L, Volume IV. M-Q, Volume V. R-Š, Volume VI. T-Ž. Martin, MS 1986-1994.

life. This was the first of its kind in Czechoslovakia, and so became a basic historiographical manual. Regarding its condensed text, simple style, and internationally accepted rules of biographical data, it can, with the help of a dictionary, be understood by foreigners. The choice of personalities in the first volumes is, however, ideologically limited. Together with its fifth volume (1992), a similar short encyclopedic manual was published in Bohemia, *The Czechoslovak Biographical Dictionary.*[24]

The events in 1989, and a new socio-political situation, demanded similar information on living or recently deceased personalities. Very quickly offered to the broad public were *Who's Who* types of manuals, though they differed not only in their extent but the quality of their processing of information.[25]

In 1993, *The Short Slovak Encyclopedia*[26] was published, culminating an effort of many years and a gap in modern Slovak encyclopedic work was filled with the first English language encyclopedia, *Slovakia and the Slovaks: A Concise Encyclopedia* published at the end of 1994.[27] The first encyclopedia to be issued in an electronic format, on CD disk, will be the *Encyclopedia of Popular Culture in Slovakia.*[28]

---

[24] ČESKOSLOVENSKÝ biografický slovník A-Ž. Edited by TOMEŠ, Josef - LÉBLOVÁ, Alena. Praha, Academia 1992.

[25] HODNÝ, Martin: Českoslovenští politici 1918-1991. Stručné životopisy. Praha, M. Hodný 1991; KTO je kto na Slovensku 1991? Compiled by ADAMEC, Vladimír and team. Bratislava, Konzorcium Encyklopédia 1991; SLOVNÍK prvního československého odboje 1914-1918. Compiled by GALANDAUER, Jan. Praha, Hermes 1993; KTO bol kto za I. ČSR. Compiled by NIŽŇANSKÝ, Eduard and team. Bratislava, Q111 1993.

[26] MALÁ slovenská encyklopédia. Prepared by Encyclopedic Institute of SAV. Bratislava, Goldpress Publishers 1993.

[27] SLOVAKIA and the Slovaks: A Concise Encyclopedia. Compiled and edited by STRHAN, Milan - DANIEL, David P. Bratislava, Encyklopedický ústav SAV a Goldpress Publishers 1994.

[28] ENCYKLOPÉDIA ľudovej kultúry Slovenska I.-II. Edited by BOTÍK, Ján - SLAVKOVSKÝ, Peter. Bratislava, Veda a Ústav etnológie SAV 1995.

BIBLIOGRAPHIES

The *Slovak National Bibliography* holds the foremost place in the development of bibliographic work in Slovakia and includes the retrospective work began by Ľudovít Vladimír Rizner[1] and the current regularly issued national bibliographies (*Slovak National Bibliography*, individual series).[2] These bibliographies list, without thematic constraints, all that is published in Slovakia. Individual historical bibliographic work began during the Second World War. In 1944 *The Bibliography of Slovak History 1939-1941*[3] was published. In 1948 an addendum was published dealing with the years 1942-1944.[4] From its foundation, historical bibliography tried to give a picture of the historical literature published in Slovakia in book and journal form and, at the same time, to deal with works about Slovak history from abroad.

The bibliography cooperatively established by historical institutions of the academy of sciences in Bratislava and Prague reflected this viewpoint. The history institutes of the Slovak Academy in Bratislava and the Czechoslovak Academy of Sciences in Prague shortly after their foundation, in 1957, started to publish annuals (and bi-annuals) dealing with the literature published since 1955. Originally the annuals were published under the title *Bibliography of*

---

[1] BIBLIOGRAFIA písomníctva slovenského na spôsob slovníka od najstarších čias do konca roku 1900 s pripojenou bibliografiou archeologickou, historickou, miestopisnou a prírodovedeckou I.-VI. Compiled by RIZNER, Ľudovít Vladimír. Turčiansky Svätý Martin, MS 1929-1934; BIBLIO-GRAFIA slovenského písomníctva do konca 19. storočia. (Doplnky k Riznerovej bibliografii.) Compiled by MIŠIANIK, Ján. Martin, MS 1971; DOPLNKY a opravy k Riznerovej bibliografii. Compiled by ORMIS, Ján V. Martin, MS 1972.

[2] Continuous bibliographies are published under the title *Slovenská národná bibliografia* by Matica Slovenská in Martin. They record everything as it is published in Slovakia. The most important is the monthly series *Slovenská národná bibliografia. Séria Knihy* (Book Series) and *Slovenská národná bibliografia. Séria Články* (Articles Series).

[3] BIBLIOGRAFIA slovenskej histórie 1939-1941. Compiled by BOKES, František - JANKO-VIČ, Vendelín - POLLA, Belo. Turčiansky Svätý Martin, MS 1944.

[4] BIBLIOGRAFIA slovenskej histórie 1942-1944 s doplnkami za roky 1939-1941. Compiled by JANKOVIČ, Vendelín. Turčiansky Svätý Martin, MS 1948.

Czechoslovak History.[5] In 1979 the name was changed,[6] and in 1993 the publisher.[7] These annuals are the most detailed historical bibliographies about Slovakia. They list all historical contributions published in Slovakia as books or articles, including translations. At the, same time, they deal with works on Slovak history published abroad. However, these foreign works were included only if they were acquired by Slovak libraries or as was possible in the existing political climate (knowledge of exile literature was obtained only sporadically). Works from historical and related scholarship were registered selectively. Articles on the occasion of anniversaries, memorials, and conferences as well as reviews are included. Usually they are registered by author, subject and location.

The delay in appearance is an inconvenience (the bibliography from 1993 deals with works from 1980-81). What is more, the volumes were published with gaps, so that the concise bibliography dealing with literature from 1955 to 1981 omits 1966-1970,[8] 1978-1979 and 1982-1989. As previously mentioned, foreign works were listed irregularly. This shortcoming is partially compensated for by Michal Lacko's *Slovak Bibliography Abroad,*[9] which deals mostly with the years 1945-75.

In the history institutes of Bratislava and Prague, other bibliographies were initiated: selective bibliographies aimed at the presentation of Czech and Slovak bibliography at international congresses (Stockholm, 1960;[10] Bucharest, 1980;[11]

---

[5] BIBLIOGRAFIE československé historie - for the year 1955, 1956, 1957, 1958, 1959-1960, 1961, 1962-1963, 1964, 1965. Praha, Nakladatelství ČSAV 1957-1972.

[6] BIBLIOGRAFIE dějin Československa - for the year 1971, 1972, 1973, 1974, 1975, 1976-1977. Praha, Academia 1982-1990.

[7] BIBLIOGRAFIE dějin Československa za léta 1980-1981. Praha, Historický ústav ČAV 1993.

[8] Literature published from 1966 to 1970 is partially approachable throuhg the bibliography: Südosteuropa Bibliographie. Band V. 1966-1970. Teil 1. Südosteuropa und grössere Teilräume, Rumänien, Ungarn, Slowakei. Edited by KRALLERT-SATTLER, Gertrud. München, R. Oldenbourg 1982.

[9] SLOVENSKÁ bibliografia v zahraničí 1945-1965. Slovak Bibliography Abroad 1945-1965. Compiled by LACKO, Michal. In: Slovak Studies 7, Cleveland - Rome, Slovak Institute 1967;

SLOVENSKÁ bibliografia v zahraničí 1966-1975. Slovak Bibliography Abroad 1966-1975. Compiled by LACKO, Michal. In: Slovak Studies 17, Cleveland - Rome, Slovak Institute 1977.

[10] 25 ans d'historiographie Tchécoslovaque 1936-1960. Edited by MACEK, Josef. Praha, Nakladatelství ČSAV 1960.

[11] HISTORIOGRAFIE v Československu 1970-1980. Výběrová bibliografie. Praha, ÚČSSD ČSAV 1980.

Stuttgart, 1985;[12] Madrid, 1990[13]). On these occasions four monograph bibliographies dealt with the literature of the years 1936-1960 and 1970-1989. Because they were aimed at the international scholarly community, the first one is in French. The others are not translated, but they contain prefaces and tables of contents in English. These bibliographies have a narrower scope than the annuals. They do not include works from abroad, chronicles, or reviews, and mention fewer periodicals. In 1988, in *Historický časopis* (The Historical Journal), a new section devoted to bibliography was established[14] including articles from basic historical periodicals and books. In this way the literature from 1986 to 1991 has been published. The goal is making information more immediately available.

The most recent major effort of Slovak historiography has been to publish a single concise retrospective bibliography which would fill the above mentioned gaps in historical bibliographies. Although a *Retrospective Bibliography of the History of Slovakia*[15] was published in 1962, it only dealt with monographs and not with journal articles. This role had to be undertaken by the bibliography started in the late sixties and early seventies in the Institute of Historical Studies of the Slovak Academy of Sciences.[16] It allows access to the literature of Slovak history from early times to 1965. Unfortunately this bibliography was never published, since it listed ideologically unsuitable works of foreign, mostly exile authorship. Currently the role of publishing it has been undertaken by the University Library in Bratislava in cooperation with the Institute of Historical Studies. The work will include approximately 18,000 entries. In the unpublished form, a concise 450-page register of author, subject and location simplifies orientation. Other bibliographies of a less universal character exist, including

---

[12] HISTORIOGRAFIE v Československu 1980-1985. Výběrová bibliografie. Praha, ÚČSSD ČSAV 1985.

[13] HISTORIOGRAFIE v Československu 1985-1989. Výběrová bibliografie. Praha, HÚ ČSAV 1990.

[14] HISTORIOGRAFIA na Slovensku. Výberová bibliografia za rok 1986. Compiled by SEDLIAKOVÁ, Alžbeta. In: HČ 36, 1988, 4, pp. 671-688; op. cit. for the year 1987 - In: HČ 37, 1989, 4, pp. 628-648; op. cit. for the year 1988 - In: HČ 38, 1990, 4, pp. 754-768; op. cit. for the year 1989 - In: HČ 39, 1991, 4-5, pp. 548-567; op. cit. for the year 1990 - In: HČ 40, 1992, 4, pp. 519-540; op. cit. for the year 1991 - In: HČ 41, 1993, 4, pp. 491-528.

[15] BIBLIOGRAFIA publikácií k miestnym a všeobecným dejinám Slovenska. Compiled by KUZMÍK, Jozef. Martin, MS 1962.

[16] BIBLIOGRAFIA slovenskej histórie do roku 1965. Compiled by JANKOVIČ, Vendelín - ŠKORUPOVÁ, Anna. Bratislava 1972. Manuscript.

The Bibliography of Modern History[17] and The History of Science and Technology.[18]

This picture of Slovak historiography has been supplemented by the publication on the twenty-fifth anniversary of the Slovak Academy of Science's Institute of Historical Studies.[19] A large part of it consists of bibliography on personalities. At the Institute of Historical Studies an extensive bibliographic work was assembled on Slovak historiographical work of 1918-1939.[20] However, it includes only articles, not monographs.

The retrospective bibliographies of the Matica slovenská occupy an important place, covering the periodical press[21] (not historical works) for a given period or on a given theme. The State Scholarly Library in Košice also carries out extensive work, including significantly that of Michal Potemra.[22]

There are also bibliographies from related branches, including archaeology[23] and ethnography.[24]

---

[17] BIBLIOGRAFIE dějin dělnického hnutí 1965, 1966. Praha, 1966-1967; NOVODOBÉ dějiny v československé historiografii. Bibliografie 1967-1986. Praha, 1968-1988.

[18] BIOBIBLIOGRAFIA prírodných, lekárskych a technických vied na Slovensku do roku 1850 I.-II. Compiled by TIBENSKÝ, Ján - HROCHOVÁ, Mária - MAUEROVÁ, Mária. Martin, MS 1976; BALNEOLOGICKÁ bibliografia Slovenska 1850-1920. Compiled by DUKA ZOLYOMI, Norbert. Piešťany, Balneologické múzeum 1980; The bibliography published periodically in the annual Z dejín vied a techniky na Slovensku 1964-1979 covers literature published from 1918 to 1976.

[19] Historický ústav SAV 1953-1978. Dvadsaťpäť rokov činnosti. Compiled by KROPILÁK, Miroslav - MATULA, Vladimír. Bratislava, HÚ SAV 1978.

[20] BIBLIOGRAFIA príspevkov k slovenským dejinám uverejnených v rokoch 1918-1939. Edited by ŠKORUPOVÁ, Anna. Martin, MS 1963.

[21] For example POĽNOHOSPODÁRSTVO na Slovensku 1918-1928. Bibliografia zo slovenských novín a časopisov I.-IV. Compiled by KÁŇAVOVÁ, Anna. Martin, MS 1982-1986; BIBLIOGRAFIA almanachov, ročeniek a zborníkov na Slovensku 1919-1944. Compiled by KOVAČIČOVÁ, Eva - ŠTVRTECKÝ, Štefan. Martin, MS 1991.

[22] For example: Slovenská historiografia v rokoch 1901-1918. Bibliografia článkov zo slovenských novín a časopisov. Compiled by POTEMRA, Michal. Košice, Štátna vedecká knižnica 1980.

[23] BIBLIOGRAFIA slovenskej archeológie - for the year 1980, 1981, 1982, 1983, 1984, 1985, 1986, 1987, 1988. Nitra, Archeologický ústav SAV 1984-1992.

[24] Národopisná literatúra na Slovensku za roky 1901-1959. Compiled by STANO, Pavol - ŽATKO, Rudolf. Martin, MS 1989; Bibliografia slovenskej etnografie a folkloristiky za roky 1960-1969, 1970-1975, 1976-1980, 1981-1985, 1986-1990. Compiled by KUBOVÁ, Milada. Bratislava, Národopisný ústav SAV 1971-1994.

REGIONAL LITERATURE

The literature on the history of villages, cities and broader regions has a long tradition in Slovakia. At present we are witnessing a renaissance in the publication of works of this kind. This consists of articles published in journals of regional history (see the chapter on "Periodicals") and books of illustrations. In these works, more often than in other kinds, there is usually a summary in multiple languages. The literature on the history of individual regions is included in historical bibliographies which usually include location listings (see "Bibliographies").

In this connection, it is necessary to mention the very active publishing of the History of Cities Section of the Slovak Historical Society of the Slovak Academy of Sciences. This section organizes conferences and symposia. From these gatherings, proceedings are published.[1]

The following items illustrate the above mentioned categories of books focused especially upon the history of particular cities.[2]

---

[1] BANSKÉ mestá na Slovensku. Compiled by MARSINA, Richard. Martin, Osveta 1990; FEUDÁLNY majetok miest na Slovensku. In: Liptov 8, 1985, pp. 9-97; NÁRODNOSTNÝ vývoj miest na Slovensku do roku 1918. Compiled by MARSINA, Richard. Martin, Osveta 1984; SPIŠSKÉ mestá v stredoveku. Compiled by MARSINA, Richard. Košice, VV 1974; STÄDTE im Donauraum. Bratislava-Pressburg 1291-1991. Compiled by MARSINA, Richard. Bratislava, Slovenská historická spoločnosť - HÚ SAV - Miestny úrad Bratislava Staré mesto 1993; VÝVOJ správy miest na Slovensku. Compiled by MARSINA, Richard. Martin, Osveta 1984.

[2] BANSKÁ ŠTIAVNICA. Compiled by VOZÁR, Jozef - GREGA, Vincent. Banská Bystrica, SV 1964; DEJINY Bratislavy. Compiled by HORVÁTH, Vladimír - LEHOTSKÁ, Darina - PLEVA, Ján. Third edition. Bratislava, Obzor 1982; NAJSTARŠIE dejiny Bratislavy. Compiled by ŠTEFANOVIČOVÁ, Tatiana. Bratislava, Elán 1993; DEJINY Levoče. Volume I. by SUCHÝ, Michal, Volume II. by CHALUPECKÝ, Ivan. Košice, VV 1974-1975; DEJINY Prešova I.-II. Compiled by SEDLÁK, Imrich. Košice, VV 1965; DEJINY Trnavy. Compiled by ŠIMONČIČ, Jozef - WATZKA, Jozef. Bratislava, Obzor 1988; HALAGA, Ondrej R.: Počiatky Košíc a zrod metropoly. Košice, VV 1993; KREMNICA. Zborník prednášok z medzinárodného sympózia. Compiled by NOVÁK, Ján. Martin, Gradus 1992; MYJAVA. Compiled by DUGÁČEK, Michal - GÁLIK, Ján. Bratislava, Obzor 1985; TRENČÍN. Vlastivedná monografia. Compiled by ŠIŠMIŠ, Milan. Bratislava, Alfa 1993; ZVOLEN. Monografia k 750. výročiu obnovenia mestských práv. Compiled by VANÍKOVÁ, Viera. Martin, Gradus 1993.

PERIODICALS

The roots of Slovak historical journals are in the second half of the nineteenth century. In 1863, the first Slovak scholarly journal, *Letopis Matice slovenskej* (Annals of the Matica slovenská), began publication. The greater part of the contributions had historical or local content. After the abolition of Matica slovenská in 1875, it ceased publication. Already in 1876, however, it resumed publication as *Slovenský letopis pre históriu, topografiu, archeológiu a etnografiu* (Slovak Annals of History, Topography, Archaeology and Ethnography) which lasted until 1882. Since it again ceased publication, the only scholarly journal in production before the First World War was *Sborník Muzeálnej slovenskej spoločnosti* (Annals of the Slovak Museum Society). This was founded in 1896 and was irregularly published and had mostly historical contributions.

After the First World War, a number of scholarly journals began to be issued which included historical articles. These included *Sborník Matice slovenskej* (Annals of Matica slovenská), *Bratislava, Sborník Filozofickej fakulty Univerzity Komenského* (Annals of the Faculty of Philosophy of Comenius University), and so on.

Sborník Matice slovenskej began publication in 1922 and in 1943 was divided into three individual annuals. One of these was the *Historický sborník* (Historical Annals), which was published till 1947. *Bratislava* was the review of the Šafárik Scholarly Society. It was published from 1927 to 1937. After the end of this society and the founding of the Slovak Scholarly Society, the journal *Historica Slovaca* was founded which is connected with the present day *Historický časopis* (Historical Journal).

For foreigners the scholarly review *Carpatica Slovaca* was designed and published in foreign languages from 1943-1944. It was published by the Slovak Academy of Sciences and Arts and devoted to disciplines of domestic interest.

This is a very brief sketch of the origins of the publication of historical periodicals. Now we would like to discuss current periodicals. Each title is followed by a few characteristics. Three periodicals, *Studia historica Slovaca, Human Affairs* and *Slovenská archeológia* (Slovak Archaeology) are published in foreign languages.

Many periodicals changed their name during publication or ceased publication and began again. Their frequency of publication also often has varied. A large proportion are partial periodicals, that is, annuals that have not been published every year. However, the numbering of these annuals assumed yearly publication.

Basic Historical Periodicals

Historická revue (Historical Review)
A popular scholarly journal. It has been published in Bratislava ten times a year since 1990.

Historické štúdie (Historical Studies)
Annals of national history and its broader international connections. This has been published since 1955 by the Institute of Historical Studies. The first two annuals were published as a supplement to the *Historický časopis,* but since the third annual, it has been published independently. Since 1984 (the twenty-seventh volume), *Historické štúdie* has been published in the form of monothematic volumes once or twice a year. The name *Historické štúdie* was given only as an additional title, and without the year. In 1993 (the thirty-fourth volume), the annual publication was renewed.

Historický časopis (Historical Journal)
The basic journal for historical interest in Slovakia. It is published by the Institute of Historical Studies. In addition to scholarly articles, it has a rich information section (jubilee articles, memorials) and section of annotations and reviews. The Historical Journal has been published since 1953 and is connected with the journal *Historica Slovaca,* with which it was published in its first seven volumes (1940-1949). Since the eighth volume, its name was changed to *Historický sborník SAVU* (Historical Annals of the Slovak Academy of Sciences and Arts). Under this name the eighth to tenth volumes were published (1950-1952). In 1953 the name was again changed to *Historický časopis.* With the name change, numbering began again from number one. Currently it is published four times a year. In 1967 the register of *Historický časopis* was published, and contained the fifteen volumes published until that time.

Slovanské štúdie (Slavic Studies)
A journal aimed at the history and culture of Slavs and other nationalities in the region of central and southeastern Europe.

This has been published since 1957. It has undergone several changes, from the original annuals, through monothematic journals and monographs (where *Slovanské štúdie* was used only as a subtitle and the year was not mentioned). Currently (since 1992) it is published twice a year with an additional monothematic issue. It is published by the Institute of Historical Studies.

Studia historica Slovaca

The foreign-language yearbook of the Institute of Historical Studies in Bratislava. It collects the latest results of Slovak historiography. The articles were printed in English, German, French and Russian, but since 1995 have been exclusively in English. It has been published since 1963.

Z dejín vied a techniky na Slovensku

(From the History of Science and Technology in Slovakia)
This annual of the Institute of Historical Studies has been published since 1962. Currently it is published in the form of monothematic yearbooks or monographs. Individual volumes are published under their own titles, where the periodical name is given only as a subtitle, and the year of publication is not mentioned.

Zborník Filozofickej fakulty Univerzity Komenského - Historica

(Annals of the Faculty of Philosophy of Comenius University - Historica)
The yearbook of the Faculty of Philosophy of Comenius University in Bratislava has been published since 1923. From the original multithematic annual, individual series, including *Historica,* developed.

Zborník Slovenského národného múzea - História

(Annals of the Slovak National Museum - History)
This is connected with the *Sborník Muzeálnej slovenskej spoločnosti,* which was founded in 1896. In the thirty-sixth and thirty-seventh volumes (1942 and 1943), the name was changed to *Sborník Slovenského národného múzea* (The Annual of the Slovak National Museum). Numbering of the volumes continued irregularly. In 1961 (volume fifty-five), the independent series *História* was founded. This series has a double numbering system. The first number is for the journal as a whole, the second for the History series. The series *Etnografia* had a similar development, and the *Archeológia* series was founded in 1991.

Periodicals from Affiliated Disciplines

Agrikultúra (Agriculture)
The annual of the Slovak Museum of Agriculture in Nitra has been published since 1962.

Biografické štúdie (Biographical Studies)
Devoted to the biographies of important Slovak personalities. It has been published since 1970 by the Matica slovenská in Martin.

Human Affairs
Containing interdisciplinary concerns of the social sciences. The journal is in English, and has been published since 1991 twice a year by the Institute of Historical Studies, Institute of Asian and African Studies and the Department of Social and Biological Communication of the Slovak Academy of Sciences.

Kniha (The Book)
The annual of the Matica slovenská in Martin on the history of book culture, it has been published since 1974.

Literárnomúzejný letopis (Annals of the Museum of Literature)
Published since 1972 by the Matica slovenská, this is the yearbook of the museum of Slovak literature.

Pamiatky a múzeá (Cultural Monuments and Museums)
This review for cultural heritage has been published since 1952. In 1961 the name was changed to *Vlastivedný časopis* (Journal of the Homeland) and in 1991 returned to the original title. It is published monthly by the Slovak National Museum, and the Institute for the Care of Historical Monuments, in Bratislava.

Slováci v zahraničí (Slovaks Abroad)
An annual publication of the Matica slovenská published since 1971.

Slovenská archeológia (Slovak Archaeology)
The basic journal of Slovak archaeologists, it has been published twice a year since 1953 by the Archaeology Institute of the Slovak Academy of Sciences in Nitra. The contributions are in Slovak, German, English, Russian and French.

Slovenská archivistika (Slovak Archival Science)
This journal of Slovak archivists has been published semi-annually since 1966. The Department of Archives of the Ministry of the Interior in Bratislava is the publisher.

Slovenská numizmatika (Slovak Numismatics)
A yearbook published since 1970, it is currently produced by the Commission for Numismatics of the Scientific Conference for Historical Sciences of the Slovak Academy of Sciences.

Slovenský národopis (Slovak Ethnology)
The basic journal of Slovak ethnologists, it has been published four times a year since 1953 by the Ethnology Institute of the Slovak Academy of Sciences in Bratislava.

Vlastivedný časopis (Journal of the Homeland)
Published monthly by the Slovak National Museum in Bratislava, 1961-1991. (See *Pamiatky a múzeá.*)

Zborník Lesníckeho, drevárskeho a poľovníckeho múzea v Antole
(Annals of the Antol Museum of Forestry, the Timber Trade, and Hunting)
An annual published since 1961.

Zborník Múzea Slovenského národného povstania
(Annals of the Museum of the Slovak National Uprising)
After the Second World War there were a number of short-lived efforts to publish a journal devoted to the Slovak National Uprising. The longest lasting of these is made up of the fifteen volumes of *Zborník Múzea SNP,* which has been published since 1976 at the Múzeum SNP in Banská Bystrica.

Zborník Slovenského banského múzea
(Annals of the Slovak Mining Museum)
Published since 1967 by the Slovak Mining Museum in Banská Štiavnica.

Periodicals on Regional History

Castrum Novum
The yearbook of the District Museum in Nové Zámky, published since 1982.

Historica Carpatica
Annual of the East Slovakia Museum in Košice, published since 1969.

Horná Nitra (Upper Nitra)
Homeland annual of the Horná Nitra Museum in Prievidza, published since 1962.

Liptov
Homeland annual of the Liptov Museum in Ružomberok, published since 1970.

Nové Obzory (New Horizons)
Social scientific annual of East Slovakia, published by the Homeland Museum of Prešov since 1959.

Stredné Slovensko (Central Slovakia)
Annual of the Central Slovakia Museum in Banská Bystrica, published since 1979.

Vlastivedné štúdie Gemera (Gemer Homeland Studies)
Yearbook published by the Gemer Homeland Society in Rimavská Sobota since 1972.

Vlastivedný zborník Považia (Považie Homeland Annals)
Published since 1972 by the Považie Museum in Žilina.

Z minulosti a prítomnosti Turca (From the Past and Present of Turiec)
Annual of the Turiec Museum of Andrej Kmeť in Martin, published since 1970.

Západné Slovensko (West Slovakia)
Homeland annual of the museums of West Slovakia. It was published by the West Slovakia Museum in Trnava from 1973-1981.

ATLASES

The development of mapmaking in Slovakia reaches back to the fifteenth century. From those days to the present it has gone through extensive change, which is manifested in works about cartography in Slovakia.[1] These provide information concerning the various divisions of Slovakia in different eras while important atlases from the last three decades accurately portray conditions to the present.

In the 1960s, an extensive historical atlas of Czechoslovakia was published.[2] It covers historical events from the oldest times to roughly the time of its publication and is the most detailed and significant historical atlas of Slovakia.

A military atlas of Czechoslovakia[3] was also published in the sixties. As usual for its type, it depicts the territory in great detail.

The basic universal geographic atlas of Slovakia is the extensive one of the Republic[4] published in the early eighties. It tries to depict not only the geography but also the socio-economic characteristics of the land. The text was published separately in Slovak and English.[5]

The latest of these extensive atlases is the ethnographic one,[6] concentrating on map depiction of chosen elements of folk culture, and covering the way of life

---

[1] PŘIKRYL, Ľubomír Viliam: Slovensko na starých mapách. Martin, Osveta 1982; PŘIKRYL, Ľubomír Viliam: Vývoj mapového zobrazovania na Slovensku. Bratislava, Veda 1977; PURGINA, Ján: Tvorcovia kartografie Slovenska do polovice 18. storočia. Bratislava, Slovenská kartografia 1972.

[2] ATLAS československých dějin. Edited by PURŠ, Jaroslav. Praha, Ústřední správa geogézie a kartografie 1965, 19 pp. 45 map units.

[3] ČESKOSLOVENSKÝ vojenský atlas. Praha, Naše vojsko 1965; ČESKOSLOVENSKÝ vojenský atlas. Seznam názvů. Praha, Naše vojsko 1966.

[4] ATLAS Slovenskej socialistickej republiky. Edited by MAZÚR, Emil - KELEMEN, Albert. Bratislava, SAV 1980, 296 maps.

[5] ATLAS Slovenskej socialistickej republiky. Textová časť. Bratislava, Veda 1982; ATLAS of the Slovak Socialist Republic. Text Part. Bratislava, Veda 1983.

[6] ETNOGRAFICKÝ atlas Slovenska. Compiled by KOVAČEVIČOVÁ, Soňa. Bratislava, Veda 1990, 535 maps.

and culture of the people for the last 150 years. Notation in English and German is included.[7]

All of these atlases were published domestically in Slovakia or the former Czechoslovakia.

Currently an interesting series of atlases on the eastern part of central Europe is being published in the United States. It will comprise ten volumes, the first of which has already appeared.[8] In addition to other central European states it also depicts Slovakia and covers the period from the fourth century until the present.

---

[7] ETHNOGRAPHIC Atlas of Slovakia. Bratislava, Etnografický ústav SAV - Veda 1994; ETNOGRAPHISCHER Atlas der Slowakei. Bratislava, Veda 1991.

[8] MAGOCSI, Paul Robert: Historical Atlas of East Central Europe. University of Washington Press 1993.

Historiography in Slovakia

PRE-HUNGARIAN PERIOD:
First to Ninth Century

The pre-Hungarian period of Slovak history is very heterogeneous. It includes the Celtic and Romano-German eras, the period of the movement of nations, Slavic origins, the Avar-Slavic period, and the era of Great Moravia. In spite of this, the character of the historiography dealing with these epochs has a specific common feature. The development of archaeological research on the whole period, on the one hand, and a stagnation of historical research, on the other, caused the analytic research of the individual periods to be marked by the archaeological approach. Questions of settlement, material culture and economic conditions were stressed and their interpretation based on archaeological material. The evaluation and interpretation of historical sources fell behind, and in most cases historical facts and realities did not provide even the basic skeleton of historical explanation. The earlier the period, the more true this is. In the post-World War II period, truly historical works dealing with the Celtic, Roman and Avar-Slavic era are very few; most of them are archaeological works which take into account, to a greater or less extent, historical development and its specific issues.

1. The Celtic Period

Articles and monographs dealing with the Celtic period in the history of Slovakia are of archaeological character, the description and analysis of archaeological locations and finds.[1] The detailed monograph on the important Celtic oppidum Pohanská of southwest Slovakia is of this type.[2]

A richer perspective on Celtic questions was inspired by revelation of Celtic Bratislava as one of the most important Celtic centers in Central Europe. Attention was devoted above all to Bratislava Celtic coinage of the Biatek

---

[1] BEŇADIK, Blažej: Obraz doby keltskej na Slovensku. In: SlArch 19, 1971, pp. 465-491; PIETA, Karol: The La Téne Period. In: Archaeological Research in Slovakia. Nitra, Archeologický ústav SAV 1981, pp. 97-112.

[2] PAULÍK, Jozef: Keltské hradisko Pohanská v Plaveckom Podhradí. Martin, Osveta 1976.

type, following many historical connections to Roman culture, from which a number of minters took their iconographic and artistic inspirations.[3] The connection with Roman culture was also found in the Celtic architecture of Bratislava.[4]

The configuration of the Bratislava Celtic oppidum, the character of its agglomeration and of the urban organism have been traced.[5]

The more broadly applicable questions of Celtic archaeology and history have been touched only sporadically by Slovak researchers; these were, above all, the questions of Celtic chronology[6] and the settlement of Celts in Slovakia.[7] Quite rich archaeological material, both old and new, from Celtic sites, made a more analytical view of the artistic development of Celts in this period in East La Téne surroundings possible.[8]

Exclusively historical issues of the Celtic period, in post-War Slovak historiography, appeared only in connection with the solution of two minor problems. Above all was the question of the extent of the Celtic territory referred to in ancient sources as Boiohaemum. The common interpretation attributing its location not only to Bohemia and Moravia but also to Slovakia was subjected to criticism which narrowed the area of Boiohaemum to southern Moravia and the adjacent region of Lower Austria.[9] This second interpretation did not receive wide currency in scientific circles. The second historical problem solved chiefly on the basis of historical sources was that of the interference of the Dacians, under the rule of Burebista, in the central Danube area, and the consequent dissolution of Boii rule in the region.[10]

---

[3] ONDROUCH, Vojtech: Keltské mince typu Biatek. Bratislava, SAV 1958; KOLNÍKOVÁ, Eva: Keltské mince na Slovensku. Bratislava, Pallas 1978.

[4] NOVOTNÝ, Bohuslav: Das oppidum in Bratislava. In: Les mouvements celtiques du Ve au Ier s. avant notre ère. Actes du XXVIIIe colloque organisé à l'ocassion du IXe Congrès Internationale des sciences Préhistoriques et Protohistoriques. Nice 1976, pp. 203-211.

[5] ZACHAR, Lev: Príspevok k problematike bratislavského oppida. In: Zb SNM 76, 1982, História 22, pp. 31-49.

[6] BEŇADIK, Blažej: Chronologické vzťahy keltských pohrebísk na Slovensku. In: SlArch 10, 1962, p. 364.

[7] TOČÍK, Anton: K otázke osídlenia juhozápadného Slovenska na zlome letopočtu. In: Archeologické rozhledy 11, 1959, p. 847.

[8] ZACHAR, Lev: Keltské umenie na Slovensku. Bratislava, Tatran 1981.

[9] ONDROUCH, Vojtech: Historische Vorausetzungen für die Limesforschung in der Tschechoslowakei. In: Limes Romanus Konferenz Nitra. Bratislava, SAV 1959, pp. 63-102.

[10] ONDROUCH, Vojtech: Historische Vorausetzungen ...; archaeological interpretion PIETA, Karol: Probleme der Erforschung der dakischen Besiedlung in der Slowakei. Traco-Dacica 3, 1982, p. 36.

Synthetic works about Celtic history in Slovakia, written within the larger context of Slovak history, conform to this trend of Celtic research from the archaeological perspective, employing only the most important historical data.[11]

2. The Romano-German Period

The basic reference work for research on the Romano-German period of Slovak history is a monograph on the "Limes" or boundary fortresses in the region of Slovakia and on the Danube.[12] This chronologically arranged, evaluated and analyzed information of ancient authors concerning Slovakia from the first to fourth centuries. In it were published the surviving inscriptions from the region, even including certain inaccuracies and shortcomings, and here at last were described from the point of view of historical and archaeological research the Roman borders of Slovakia and its individual fortresses.

An illustration drafted by Vojtech Ondrouch was added and revised after the Second World War, thanks to archaeological research on the most important sites, such as Stupava, Pác, Milanovce and Bratislava - Rusovce, Devín, Dúbravka.[13] Besides analytical books and articles, this research enabled the evaluation of the most important artistic relics from the Roman period.[14] It also made possible articles about the connection of the Slovak region with developed

---

[11] BEŇADIK, Blažej: Vojenská demokracia u keltských a germánskych kmeňov. In: Dejiny Slovenska I. Edited by HOLOTÍK, Ľudovít - TIBENSKÝ, Ján. Bratislava 1961, pp.51-57; BEŇADIK, Blažej: Doba laténska. In: Slovensko I. Dejiny. Edited by TIBENSKÝ, Ján. Bratislava, Obzor 1971, pp. 103-122; CHROPOVSKÝ, Bohuslav: Slovensko v protohistorickom období. In: Dejiny Slovenska I. Edited by MARSINA, Richard. Bratislava, Veda 1986, pp. 41-49.

[12] ONDROUCH, Vojtech: Limes Romanus na Slovensku. Bratislava, Učená spoločnosť Šafárikova 1938.

[13] For a review of individual sites and discoveries see: KOLNÍK, Titus: Prehľad a stav bádania v dobe rímskej a sťahovania národov. In: SlArch 19, 1971, pp. 449-558; KOLNÍK, Titus: The Roman and Great Migrations Periods. In: Archaeological Research in Slovakia, pp. 113-132; KOLNÍK, Titus: Archeologický výskum v Bratislave-Dúbravke. In: Najstaršie dejiny Bratislavy. Edited by HORVÁTH, Vladimír. Bratislava, Archív mesta Bratislavy 1987, pp. 75-88; KRASKOVSKÁ, Ľudmila: Gerulata - Rusovce. Rímske pohrebisko I. Bratislava, SNM 1974; PICHLEROVÁ, Magda: Gerulata - Rusovce. Rímske pohrebisko II. Bratislava, SNM 1981.

[14] ONDROUCH, Vojtech: Bohaté hroby z doby rímskej na Slovensku. Bratislava, SAV 1957; DEKAN, Ján: Apoteóza slobody na antickej mise zo Stráží. Bratislava, Pallas 1979; KOLNÍK, Titus: Neskoroantická pyxida z Čiernych Kľačian (ikonografia, datovanie a vzťahy k Veľkej Morave). In: SlArch 31, 1983, pp. 17-84; KOLNÍK, Titus: Rímske a germánske umenie na Slovensku. Bratislava, Tatran 1984.

Roman and Roman-provincial craft and trade centers, as reflected in imported material.[15]

Archaeological research was also stimulated by more developed knowledge in epigraphy[16] and numismatics.[17]

Significant for Romano-German period historiography is the growth of archaeological and historical articles devoted to specific key problems of ancient history in Slovakia. An article devoted to the analysis of the famous Ptolemy map from the second century, showing the regions above the Danube, expresses the author's doubts about the widely believed identification of Ptolemy's Leukaristos with the Roman Laugaritio, that is, with contemporary Trenčín. He points out the alternative possibilities for the site of this city (in Poland).[18] An important problem to which Slovak archaeology and historiography long devoted attention was the question of the boundaries of the Roman Empire and the trans-Danubian territory of the barbarians.[19] This re-opened the question entertained by František Křížek before the War, that the Roman boundaries were formed not by the Danube but the Little Danube, so that Slovak territory was a part of the Empire. This point of view remained hypothetical even after detailed research of the data from Ptolemy.[20]

Attention was also devoted to the question of the relations with Rome of the German states north of the central Danube, especially the "kingdoms" of Marobud and Vannius. The question of the site of Marobud was examined,

---

[15] KREKOVIČ, Eduard: Rímska importovaná keramika na Slovensku. In: SlArch 29, 1981, pp. 341-376; HEČKOVÁ, Jana: Podiel výrobných centier rímskych provincií na spoločensko-ekonomickom vývoji naddunajského barbarika vo svetle rímskych importov. In: SlArch 30, 1982, pp. 5-77; KREKOVIČ, Eduard: Rímske importy na Slovensku. In: Památky archeologické 78, 1987, pp. 231-282.

[16] ČEŠKA, Josef - HOŠEK, Radislav: Inscriptiones Pannoniae Superioris in Slovacia Transdanubiana asservata. Brno, Univerzita J. E. Purkyně 1967; HOŠEK, Radislav: Tituli latini Pannoniae superioris annis 1967-1982 in Slovacia reperti. Praha, Academia 1985.

[17] ONDROUCH, Vojtech: Nálezy keltských, antických a byzantských mincí na Slovensku. Bratislava, SAV 1964; KOLNÍKOVÁ, Eva: Rímske mince na Slovensku. Bratislava, Tatran 1980; MINAROVIČOVÁ, Elena: Rímske mince v zbierkach Slovenského národného múzea v Bratislave. Bratislava, SNM 1990.

[18] PŘIKRYL, Ľubomír V.: Leukaristos (Laugaritio) v diele Klaudia Ptolemaia. In: Laugaricio. Zborník historických štúdií k 1800. výročiu rímskeho nápisu v Trenčíne. Košice, VV 1980, pp. 13-26.

[19] DEKAN, Ján: Stand und Aufgabe der Limesforschung in der Slowakei. In: Limes Romanus Konferenz (see note 9), pp. 15-26.

[20] KŘÍŽEK, František: Das Problem der römischen Grenzen an Nordpannonischen Limes. In: Limes Romanus Konferenz, pp. 49-62; PÜSPÖKI-NAGY, Péter: Limes Romanus na Slovensku. In: Zb FFUK Historica 21, 1970, pp.129-175.

the author locating it in Moravia and adjacent Austrian territory, while previous interpretation placed it in southwest Slovakia.[21] The combination of archaeological finds and historical research allows a greater variety of opinions on the location of Vannius.[22]

Further, older archaeological and epigraphic artifacts were re-evaluated, particularly the inscription on Trenčín Rock, which was left there in 169 A.D.[23] by the army of Emperor Marcus Aurelius, and new epigraphic artifacts, which were integrated into the whole historical context. The most important find was the epitaph from Boldog which spoke about a Roman soldier, tradesman and interpreter active deep in the territory of the Quadus tribe, and was evidence for the different forms of civil and military co-existence of the Roman Empire with barbaric tribes north of the central Danube.[24] Although somewhat schematic, research on the socio-economic structure of Slovakia and its connection with the rest of the ancient world was carried out.[25]

On the basis of broader archaeological knowledge and a deeper study of written documents, the first extensive monographic synthesis of Slovak history in the Roman era was possible from an historical point of view: evaluating the historical development from the first to fourth century; drafting an ethnic map of the Slovakia of that time, emphasizing the focal points of development; the kingdom of Marobud (located correctly in Slovakia) and Vannius; and evaluating the renewal of German power in Slovakia in the third century. This work, with new finds, gave an overview of the border system, as well as taking note of the special development in barbarian lands outside of the reach of Roman power[26]. After the publication of this book, a new analytical view was possi-

---

[21] ONDROUCH, Vojtech: Historische Voraussetzungen ... (see note 9), pp. 63-102.

[22] KOLNÍK, Titus: Anfänge der germanischen Besiedlung in der Südslowakei und das Regnum Vannianum. In: Ausklang der Laténe Zivilisation und Anfänge der germanischen Besiedlung im mittleren Donaugebiet. Bratislava, SAV 1970, pp. 143-171.

[23] SZÁSZOVÁ, Helena: Trenčiansky rímsky nápis vo vedeckej a populárno-vednej literatúre. In: Laugaricio ... (see note 18), pp. 13-26.

[24] KOLNÍK, Titus: Rímsky nápis z Boldogu. In: SlArch 25, 1977, pp. 481-500; KOLNÍK, Titus: Atilius Primus - interprex, centurio und negotiator. Eine bedeutende Grabinschrift aus dem 1. Jahrhundert u.Z. im queadischen Limes-Vorland. In: Acta archaeologica Hungarica 30, 1978, pp. 61-75.

[25] ONDROUCH, Vojtech: Hospodársky a spoločenský vývin Slovenska v dobe rímskej. In: Historický sborník SAVU 10, 1952, pp. 311-323; ONDROUCH, Vojtech: K hospodárskym a kultúrnym stykom Slovenska v dobe rímskeho panstva v Podunajsku. In: HČ 2, 1954, pp. 215-231.

[26] PELIKÁN, Oldřich: Slovensko a rímske impérium. Bratislava, SVKL 1961.

ble, stressing the diversity of the relationship of Rome with the Danubian barbarian environment.[27]

Looking at a broad geographical context, articles were devoted to Roman municipal administration and town histories in Pannonia based on comparison between ancient epigraphic and historical material as well as archaeological evidence.[28]

Slovak territory outside of Roman provincial borders was not neglected. These areas, free of the influence of Roman culture and civilization, retained the traditions of previous developments anchored in the La Téne era.[29]

3. Period of the Migration of Peoples

This period of the history of Slovakia is so far absent from the historical literature. It has only been researched sufficiently from the archaeological perspective. The archaeological research has devoted itself to differentiating the ethnic groups that during this migration left their traces in Slovakia (particularly the Langobards and Huns).[30]

4. The Arrival of the Slavs and the Avaro-Slavic Period (Fifth to Eighth Centuries)

The basis for what we know about this period is the archaeological research that produced information about individual sites, material culture, and socio-

---

[27] KOLNÍK, Titus: Novšie archeologické nálezy k pobytu Rimanov na Slovensku. In: Laugaricio ... (see note 18), pp. 37-72.

[28] VALACHOVIČ, Pavol: Rímska municipálna správa v západnej a južnej Panónii v 1.-3. storočí n.l. In: HČ 37, 1989, pp. 95-119; VALACHOVIČ, Pavol: Rímska municipálna správa v Panónii v mestách na dunajskom limite v 1.-3. storočí n.l. In: Zb FFUK Historica 35-36, 1985-1986, pp. 23-47; VALACHOVIČ, Pavol: Ammianus Marcellinus a mestá v Panónii v 4.storočí n.l. In: Zb FFUK Historica 37, 1987, pp. 3-13.

[29] PIETA, Karol: Die Púchov Kultur. Nitra, Archeologický ústav SAV 1982.

[30] An overview of ancient finds: KOLNÍK, Titus: Prehľad a stav bádania o dobe rímskej a sťahovaní národov. In: SlArch 19, 1971, pp. 534-539; concerning the incursions into Slovakia by the Huns see: KOLNÍKOVÁ, Eva: Nález neskororímskych solidov v Bíni, okr. Nové Zámky. (K minciam z doby sťahovania národov na Slovensku.) In: Numizmatický zborník 10, 1967-1968, pp. 5-50; for the newest discoveries and interpretations see: ŠTEFANOVIČOVÁ, Tatiana: Osudy starých Slovanov. Martin, Osveta 1989, pp. 11-17, 25-27; PIETA, Karol: Die Völkerwanderungszeit in der Slowakei. In: Germanen, Hunnen und Awaren. Schätze der Völkerwanderungszeit. Nürnberg 1987, pp. 383-414; NOVOTNÝ, Bohuslav: Šarovce. Bratislava, SAV 1975.

economic and territorial conditions.[31] It is also possible to trace from an historical perspective the heightened interest in the narrative documents from this period, translated and published in part. This involved in particular fragments of the most important Latin authors (Jordanes, Fredegar and P.D.) and the Greek-Byzantine ones (Prokopios, Menander, Pseudo-Maurikios, Theophylaktus and Simokattes).[32] The drawbacks of this publication are disconnected fragments that are too brief, making it impossible to evaluate the whole informational context, and an insufficient critical apparatus which is limited to the most basic guidance and explanation.

With the connection of archaeological research and the study of written sources, it was possible to answer many of the questions of the Slavic and Avaro-Slavic period on a comparative and interdisciplinary basis. Attention was devoted chiefly to Slavic ethno-genesis and the arrival of Slavs on Slovak territory. Information on the presence of Slavs in the Danube territory[33] was analyzed on a number of occasions, while archaeological results, especially, allowed the currently accepted conclusion that the Slavic tribes were arriving in Slovakia during the fifth century, presumably in two main waves: one connected to the Prague ceramic types, and the other to an older one[34]. Analysis of

---

[31] An overview of ancient research, finds and interpretations published in: DEKAN, Ján: Vývoj a stav archeologického výskumu doby predveľkomoravskej. In: SlArch 19, 1971, pp. 559-580; ČILINSKÁ, Zlata: The Pre-Great Moravian Period. In: Archaeological Research in Slovakia, pp. 133-150; information concerning individual finds and sites were published in: Významné slovanské nálezy na Slovensku. Bratislava, SAV 1978.

[32] RATKOŠ, Peter: Pramene k dejinám Veľkej Moravy. Bratislava, SAV 1964 and 1968.

[33] DEKAN, Ján: Začiatky slovenských dejín a Ríša veľkomoravská. Bratislava, SAVU 1951; KUČERA, Matúš: Typológia včasnostredovekého štátu na strednom Dunaji. In: ČSČH 27, 1979, pp. 856-884; KUČERA, Matúš: Veľká Morava a začiatky našich národných dejín. In: HČ 33, 1985, pp. 163-200.

[34] BIALEKOVÁ, Darina: Nové včasnoslovanské nálezy z juhozápadného Slovenska. In: SlArch 10, 1962, pp. 109-120; BIALEKOVÁ, Darina: Zur Datierung der oberen Grenze der Prager Typus in der Südwestslowakei. In: Archeologické rozhledy 20, 1968, pp. 619-625; FUSEK, Gabriel: Zur Problematik der frühslawischen Besiedlung in der West- und Mittelslowakei. In: Interaktionen der mitteleuropäischen Slawen und anderen Ethnika im 6.-10. Jahrhundert. Nitra, Archeologický ústav SAV 1984, pp. 105-107; TOČÍK, Anton: Význam posledných archeologických výskumov na Slovensku pre najstaršie dejiny Slovanov a Veľkej Moravy. In: HČ 3, 1955, pp. 410-421. For a different view, that the Prague type is a general stage in the development of the Slavs, see: KUDLÁČEK, Jozef: K začiatkom slovanského osídlenia na území Československa. In: HČ 4, 1958, pp. 72-92; TOČÍK, Anton: Slováci na strednom Dunaji v 5.-8. storočí. In: O počiatkoch slovenských dejín. Compiled by RATKOŠ, Peter. Bratislava, SAV 1965, pp. 20-35; FUSEK, Gabriel: Archeologické doklady k najstaršiemu slovanskému osídleniu Slovenska. In: Slavica Slovaca 28, 1993, pp. 30-35.

sources (Priscus, and Nestor's chronicle) from an historical point of view, skeptically accepted the possibility of autochthonous development of the Slavs in the central Danube region.[35] It was impossible to prove the presence of the eastern Slavic tribal union of the Ants in an acceptable way.[36]

In the last thirty years, archaeological research has solved the important question of the penetration of Avars in the territory of Slovakia in the sixth and seventh centuries and observed that in this period it is possible to conclude that they occupied the narrow territory of the region adjacent to the Danube.[37] Connected with this is the often discussed question of the so-called empire of Samo, the first Slavic tribal union (ca. 623-658): its location and connection to the Avars. Generally accepted in the Slovak archaeological and historical literature is the theory that the Samo empire spread on the territory of southwest Slovakia and southern Moravia.[38] The attempt to narrow the occupation to southern Moravia and Lower Austria[39] was not accepted. A single version of the genesis and foundation of the Samo empire is widespread in Slovak historiography; however, it depends too much on the Frankish chronicler Fredegar, though it is obvious that his account bears folk and traditional elements, and is not integrated and trustworthy. There is no doubt that the Samo empire was founded as a response to the violent rule of the Avars in the Danubian region and that this resistance was successful.[40] The growth of the power of the empire of Samo was accompanied by a confrontation with the empire of the Franks.[41]

---

[35] AVENARIUS, Alexander: Začiatky Slovanov na strednom Dunaji: autochtonistická teória vo svetle súčaného bádania. In: HČ 40, 1992, pp. 1-16.

[36] ČILINSKÁ, Zlata: K otázke príchodu Antov na stredný Dunaj. In: Sborník prací Filosofické fakulty Brněnské university, Brno 1989-1990, pp. 19-25.

[37] EISNER, Ján: Děvínská Nová Ves - slovanské pohřebiště. Bratislava, SAV 1952; ČILINSKÁ, Zlata: W kwestii pobytu Awarów v Karpatach slowackich. In: Acta archaeologica Carpatica 4, 1962, pp. 159-175.

[38] ČILINSKÁ, Zlata: Zur Frage des Samos Reiches. In: Rapports du III⁰ Congrés Internationale d'Archéologie Slave 2, Bratislava, SAV 1980, pp. 79-86; KUČERA, Matúš: Veľká Morava a začiatky našich národných dejín. In: HČ 33, 1985, p. 176 ff.; KUČERA, Matúš: Postavy veľkomoravskej histórie. Martin, Osveta 1986.

[39] AVENARIUS, Alexander: Slovania v severozápadnom pomedzí Avarského kaganátu. In: Zborník prác Ľ. Kraskovskej k životnému jubileu. Bratislava, SNM 1984, pp. 151-158.

[40] Compare with the work cited in note 38. CHROPOVSKÝ, Bohuslav: Slovensko na úsvite dejín. Bratislava, Obzor 1970; DEKAN, Ján: Začiatky slovenských dejín ... (see note 33); some doubts about the veracity of the interpretation of Fredegar were raised by ŠTEFANOVIČOVÁ, Tatiana: Osudy starých Slovanov, p. 34 ff.; SEDLÁK, Vincent: Historicko-spoločenský vývin Slovanov v dunajsko-karpatskej oblasti (so zreteľom na predkov Slovákov). In: Slavica Slovaca 27, 1992, pp. 177-186.

[41] AVENARIUS, Alexander: Die Awaren in Europa. Bratislava-Amsterdam, Hakkert 1974.

The relations between these two empires is traced in archaeological material, mainly finds of Frankish (western) arms.[42]

For the second half of the seventh and the whole of the eighth century, written documents about the history of Slovakia in the Avaro-Slavic period are absent; thus tracing the fate of Slovakia was based exclusively on archaeological finds. By this means primarily questions of the change in material culture were solved. At places where beaten tin ornaments existed appeared molded bronze ornaments with new (floral, zoomorfic and anthropomorfic) motifs. An analysis of this change found that this was an expression of the development of the civilization and not (according to Slovak archaeologists) caused by the arrival of a new ethnic group in Pannonia[43] or a second wave of Avar incursions.

Archaeological material shows that despite the further expansion of the Avar race to northern Slovakia and the stronger Avar presence in this region,[44] Avar society gradually developed into more settled forms of life. Their own agriculture and craft began to play a larger role in their economy,[45] compared to earlier times when they plundered the Byzantine and Frankish empires. Although these invasions also took place in the seventh century, they were less frequent. Byzantine coins and luxury goods still came as a *tributum pacis* from

---

[42] ZÁBOJNÍK, Jozef: K výskytu predmetov západného pôvodu na pohrebiskách z obdobia avarskej ríše v Dunajskej kotline. In: SlArch 36, 1978, pp. 193-211; MINÁČ, Vladimír: O osídlení Bratislavskej brány v 7.-8. stor. In: Zb SNM 72, Historica 18, 1978, pp. 61-81.

[43] DEKAN, Ján: Les motifs figuraux humains sur les bronzes moulés de la zone danubienne centrale a l'epoque prècèdant l'empire de la Grand Moravie. In: SHS 2, 1964, pp. 52-102; DEKAN, Ján: Herkunft und Ethnizität der gegossenen Bronzenindustrie des 8. Jahrhunderts. In: SlArch 20, 1972, pp. 317-452.

[44] For the analysis of individual gravesites: ČILINSKÁ, Zlata: Slawisch-awarisches Gräberfeld in Nové Zámky. Bratislava, SAV 1966; ČILINSKÁ, Zlata: Frühmittelalterliches Gräberfeld in Želovce. Bratislava, SAV 1973; KRASKOVSKÁ, Ľudmila: Slovensko-avarské pohrebisko pri Záhorskej Bystrici. Bratislava, SNM 1972; TOČÍK, Anton: Slawisch-awarisches Gräberfeld in Holiare. Bratislava, SAV 1968; TOČÍK, Anton: Slawisch-awarisches Gräberfeld in Štúrovo. Bratislava, SAV 1968.

[45] DEKAN, Ján: Vývoj a stav archeologického výskumu doby predveľkomoravskej (see note 31), pp. 574-575; ČILINSKÁ, Zlata: Sociálno-ekonomická problematika vo svetle pohrebísk juhozápadného Slovenska. In: O počiatkoch slovenských dejín, p. 49; ČILINSKÁ, Zlata: Anfänge des spezializierten Handwerks und Handels bei altslawischen Gesellschaft in der Slowakei. In: SlArch 34, 1986, p. 299 ff; ČILINSKÁ, Zlata: The development of the Slavs North of the Danube during the Avar Empire and their Social - Cultural Contribution to Great Moravia. In: SlArch 13, 1983, pp. 237-275; ZÁBOJNÍK, Jozef: On the Problems of Settlements of the Avar Khaganates Period in Slovakia. In: Archeologické rozlety 40, 1988, pp. 401-437.

Byzantium.[46] More intensive Avar-Slavic symbiosis gradually developed contributing to the decline of the Avars as a separate ethnic group in central Europe. We can trace this final end of the Avar empire in written sources, particular Frankish chronicles. Their analysis shows reference to the Avars disappearing in 822 which argues against claims of Avaro-Hungarian continuity. Examination of the last information on the Avars concerns their conversion to Christianity (the baptism of Kapkan Theodore); the invasion of the army of Charles the Great and his son Pippin against the Avars in 796 and 803; and the synod of the Frankish church, considering in 796 the possibility or necessity of Christianization of the invaded Avar territory.[47]

5. The Great Moravian Period

Written sources provide the basis for analysis of the Great Moravian period in Slovak history. This is in contrast to previous periods, when archaeology was necessary for full elaboration. In the above mentioned work by Peter Ratkoš, the whole documentary basis was made available, including Byzantine chronicles, Latin annals, letters, documents, and Slavic historical and hagiographic sources. However, even in this book the broader historical commentary is missing. The publication of the Life of Methodius, as well as some later sources, with an apparatus of explanatory notes, filled this gap.[48]

The scholarly edition of Great Moravian documentary material and letters, in the context of the first Slovak collection of charters (*Codex diplomaticus ...*) , was supported by the critical evaluation of historically doubtful material (chiefly the letter of 869 from Pope Hadrian II to Rastislav, Svätopluk and Koceľ), and also by the study of copies of lost letters which are possibly of Great Moravian origin.[49] It is the most reliable modern critical edition of Latin letters in Great Moravian history.[50]

---

[46] SVOBODA, Bedřich: Poklad byzantského kovotepce v Zemianskom Vrbovku. In: Památky archeologické 44, 1953, p. 33 ff.; RADOMERSKÝ, Pavol: Byzantská mince z pokladu v Zemianskom Vrbovku. In: Památky archeologické 44, 1953, p. 109 ff.

[47] RATKOŠ, Peter: Historiche-Quellen und die sogenannte Awarisch-magyarische Kontinuität. In: Študijné zvesti Archeologického ústavu 16, 1968, pp. 183-192.

[48] PAULÍNY, Eugen - ONDRUŠ, Šimon: Život a dielo Metoda prvoučiteľa národa slovienskeho. Bratislava, Tatran 1985.

[49] MARSINA, Richard: Štúdie k slovenskému diplomatáru I/1. In: HŠt 16, 1971, pp. 5-108; MARSINA, Richard: Veľkomoravské deperditá. In: SlArchiv 6, 1971, pp. 18-44.

[50] Codex diplomaticus et epistolaris Slovaciae I. Edited by MARSINA, Richard. Bratislava, SAV 1971.

Although the elaboration of the Great Moravian period is largely accomplished through historical analysis of written material, archaeology has a significant contribution to make. In addition to reviews of the literature compiling basic works devoted to individual sites,[51] other work was done summarizing the whole situation of material culture, settlement, the economy, and the life of Great Moravian society, comparing this information to historical data.[52] Some Slavic Great Moravian sites were analyzed, whose importance lay in the wider Slavic agglomeration and its life (Pobedím),[53] and showed the contribution of Great Moravian architecture (Ducové, Devín, and particularly Bratislava Castle).[54] Archaeological research on the Great Moravian legacy led to a less formal treatment of the art of Great Moravia.[55]

Slovak archaeologists and historians (mostly in the 1950s but also later) devoted much attention to the economic and social questions of the history of Great Moravian society.

Thus, from the beginning of the sixties[56] was constructed a concept of the role of a synthetic history of Slovakia, reflecting the results of discussions between archaeologists and historians concerning the form of the Great Moravian state. They tried to answer the questions of the structure and social stratification of society, often reflecting a priori morals rather than the quality of the sources, which even today appear unable to support these ideas.[57] Together with these

---

[51] Významné slovanské náleziská na Slovensku. Compiled by CHROPOVSKÝ, Bohuslav. Bratislava, Veda 1978; for an overview of Great Moravian sites see CHROPOVSKÝ, Bohuslav: Vývoj a stav archeologického výskumu doby veľkomoravskej. In: SlArch 19, 1971, pp. 581-601.

[52] CHROPOVSKÝ, Bohuslav: Slovensko na úsvite dejín. Bratislava, Obzor 1970; ŠTEFANO-VIČOVÁ, Tatiana: Osudy starých Slovanov, (see note 30).

[53] VENDTOVÁ, Viera: Slovanské osídlenie Pobedima a okolia. In: SlArch 17, 1969, pp. 119-237; BIALEKOVÁ, Darina: Pobedim - slovanské hradiská a sídliská z 9. storočia. Nitra, Archeologický ústav SAV 1975.

[54] RUTTKAY, Alexander: Ducové. Veľkomoravský veľmožský dvorec a včasnostredoveké pohrebisko. Nitra, Archeologický ústav 1975; ŠTEFANOVIČOVÁ, Tatiana: Bratislavský hrad v 9.-12. storočí. Bratislava, Obzor 1975; PLACHÁ, Veronika - HLAVICOVÁ, Jana - KELLER, Igor: Slovanský Devín. Bratislava, Obzor 1990.

[55] DEKAN, Ján: Veľká Morava. Doba a umenie. Bratislava, Tatran 1976.

[56] RATKOŠ, Peter: Počiatky feudalizmu na Slovensku. In: Dejiny Slovenska I. Bratislava 1961, pp. 85-118.

[57] RATKOŠ, Peter: Počiatky feudalizmu na Slovensku. In: HČ 2, 1954, pp. 252-276; KRAJČO-VIČ, Rudolf: Počiatky feudalizmu u nás vo svetle jazykových faktorov. In: HČ 6, 1956, pp. 222-234; KUČERA, Matúš: Problémy vzniku a vývoja feudalizmu na Slovensku. In: HČ 22, 1974, pp. 856-883; RATKOŠ, Peter: Slovensko v dobe veľkomoravskej. Košice, VV 1988.

questions, research was done on the ethnic origin of the Great Moravian inhabitants, with scholars coming to more or less unambiguous results on the nature of "Great Moravian" nationality.[58]

There was also attention given to Great Moravia's territorial scale and expansion, especially in the period of Svätopluk. In connection with this, information from Constantine Porphyrogennetos on the location of Great Moravia was analyzed, though the conclusion was ambiguous.[59] Research on the possible border of Great Moravia with Bulgaria was built on a broader basis, and on analysis of written documents connected with the period of Svätopluk, which led to the not absolutely certain conclusion that the ruler's empire crossed the Danube and reached the Tisa River.[60]

In the broader geo-political and historical framework were articles dealing with the importance of this state for the history of Slovakia.[61]

In the course of the sixties and seventies, the problems of the political history of the Great Moravian state comes even more to the foreground. From this perspective the first post-War analysis of the history of this period was written, which didn't need to concern itself with questions of material culture, because these formed the contents of an independent unit.[62] With this division analytical problems were well served since interpretation did not need to be submerged in details or raised to excessively universal formulations, but could concentrate on analysis of written documents. It is interesting that the author paid little attention to the issues of the mission of Cyril and Methodius, since this forms a part of all other treatments of Great Moravia. The author of an article from the early seventies on Great Moravia proceeds in a similar fashion. In contrast to all other interpretations, this article has the advantage of not dividing into special chap-

---

[58] RATKOŠ, Peter: K otázke etnického charakteru Veľkej Moravy. In: O vzájomných vzťahoch Čechov a Slovákov, pp. 23-37; KUDLÁČEK, Jozef: K otázke o vznikaní národnosti na našom území. In: HČ 4, 1956, p. 397 ff; KRAJČOVIČ, Rudolf: Problém vzniku slovenského národa z jazykového hľadiska. In: HČ 5, 1957, pp. 483-492; DEKAN, Ján: Veľká Morava a problém staromoravskej národnosti. In: HČ 20, 1972, pp. 173-185.

[59] DEKAN, Ján: Príspevok o otázke politických hraníc Veľkej Moravy. In: Historica Slovaca 5, 1948, pp. 206-209; RATKOŠ, Peter: Pramene... (see note 32), p. 310 note 1.

[60] Dejiny Slovenska I. Bratislava 1986, pp. 88-163. RATKOŠ, Peter: Územný vývoj Veľkej Moravy. Fikcie a skutočnosť. In: HČ 3, 1955, pp. 200-220.

[61] KUČERA, Matúš: Veľká Morava a začiatky našich národných dejín. In: HČ 33, 1985, pp. 163-199; KUČERA, Matúš: Veľká Morava a slovenské dejiny. In: Velká Morava a počátky česko-slovenské státnosti. Bratislava, Obzor 1985, pp. 245-272.

[62] Slovensko v praveku. Compiled by VARSIK, Branislav. Bratislava, SAVU 1947; DEKAN, Ján: Začiatky slovenských dejín a Ríša veľkomoravská. Bratislava, SAVU 1951.

ters political, economic, social and cultural development, but treats them together.[63] Similarly to the next synthesis from the mid-eighties, here we can trace an effort towards uniform interpretation of the whole Great Moravian history, including issues following the death of Svätopluk.[64] The attempt to fill in minor details of political development at the close of the Great Moravian state is apparent also in a more recent book devoted to this period.[65] The history of politics and other aspects of Great Moravian society (e.g. cultural relations) were discussed in individual smaller treatments of particular rulers and other figures of the period. This book gives a thorough picture of different aspects of Great Moravian history and in addition tries to capture and evaluate the role of individual actors in its events.[66]

Slovak historiography has devoted special attention to questions of culture and church, particularly the effects of Cyril and Methodius' mission. As far as preceding events, little has been written about the Irish-Scottish and Frankish missions, and this has tended to concentrate on linguistic and literary history. Similarly, treatment of Benedictine activity before or contemporary with Cyril and Methodius on Slovak territory has only reached a draft stage with ambiguous results.[67]

Concerning the mission of Cyril and Methodius, there was analysis of questions connected with their Byzantine education and cultural profile, and their roots in the Byzantine theological and philosophical tradition which they carried to Great Moravia. There was also treatment of the modification of Byzantine culture in new surroundings. Tracing of Byzantine cultural penetration in the material culture followed.[68]

Analysis addressed both the broad scale and individual documents and artifacts.[69] The *Freising fragments* received significant attention and their examina-

---

[63] Slovensko. Dejiny. Bratislava, Obzor 1971, pp. 173-210.

[64] Dejiny Slovenska I. Bratislava, Veda 1986, pp. 118-124.

[65] KUČERA, Matúš: Postavy veľkomoravskej histórie. Martin, Osveta 1985.

[66] RATKOŠ, Peter: Slovensko v dobe Veľkomoravskej. Košice, VV 1988.

[67] PAULÍNY, Eugen: Slovesnosť a kultúrny jazyk Veľkej Moravy. Bratislava, SVKL 1964; RATKOŠ, Peter: Kristianizácia Veľkej Moravy pred misiou Cyrila a Metoda. In: HČ 19, 1971, pp. 71-83.

[68] AVENARIUS, Alexander: Byzantská kultúra v slovanskom prostredí v 6.-12. storočí. Bratislava, Veda 1992; AVENARIUS, Alexander: Byzantský podiel na vytváraní veľkomoravskej kultúry. In: HČ 33, 1985, pp. 240-256; ŠTEFANOVIČOVÁ, Tatiana: K byzantským prvkom v šperkárstve predveľkomoravského obdobia v oblasti Bratislavy. In: Zborník prác Ľ. Kraskovskej. Bratislava, SNM 1984, pp. 211-215; VARSÍK, Vladimír: Byzantinische Gürtelschallen im mittleren und unteren Donauraum im 6. und 7. Jahrhundert. In: SlArch 40, 1992, pp. 77-108.

[69] PAULÍNY, Eugen: Slovesnosť a kultúrny jazyk Veľkej Moravy. Bratislava, SVKL 1964.

tion proved their translation from Upper German origin, making them the most important evidence of the penetration of western missionaries into Slovak territory.[70]

Issues concerning the church also drew attention. Within Marsina's chronologically broader article, he analyzes information about the origins of the Nitra bishopric, particularly in connection with the activities of Bishop Viching,[71] and issues of the Slavic liturgy. On the basis of diplomatic history, he questions the authenticity of the letter from the Pope in 869 permitting the Slavic liturgy in Great Moravia as it is preserved in the Life of Methodius.[72]

Research, primarily of cultural and historical issues of Great Moravia, led to the production of analytical books. In addition to a brief popular review[73] on the occasion of Methodius' anniversary, a book treating the issues of Cyril and (primarily) Methodius' mission in the larger context of Great Moravian history and culture, employing results of analytical study on Great Moravian written documents, is so far the most complex approach to these issues.[74]

Several articles have been devoted to the issues of the Great Moravian legacy. These analyze its tradition in the context of the Hungarian state[75] and deal with Benedictine mission activity in Nitra during and after the Great Moravian period.[76]

[70] ISAČENKO, Alexander: Jazyk a pôvod Frizinských pamiatok. Bratislava, SAVU 1943; ISAČENKO, Alexander: Začiatky vzdelanosti vo Veľkomoravskej ríši. Turčiansky Sv. Martin, MS 1948.

[71] MARSINA, Richard: Nitrianske biskupstvo a jeho biskupi od 9. do polovice 13. storočia. In: HČ 41, 1993, pp. 529-543.

[72] MARSINA, Richard: Povolenie slovanskej liturgie na Veľkej Morave. In: HČ 18, 1970, pp. 4-16; RATKOŠ, Peter: Slavische liturgische Sprache im Lichte der päpstlichen Politik in den Jahren 869-880. In: SHS 7, 1974, pp. 185-204.

[73] BAGIN, Anton: Apoštoli Slovanov. Cyril a Metod a Veľká Morava. Bratislava, Spolok sv. Vojtecha 1987.

[74] MARSINA, Richard: Metodov boj. Bratislava, Obzor 1985.

[75] RATKOŠ, Peter: Anonymove Gesta Hungarorum a ich pramenná hodnota. In: HČ 31, 1983, pp. 825-870; STEINHÜBEL, Ján: Veľkomoravská historická tradícia naddunajských Slovanov. In: HČ 38, 1990, pp. 693-705.

[76] KÚTNIK, Jozef: O pôvode pustovníka Svorada. (K počiatkom kultúrnych dejín Liptova.) In: Nové obzory 11, 1969, pp. 5-122.

Studia historica Slovaca XX, 1995

SLOVAK HISTORIOGRAPHY ON THE MIDDLE AGES:
Early Tenth to the Early Sixteenth Century

Around 906, a large part of the territory of present-day Slovakia came under the sway of the old Hungarian tribal union. Subsequently the whole territory became part of the Hungarian state and fell under Magyar hegemony. The originally exclusively Slavic character of the inhabitants of Slovak territory, the precursors of contemporary Slovaks, was changed by the old Magyar tribal union so that in southern Slovakia numerous Magyars settled, whose descendants live there to the present. Already at the tenth century, the previously second most important Great Moravian center of Nitra became the seat of the appanage dukes of the Arpád family and remained such into the twelfth century. In the eleventh century, southwestern Slovakia became the target of military adventures from the German Empire which was seeking to make a vassal state of Hungary. During the second half of the twelfth century, Germans settled the Spiš district. From the thirteenth century are found German settlers in towns with city privileges. Slovakia was among the most urbanized parts of the Kingdom of Hungary. Based on available sources, the settlement of Slovakia can be traced in greater detail only from the beginning of the thirteenth century. From those times, we can prove more concretely intensive mining enterprises, although the extraction of precious metal ores, as well as of iron and copper, were undoubtedly older. In the fifteenth century, Slovakia was the territory upon which took place most of the dynastic struggles for the Hungarian crown.[1]

The real growth of Slovak historiography dealing with the Middle Ages only occurred in the 1950s. Thus I will concentrate mostly on this period, mentioning chiefly books, and only the most important articles from journals and annals. Before starting with an evaluation of editions of narrative and diplomatic sources on Slovak history, it is necessary to provide a few theoretical historiographical remarks. Slovak history is not the same as the history of a "Slovak" state since, from the earliest times the Slovaks have been a part of state units

---

[1] Compare with the older review MARSINA, Richard: L'Historiographie Slovaque du Moyen âge en 1960-1977. In: SHS 11, 1980, pp. 69-99.

over which people of other languages had hegemony. The subject of Slovak history must be understood as the research of the territory and the inhabitants of Slovakia.[2] During the course of the struggle of the Communist Party with so-called bourgeois nationalism, the term Slovak history became unacceptable and officially ceased to exist during the early 1950s. It was replaced by the concept of Czechoslovak history which is, in scholarly terms, equally anachronistic or incorrect. It lacks both a territorial and a national subject since Czechoslovakia did not exist until 1918 and a Czechoslovak "nation" did not exist as a specific ethnic group. Thus, it is not possible to speak of Czechoslovak history prior to 1918.[3]

Much attention was devoted to research on settlement and development of towns in the Middle Ages, from the urban development, legal, economic (including mining) and social points of view. Little was devoted to solving the questions of economic history in the more narrow sense or to politics, and hardly any to research of the nobility. Only in recent years has research intensified on the church, and few significant results have been produced on the development of medieval culture (codicological literature and schools). Work on the development of architecture and the arts has had better results (the focus of the research of a special discipline). The editions of medieval sources on the history of the Slovak region, written nearly exclusively in Latin, were until 1918 included in general Hungarian editions. Two regions of Slovakia, the counties of Spiš and Šariš, already had resource editions in print by the eighteenth century.[4] In the late 1930s, there was an attempt to publish so-called *Slovenský diplomatár,* including the documents of only some municipal and family archives.[5] Contemporaneously, editions appeared containing our oldest documents, written in Slovacized Czech (coming from the fifteenth century), and the translation

---

[2] RAPANT, Daniel: Národ a dejiny. In: Prúdy 8, 1924, pp. 470-477; compare also Československé dejiny. Problémy a metódy. In: Od pravěku k dnešku. Sborník k narozeninám Josefa Pekaře II. Praha 1930, pp. 531-563.

[3] MARSINA, Richard: Slovenské dejiny (1. K otázke pomenovania). In: HČ 38, 1990, pp. 625-638.

[4] WAGNER, Carolus (Ed.): Analecta Scepusii sacri et profani I.-II. Vindobonae 1774; III.-IV. Posonii-Cassoviae 1778; WAGNER, Carolus: Diplomatarium comitatus Sarosiensis. Cassoviae 1780; compare also BÁRDOSY, Joannes - SCHMAUK, Michael (Ed.): Supplementum analectorum terrae Scepusiensis. Leutschoviae 1802; SCHMAUK, Michael - HRADSZKY, Josephus (Ed.): Supplementum analectorum terrae Scepusiensis II. Szepesváraliae 1889; WEBER, Samu (Ed.): Supplementum analectorum terrae Scepusiensis III. Löcse 1908.

[5] JERŠOVÁ-OPOČENSKÁ, Mária: Slovenský diplomatár. In: Príloha Sborníka Muzeálnej spoločnosti slovenskej 25-30, 1931-1936.

of the Magdeburg law from German of 1473[6] (for in those days the leaders of the applicable city council did not speak sufficient German). Slightly later documents from the family archive of Okoličáni (1248-1487) was published. The critical preparation work for this edition was analysis of the forgeries produced by Ján of Madočany, who lived in the second half of the fourteenth century,[7] for a number of his falsifications are included in this archive to the present. Another volume of Slovak written documents, from the fifteenth and sixteenth centuries, was also published, and there was a thematic edition of documents dealing with the uprisings of miners in Banská Bystrica in 1525-1526.[8]

In the later fifties, a plan was created for systematic publication of the oldest documentary and letter sources of the history of Slovakia to the end of the thirteenth century.[9] After many years of study in domestic and foreign archives, scholars recorded all the documents up to 1387 (in foreign archives up to 1526), and started to elaborate the first part of the Slovak collection of charters, containing documents from the earliest times (805) to 1235. This was finished in the first half of 1966, and published five years later.[10] For the preparation of the Slovak *Codex diplomaticus,* one of the guides to origin and authenticity was the hand of the writer, which demanded research of many original documents not published in this collection of charters because, for instance, only one third of the documents from the Hungarian Royal Office are included.

From this heuristic base, the beginning of publication of documents and letters from the fourteenth century was made possible, though because of their

---

[6] CHALOUPECKÝ, Václav (Ed.): Kniha Žilinská. Bratislava, Učená společnost Šafaříkova 1934; CHALOUPECKÝ, Václav: Středověké listiny ze Slovenska. Bratislava-Praha, Melantrich 1937.

[7] HÚŠČAVA, Alexander (Ed.): Archív zemianskeho rodu z Okoličného. Bratislava, Academia scientiarum et artium Slovaca 1943; HÚŠČAVA, Alexander: Ján Literát a liptovské falzá. Bratislava, USŠ 1936.

[8] VARSIK, Branislav (Ed.): Slovenské listy a listiny z XV. a XVI. storočia. Bratislava, Vydavateľstvo SAV 1956; RATKOŠ, Peter (Ed.): Dokumenty k dejinám baníckeho povstania 1525-1526. Bratislava, Vydavateľstvo SAV 1957; GÁCSOVÁ, Alžbeta (Ed.): Dokumenty k protifeudálnym bojom slovenského ľudu (1113-1848). Bratislava, Vydavateľstvo SAV 1955.

[9] MARSINA, Richard: O potrebe a zásadách vydávania Slovenského diplomatára. In: HČ 5, 1957, pp. 297-314; compare also MARSINA, Richard: Urkundenbuch der Slowakei und sein Program. In: SHS 3, 1965, pp. 263-285; MARSINA, Richard: Diplomatická medievistika na Slovensku (Predmet, stav a úlohy). In: SlArchiv 2, 1967, pp. 29-46.

[10] MARSINA, Richard (Ed.): Codex diplomaticus et epistolaris Slovaciae (CDSI) I. 805-1235. Bratislava, Academia scientiarum Slovaca 1971. XLVIII + 472 pp. + XXV illustrative tables.

quantity they had to be published in the form of abstracts. The first part contains abstracts from letters and documents from 1301 to 1314.[11] A second volume of both basic editions was published, containing material from 1235-1260, and a second volume of the abstracts, from 1315-1323.[12] Of the oldest grants of privileges to towns in Slovakia a first volume was published containing those from 1238-1350.[13] The preparation of this edition is still in process, but because of unavailability of sufficient financial resources there is little hope of publishing the finished volumes.

In parallel with the preparation of the Slovak *Codex diplomaticus,* the validity of many documents was researched, the results of which were published in *Studies for the Slovak Collection of Charters I/1-2.*[14] *Studies for the Slovak Collection of Charters II.* includes paleographic and diplomatic evaluation, and tries to describe the beginnings of many publishing institutions active in later centuries of the Middle Ages ("trustworthy places" and counties).[15] In addition to the studies for the Slovak collection of charters there were also prepared different studies addressing the authenticity of documents. The two oldest originals preserved in Slovakia, from the Zobor monastery in 1111 and 1113,[16] were very carefully analyzed. Subjects of research were questionable sections of the Podolinec document from 1244; the Bardejov document of 1247; different executions of the founding charter of Premonstratensian abbey in Turiec (Kláštor pod Znievom); the privilege for Spišské Vlachy from 1243; the question of the precise dating of privileges for Spiš towns; and the oldest preserved documents of the cloister in Klíž.[17] Within preparatory work (of

---

[11] SEDLÁK, Vincent (Ed.): Regesta diplomatica nec non epistolaria Slovaciae (RDSI) I. 1301-1314. Bratislavae, Academia scientiarum Slovaca 1980. 651 pp. + 16 illustrative tables.

[12] MARSINA, Richard (Ed.): CDSI II. 1235-1260. Bratislavae, Obzor 1987. XXXII + 608 pp. + XXV illustrative tables; SEDLÁK, Vincent (Ed.): RDSI II. 1315-1323. Bratislavae, Academia scientiarum Slovaca 1987. 634 pp. + 4 illustrative tables.

[13] JUCK, Ľubomír (Ed.): Výsady miest a mestečiek na Slovensku I. 1238-1350. Bratislava, Veda 1984.

[14] MARSINA, Richard: Štúdie k Slovenskému diplomatáru I/1. In: HŠt 16, 1971, pp. 5-108; I/2. In: HŠt 18, 1973, pp. 5-119.

[15] MARSINA, Richard: Štúdie k Slovenskému diplomatáru II. Bratislava, Veda 1989.

[16] MARSINA, Richard: K problematike najstarších zoborských listín. I. In: HŠt 7, 1961, pp. 202-220; II.-V. In: SbFFUK Historica 14, 1963, pp. 1-36.

[17] BEŇKO, Ján: Problém pravosti podolineckej listiny z r. 1244. In: SlArchiv 3, 1968, pp. 312-329; VARSIK, Branislav: K otázke falza bardejovskej listiny z r. 1247. In: SlArchiv 10, 1975, pp. 141-150; AVENARIUS, Alexander: Problém pravosti privilégia pre turčiansky kláštor z r. 1252. In:Sb FFUK Historica 16, 1965, pp. 111-129; RATKOŠ, Peter: Privilégium Spišských Vlách z r. 1243 a Turnianske

which only a summary was published), the office of King Andrew III[18] was analyzed through paleographic and diplomatic methods. The validity of additional documents from the fourteenth century was analyzed.[19] Only in brief summaries are discussions about the first period of Hungarian diplomatic development (in the eleventh and twelfth centuries) and development of documentary writing in Slovakia in the Middle Ages.[20]

Public notary functions in Slovakia (in the Hungarian Kingdom) of the Middle Ages were executed by the so-called "trustworthy places." The paleographical-diplomatic analysis of the oldest of the documents at these locations (until 1350) was done in Turiec (Kláštor pod Znievom) and in Jasov.[21] While in the earliest periods the publishers of the documents were the heads of district administration ("župani"), from the end of the thirteenth century we can begin to speak of regional documents ("župná listina"). Document production until 1526, from Nitra, Tekov, Zemplín and Abov counties, was researched and analyzed.[22] In the second half of the thirteenth century, documentation of cities begins in Slovak territory. The development of documentation in Trnava until 1526 has been analyzed, Trnava having the oldest preserved town privileges in Slovakia. Anna Buzinkayová performed paleographical-diplomatic analysis of office activity from Ján Jiskra from Brandýs.[23]

---

prédium. In: SlArchiv 16, 1979, pp. 73-86; ULIČNÝ, Ferdinand: Výsady spišských miest z roku 1271. In: SlArchiv 16, 1981, pp. 88-96; LUKAČKA, Ján: Klížska listina z r. 1293. In: SlArchiv 17, 1982, pp. 128-135.

[18] SULITKOVÁ, Ludmila: Kancelář posledního Arpádovce Ondřeje III., její činnost a personální obsazení. In: HŠt 25, 1981, pp. 175-216.

[19] BEŇKO, Ján: Listina z r. 1301 na Plaveč. In: SlArchiv 16, 1981, pp. 82-93.

[20] MARSINA, Richard: Prvé obdobie uhorského diplomatického vývinu. In: SlArchiv 25, 1990, pp. 8-20; MARSINA, Richard: Vývoj listinného písma v stredoveku na Slovensku. In: SlArchiv 26, 1991, pp. 21-35.

[21] HOLOŠOVÁ, Alžbeta: Činnosť hodnoverného miesta v Turci do roku 1350. In: SlArchiv 25, 1990, pp. 56-81; VÁŇOVÁ-BODNÁROVÁ, Milica: Činnosť hodnoverného miesta Jasov do roku 1350. In: Historica Carpatica, História 9, 1978, pp. 279-314.

[22] NOVÁKOVÁ, Veronika: Nitrianska stolica do roku 1526. In: SlArchiv 19, 1984, pp. 35-58; NOVÁKOVÁ, Veronika: Vývoj správy a spísomňovania v Tekovskej stolici do roku 1526. In: SlArchiv 23, 1988, pp. 34-53; NOVÁKOVÁ, Veronika: Vývoj správy a spísomňovania v Abovskej stolici do r. 1526. In: SlArchiv 27, 1992, pp. 56-79; ULIČNÝ, Ferdinand ml.: Listiny Zemplínskej stolice do roku 1526. In: SlArchiv 23, 1988, pp. 89-110.

[23] ČORDÁŠOVÁ, Silvia: Vývoj spísomňovania v Trnave do r. 1526. In: SlArchiv 10, 1975, pp. 102-121; A critical study of the basic privileges of the town of Trnava HÚŠČAVA, Alexander: Najstaršie výsady mesta Trnavy. Bratislava, Universum 1939; BUZINKAYOVÁ, Anna: Písomnosti a kancelária Jána Jiskru z Brandýsa. In: SlArchiv 17, 1982, pp. 64-91.

Only Bratislava and Banská Bystrica have published, in recent decades, their inventories of thousands of medieval documents. For Bardejov and Prešov similar inventories were carried out, but only published in part. To the present these parts are available to researchers for study only in the archives.[24]

In heraldry, primary attention was devoted to town coats of arms, which the Heraldic Commission, acting under the Department of the Archives of the Ministry of the Interior, tried to clear of later accretions and return to the original medieval forms.[25] In connection with the research of county documentation, a parallel investigation of administrative development (e.g., in Šariš county) took place.[26] Attention was also devoted to old terminology of regional administrative units and medieval villages in Slovakia.[27]

Much less attention naturally was paid to practically non-existent narrative sources. The most notable exceptions are the legend of Ss. Svorád-Ondrej and Benedict and the chronicle from Spišská Sobota although these attracted only little attention, limited to solving the question of the origin of the cult of these saints. Work was done on the circumstances of the origin of the so-called Pray codices, which rested through the centuries in the library of the Bratislava Chapter, and part of whose contents are the Bratislava annals. Slovakia and Slovaks play a role in the pan-Hungarian chronicles, of which the current author made a brief overview.[28] Special attention was devoted to the chronicle of an

---

[24] LEHOTSKÁ, Darina and team: Inventár stredovekých listín, listov a iných príbuzných písomností. Archív mesta Bratislavy. Praha, Archivní správa MV 1956; HORVÁTH, Vladimír: Inventár listín a listov 2. (1501-1536). Archív mesta Bratislavy. Bratislava, Slovenská archívna správa 1966; MATULAY, Ctibor: Banská Bystrica. Katalóg administratívnych a súdnych písomností. (1020) 1255-1536. Bratislava, Slovenská archívna správa 1980.

[25] NOVÁK, Jozef: Slovenské mestské a obecné erby. Martin, Osveta 1972; VRTEĽ, Ladislav: O zástave v erbe Nitry. In: SlArchiv 25, 1990, pp. 35-46.

[26] ULIČNÝ, Ferdinand: Administratívny vývin Šarišskej župy do 18. storočia. In: SlArchiv 25, 1990, pp. 82-103.

27 SOKOLOVSKÝ, Leon: Grad-španstvo-stolica-župa. In: SlArchiv 15, 1981, pp. 94-118; SOKOLOVSKÝ, Leon: Terminológia dejín správy stredovekej dediny na Slovensku. In: HČ 33, 1985, pp. 506-528.

[28] RATKOŠ, Peter: Vznik kultu Ondreja-Svorada a Benedikta vo svetle záhrebských pamiatok. In: Historijski zbornik 29-30, 1976-1977, pp. 77-86; compare also HOLINKA, Rudolf: Sv. Svorád a Benedikt; světci Slovenska. (Rozbor a text legendy z konce XV. století.) In: Bratislava 8, Bratislava, Učená společnost Šafaříkova 1934, pp. 304-352; RATKOŠ, Peter: Nový pohľad na vznik a funkciu Prayovho kódexu. In: SlArchiv 1, 1966, pp. 98-120; MARSINA, Richard: Stredoveké uhorské rozprávacie pramene a slovenské dejiny. In: Zb SNM 78, História 24, 1984, pp. 167-195.

anonymous Hungarian author and its problematic contents, and to the origin of the author of the biography of King Louis I, Ján of Šarišské Sokolovce.[29]

In Slovak historiography, research on settlement patterns received considerable interest. Neither Slovakia nor the Slovaks possess an uninterrupted state tradition. Since the second third of the ninth century they have always been part of a foreign hegemonous states unit. This was the cause, from the turn of the century, of the beginning of the notion of the non-existence of Slovaks as an integral society in the past. Thus, for example, the Hungarian historian János Karácsonyi already before World War I proposed that the ninth century inhabitants of this region were killed or assimilated, that before the thirteenth century central and northern Slovakia were uninhabited, and that Slovaks were formed into a national society from nearby Slavic immigrants.[30] The Czech historian Václav Chaloupecký, active at the university in Bratislava, also considered the territory of northern and central Slovakia as uninhabited before the thirteenth century.[31] Scholarly reaction on the Slovak side to these positions came only after the publication of work by Chaloupecký's student Alexander Húščava, about the settlement of Liptov, in which he concurred that it began only in the thirteenth century.[32] The first to disagree with these conclusions was Daniel Rapant. His position was supported by another Czech professor in Slovakia, Vladimír Šmilauer, who came to his conclusions on the basis of detailed research on the names of bodies of water, in which he pointed out that in central and northern Slovakia are many linguistic forms from before the thirteenth century, among which appear names of pre-Slavic origin.[33]

The first modern book about the settling of a whole northern Slovak county is

---

[29] RATKOŠ, Peter: Anonymove Gesta Hungarorum a ich pramenná hodnota. In: HČ 31, 1983, pp. 825-870; KUMOROVITZ, Lajoš Bernát: Kancelárska činnosť magistra Jána zo Šarišských Sokoloviec, kronikára Ľudovíta I. In: SlArchiv 16, 1981, pp. 47-75.

[30] KARÁCSONYI, János: Halavány vonások hazánk Szent István korabeli határairól. In: Századok 35, 1901, pp. 1039-1058.

[31] CHALOUPECKÝ, Václav: Staré Slovensko. Bratislava, Filozofická fakulta Univerzity Komenského 1923.

[32] HÚŠČAVA, Alexander: Kolonizácia Liptova do konca 14. storočia. Bratislava, Filozofická fakulta Univerzity Komenského 1930.

[33] RAPANT, Daniel: O starý Liptov. In: Bratislava 7, Bratislava 1933, pp. 515-541 (A paper which was also published separately); ŠMILAUER, Vladimír: Vodopis starého Slovenska. Bratislava-Praha, Učená společnost Šafaříkova 1932.

about Turiec,[34] and the second about the most northern county, Orava, whose northern part on the Polish border was settled quite late.[35] Among other works published since the sixties an important role was played by thorough medieval documentary bases from foreign archives (till 1526). This research was performed mainly in the Hungarian National Archive (Magyar Országos Levéltár) in Budapest and in the Ostrihom (Esztergom) Archive, as a beginning of preparation of editions of medieval documents on the territory of Slovakia (*Diplomatary, Registry,* etc.) in the Institute of Historical Studies of the Slovak Academy of Sciences. Most of the documents of the thirteenth century and nearly half of those from the fourteenth and fifteenth centuries are in these archives.

Among the individual regions the most attention was devoted to the settlement of eastern and northern Slovakia. The largest work is the three-volume work on the settlement of the Košice basin, which deals with its topic broadly, taking in adjacent regions, and, in the third volume, settlement patterns in other parts of Slovakia are treated.[36] In some smaller regions mostly in northern Slovakia in recent decades, many historians concerned themselves with the research of settlement so that a confrontation of views began to appear. A work dealing with the settlement of the whole of northern Slovakia exists, as well as works on Orava and Liptov, and recent analyses of the settling of Liptov and Šariš, supported by a broader heuristic basis than the older opinions and works and bringing new views on the settlement of northern Slovakia.[37] From western and central Slovakia, interest centered on the original Slovak settlement between Bratislava and Modra, on the great numbers killed during the Tatar invasion (1241-1242), and the settling of Germans in Bratislava county in the thirteenth and fourteenth centuries.[38] On a broader heuristic basis, new analysis

---

[34] ŠIKURA, Ján st.: Miestopisné dejiny Turca. Bratislava, Academia scientiarum et artium Slovaca 1944; the author could also be backed up by the work by MÁLYUSZ, Elemér: Turócz megye kialakulása. Budapest, Budavári tudományos társaság 1922, from which it was revealed that in Turiec already in the ninth century there were approximately thirty villages which largely continued to exist afterwards.

[35] KAVULJAK, Andrej: Historický miestopis Oravy. Bratislava, Vydavateľstvo SAV 1955.

[36] VARSIK, Branislav: Osídlenie Košickej kotliny I.-III. Bratislava, Vydavateľstvo SAV 1964, 1973, 1977.

[37] BEŇKO, Ján: Osídlenie severného Slovenska. Košice, VV 1985; ULIČNÝ, Ferdinand: Dejiny osídlenia Liptova do konca 16. storočia. In: Liptov 7, 1983, pp. 39-90; Liptov 8, 1985, pp. 133-208; Liptov 9, 1987, pp. 61-149 ; ULIČNÝ, Ferdinand: Dejiny osídlenia Šariša. Košice, VV 1990.

[38] VARSIK, Branislav: Z osídlenia západného a stredného Slovenska v stredoveku. Bratislava, Veda 1984.

of names of bodies of water in the Slovak region has begun.[39] Already some decades ago, work on the linguistic origin of local names in southern Slovakia and adjacent territories was published. Although this work was criticized for its political approach, and not all its conclusions are accepted, it observed that the names of the same origin in western and in southern Slovakia appear also in the northern half of the trans-Danubian region, in modern-day northern and eastern Hungary, in western Romania, and in the trans-Carpathian Ukraine.[40] For determining the oldest settling of the region and its continuity, in recent decades, besides documents, archaeology dealing with Slavic settlement has played a significant part.[41] Attempts to bring together knowledge of the development and continuity of the settling of Slovakia show that we cannot speak of central and northern Slovakia being uninhabited before the thirteenth century.[42]

In addition to the above mentioned books which sometimes synthesize the results of previously published research significant articles have appeared.[43] It is necessary to emphasize those trying to solve the question of the origin of the institution of "Szolgagyör" which in the early Middle Ages had spread to many parts of the Hungarian Kingdom; and also those dealing with the territory originally belonging to the Bratislava Castle district administration.[44] Other important articles include research on the oldest settlement of northwestern Slovakia, development of the settlement of central and northern Ponitrie and, with the help of local names, Slovak settlement in the southern region of central Slovakia.[45] Attention was also devoted to research of the settling of Zvolen

---

[39] VARSIK, Branislav: Slovanské (slovenské) názvy riek na Slovensku. Bratislava, Veda 1990.

[40] STANISLAV, Ján: Slovenský juh v stredoveku. I.-III. (maps) Turčiansky Svätý Martin, MS 1948. Other monographs by linguists also devote attention to the etymology and history of local name origins: KRAJČOVIČ, Rudolf: Svedectvo dejín o slovenčine. Martin, MS 1980; NOVÁK, Ľudovít: K najstarším dejinám slovenského jazyka. Bratislava, Veda 1980.

[41] CHROPOVSKÝ, Bohuslav (Ed.): Významné slovanské náleziská na Slovensku. Bratislava, Veda 1978.

[42] Slovenský ľud po rozpade Veľkomoravskej ríše. Compiled by MARSINA, Richard. Bratislava, Veda 1984.

[43] Compare earlier studies of settlements cited in note 1, mostly pp. 74-79.

[44] SEDLÁK, Vincent: K otázke vzniku a pôvodu inštitúcie "Szolgagyör". In: HŠt 12, 1967, pp. 155-185; SEDLÁK, Vincent: Bratislavské hradné županstvo a Bratislava do roku 1291. In: Bratislava 6. Bratislava, Osveta a Mestské múzeum 1970, pp. 35-59.

[45] MARSINA, Richard: Osídlenie Hornej Trenčianskej pred Tatárskym vpádom. In: Sb FFUK Historica 15, 1964, pp. 47-70; LUKAČKA, Ján: Vývin osídlenia stredného a severného Ponitria do 15. storočia. In: HČ 33, 1985, pp. 817-840; VARSIK, Branislav: Slovanské osídlenie v Gemeri a pôvod názvu rieky Blh. In: HČ 35, 1987, pp. 592-601; VARSIK, Branislav: Osídlenie Novohradu a Ipeľskej kotliny vo svetle miestnych názvov. In: HČ 40, 1992, pp. 17-31.

county. In addition the arrival of German settlers in Záhorie was dated more precisely utilizing more complete heuristic principles.[46] A concise view on the medieval village was also elaborated, taking into account all aspects of its material culture.[47]

Slovak medievalists also devoted a good deal of attention to the histories of towns. A large proportion of the most important or first category towns in the Hungarian Kingdom were on Slovak territory. Perhaps this was connected to the frontier role of Slovakia in the north and west and with the orientation of the most significant international trade routes (the Danubian, Czech-Hungarian, Baltic-Balkan, and Silesian-Hungarian) but also because mining towns were based on the rich copper and iron ore deposits there. Thus, plentiful documentary resources were preserved, which from the fifteenth century enable the analysis of the histories of towns. A great number of books of this kind were published, of which the most important have been mentioned in the chapter on regional history.[48] Of books given over exclusively to medieval history in these towns only a few were published. The volume on Kremnica deals with the origin of mining and its first century and with urban life after town privileges were received.[49] That on Košice makes an important contribution to knowledge about Baltic-Balkan trade.[50] One special book analyzes the citizens of Bardejov on the basis of the tax registry.[51] The result of many decades of work is the book on Košice from 1230 to 1312, which tries to create a detailed picture of the era before it gained town privileges.[52] The Marxist effort to stress the "mover of history–the class struggle" transformed the revolt of miners in Banská Bystrica in 1525-1526 into an uprising to which a special book was devoted[53] (also

---

[46] ĎURKOVÁ, Mária: Sídliskové pomery na Vígľašskom panstve do začiatku 16. storočia. In: HČ 41, 1993, pp. 23-35; SEDLÁK, Vincent: Začiatky nemeckého osídlenia Záhoria. In: HČ 41, 1993, pp. 233-243.

[47] HABOVŠTIAK, Alojz: Stredoveká dedina na Slovensku. Bratislava, Veda 1985.

[48] Compare also note 1, pp. 79-85. Compare the review of the development of towns in Slovakia in the Middle Ages by MARSINA, Richard: Pour l'histoire des villes en Slovaquie au Moyen âge. In: SHS 8, 1975, pp. 21-72

[49] LAMOŠ, Teodor: Vznik a počiatky banského a mincovného mesta Kremnice 1328-1430. Banská Bystrica, SV 1968.

[50] HALAGA, Ondrej R.: Košice-Balt. 1275-1526. Košice, VV 1975.

[51] GÁCSOVÁ, Alžbeta: Spoločenská štruktúra Bardejova v 15. stor. a v prvej polovici 16. stor. Bratislava, Vydavateľstvo SAV 1972; GÁCSOVÁ, Alžbeta: Spoločenská štruktúra Kežmarku v 15. stor. a v prvej pol. 16. storočia. In: HČ 19, 1971, pp. 357-384.

[52] HALAGA, Ondrej R.: Počiatky Košíc a zrod metropoly. Košice, VV 1993.

[53] RATKOŠ, Peter: Povstanie baníkov na Slovensku v roku 1525-1526. Bratislava, Vydavateľstvo SAV 1963.

a special volume of resources already mentioned). Individual volumes containing papers presented at conferences were published on the 700th anniversary of the granting of collective privileges to the Spiš towns in 1271, and on the 700th anniversary of the granting of basic privileges to the current capital of Slovakia, Bratislava, in 1291.[54] An overview of the development of crafts and their specialization in Slovakia, to the beginning of the sixteenth century, contains work on guilds. The final stages of extracting and processing copper in the late fifteenth and early sixteenth century, by the fusion of Fugger and Thurzo capital, also has been the subject of its own book.[55] In many towns archaeological research was conducted and only one book was published based on the research conducted in Bratislava.[56] The analysis of the building of urban areas had its way prepared by earlier work.[57] In many towns of Slovakia, the plans of original medieval fortresses and fortifications were preserved, and many of these structures have been preserved or restored in recent decades.[58]

In annals and periodicals, a great number of contributions on the history of medieval towns in Slovak territory were published, of which it is possible to mention only a few. An outline of the development of towns in Slovakia in the Middle Ages was laid out and an essay on the possible influences on the genesis of towns in Slovakia was published. On the basis of existing books and primary documents, Ľubomír Juck outlined the intensity and orientation of trade in cities in the fourteenth century, and Július Bartl turned his attention to the repeatedly researched decrees for towns of King Sigismund of 1405.[59] Only recently have historians looked at the history of Jews in Slovakia, who for the most part lived in towns. Bratislava was the only town in the whole of the Hungarian Kingdom which had in its basic privileges (1291) a special article

---

[54] Spišské mestá v stredoveku. Compiled by MARSINA, Richard. Košice, VV 1974; Städte im Donauraum. Compiled by MARSINA, Richard. Bratislava, Slovenská historická spoločnosť 1993.

[55] ŠPIESZ, Anton: Remeslo na Slovensku v období existencie cechov. Bratislava, Vydavateľstvo SAV 1972; VLACHOVIČ, Jozef: Slovenská meď v 16. a 17. storočí. Bratislava, Vydavateľstvo SAV 1964.

[56] POLLA, Belo: Bratislava, západné suburbium. Košice, VV 1979.

[57] MENCL, Václav: Středověká města na Slovensku. Bratislava, Učená společnost Šafaříkova 1938; ZALČÍK, Tibor: Urbanizmus stredovekého mesta na Slovensku. Bratislava, Pallas 1973.

[58] ŠÁŠKY, Ladislav: Kamenná krása našich miest. Martin, Osveta 1981.

[59] MARSINA, Richard: Pour l'histoire des villes en Slovaquie au Moyen âge. (see note 48); KUČERA, Matúš: Genéza miest na Slovensku. In: Archaeologia historica 3, 1978, pp. 147-164; JUCK, Ľubomír: Obchod v mestách na Slovensku v 14. storočí. In: HČ 35, 1987, pp. 256-278; BARTL, Július: Dekréty kráľa Žigmunda z r. 1405 a ich význam pri formovaní meštianskeho stavu v Uhorsku. In: HČ 40, 1992, pp. 281-296.

concerning Jews (or rather the Jewish community), giving them the same rights as other burghers. This situation was only applicable to western Slovak towns, as in central Slovak mining and eastern Slovak towns, Jews were not allowed to settle.[60]

In addition to cities, already in the fourteenth and fifteenth centuries smaller towns existed, whose smallness was a function of their legal status in the second category, though only some of them were subject towns. An attempt was made to concretely categorize towns and small towns for east Slovakia and Trenčín and Liptov counties.[61] Great attention was paid to the history of Košice, researching the beginning of distant trade and regulations of storage, as well as to Slovak-Russian trade connections, the struggle of Košice against the oligarchs, and the close trade agreements between Kraków and Košice (already from the fourteenth century).[62] Among towns in Slovakia, Košice owned the most extensive feudal lands in its surroundings as well as in the vineyards of the distant Tokay region. The extent and trends of medieval trade were researched also in the context of Bratislava and Bardejov.[63] Zvolen is among the towns that received their privileges in the first phase of granting in the region, around 1238, and in the time before the grant, it was the region's only seat of administration of the royal lands, and it was the location of a royal chapel.[64] The course of the quarrel of Banská Bystrica with the Thurzo-Fugger Mining Company, over the former's demand for tribute on the basis of its privilege, is an interesting

---

[60] MARSINA, Richard: Das Judentum in der Slowakei im Mittelalter. In: Juden im Grenzraum. Eisenstadt 1993, pp. 23-35.

[61] ULIČNÝ, Ferdinand: Začiatky mestečiek na východnom Slovensku. In: HČ 38, 1990, pp. 253-272; BARTL, Július: Mestá a mestečká Trenčianskej stolice v stredoveku. In: HČ 36, 1988, pp. 906-927; BARTL, Július: K vývoju miest a mestečiek Liptova v stredoveku. In: Liptov 8, 1985, pp. 45-68.

[62] HALAGA, Ondrej R.: Slovensko-ruské styky v období feudalizmu 1. In: Historica Carpatica 1, 1969, pp. 67-91; HALAGA, Ondrej R.: Počiatky diaľkového obchodu cez stredné Karpaty a košického práva skladu. In: Historica Carpatica 4, 1973, pp. 3-28; VARSIK, Branislav: Vznik a začiatky Košíc. In: Historica Carpatica 11, 1980, pp. 152-168; VARSIK, Branislav: K boju medzi košickými mešťanmi a Omodejovcami. In: Historický sborník SAVU 10, 1952, pp. 221-225; HALAGA, Ondrej R.: Boj Košíc proti oligarchii Omodejovcov a Matúš Trenčiansky. In: HČ 34, 1986, pp. 326-348; HALAGA, Ondrej R.: Pakty vzájomnosti obchodných stredísk Krakova a Košíc. In: HČ 36, 1988, pp. 159-174.

[63] ULIČNÝ, Ferdinand: Feudálne majetky Košíc v 14.-17. storočí. In: Historica Carpatica 22, 1991, pp. 25-45; BARTL, Július: Bratislavský obchod v stredoveku. In: Sb FFUK Historica 16, 1964, pp. 87-112; DEÁK, Ladislav: Bardejovský obchod a bardejovská obchodná cesta v prvej polovici 15. stor. In: Sb FFUK Historica 14, 1962, pp. 107-134.

[64] MARSINA, Richard: K najstarším dejinám Zvolena. In: HČ 37, 1989, pp. 793-805.

episode.[65] The issue of collective territorial privileges and their relation to Slavic common law also received attention.[66]

In addition to syntheses mentioned in the second chapter, there were also specialized books. Studies of economic and social development in the tenth to thirteenth centuries draw attention to the difficulty of the transition of the economy and society after the arrival of the Old Magyars to the Danube basin and the gradual creation of the hegemonic Hungarian Kingdom.[67] In 1328 in the mining town of Kremnica, the mint was founded that operates to the present.[68] The cultivation of vineyards and production of wine spread in the southern parts of Slovakia in the Middle Ages (perhaps in some locations with continuity from Roman times). This can be traced in documents from the thirteenth century, but in greater detail only from the fifteenth. In earliest times hand millstones ground corn since water mills were built only later.[69]

Because of geographical proximity, Slovakia suffered under all the invasions by the Hussite army into the Hungarian Kingdom (1428-1434), which plundered the economic basis of King-Emperor Sigismund. Politically unstable conditions continued from the beginning of the 1440s, allowing dynastic quarrels.[70] The historiographical attempt to present the Czech king and emperor Charles IV as a figure of Slovak history (shown by the book title *Pater Patriae*) foundered on insufficient evidence and Charles was superseded by Matúš Čák Trenčiansky.[71]

Among studies of political history are my contribution on the development of Slovakia in the beginning of the eleventh century, and the battles of the Arpád dynasty with the Czech Přemyslids in the third quarter of the thirteenth century

---

[65] GRAUS, Igor: Zápas o banskobystrické mestské výsady na začiatku 16. storočia. In: HČ 42, 1994, pp. 3-20. Compare also SKLADANÝ, Marián: Najstarší doklad o podnikateľskej činnosti Jána Thurzu v stredoslovenských banských mestách. In: HŠt 19, 1974, pp. 237-265.

[66] RATKOŠ, Peter: Dedičské právo v turčiansko-liptovských privilégiách 13. storočia. In: HŠt 11, 1966, pp. 79-90; HALAGA, Ondrej R.: Turčiansko-liptovské privilégiá (1257, 1265) a slovanské zvykové právo. In: Právnické štúdie 15, Bratislava 1967, pp. 717-733.

[67] KUČERA, Matúš: Slovensko po páde Veľkej Moravy. Bratislava, Vydavateľstvo SAV 1974.

[68] Kremnická mincovňa. 1328-1978. Compiled by KAZIMÍR, Kazimír and team. Martin, Osveta 1978.

[69] KAZIMÍR, Štefan: Pestovanie viniča a produkcia vína na Slovensku v minulosti. Bratislava, Veda 1986; HANUŠIN, Ján: Najstaršie vodné mlyny na Slovensku (do konca 13. stor.). In: Dějiny věd a techniky 12, Praha 1979, pp. 9-23.

[70] VARSIK, Branislav: Husitské revolučné hnutie a Slovensko. Bratislava, Vydavateľstvo SAV 1965; ŠPIRKO, Jozef: Husiti, jiskrovci a bratríci v dejinách Spiša. Spišská Kapitula, Spišský dejepisný spolok 1937.

[71] KUČERA, Matúš: Pater patriae. Bratislava, Tatran 1981.

which took place almost exclusively in southwestern Slovakian territory.[72] In the disordly twenty years after the extinction of the Arpád family, Charles Robert Anjou struggled over real power at first with the Czech and then the Bavarian pretender to the Hungarian throne, and finally with the Hungarian oligarchs. He also attempted to regularize conditions. This era is the subject of several studies.[73] In the first half of the fifteenth century Slovakia played an important role as the Hungarian frontier with the Polish Kingdom, in development of mutual relations. It also suffered from the invasions of the Polish army and the dynastic struggles for the Hungarian throne.[74]

The Stibors, a Polish noble family, supported the Emperor Sigismund of Luxembourg against revolts by the nobles, against the invading Hussites and played a significant role in the history of the Hungarian Kingdom, especially in the territory inhabited by the Slovaks.[75] Despite of the view expressed in Hungarian historiography that the nobles of the Hungarian Kingdom were exclusively Magyar, detailed studies show that in Upper Hungary, i.e., Slovak counties, from the thirteenth century (when documentation becomes available) there were numerous families of Slovak origin among the lower nobility.[76]

In the past decades, little attention was devoted to the history of the church and religious institutions, a situation which recently has begun to change. Ninety percent of the area of the archdiocese of the Hungarian primate, the Archbishop of Ostrihom (Esztergom), was on Slovak territory, as well as the majority of his lands. Here also were the majority of the seats of his predialists, that is, the members of his obligatory military contingent.[77] The Christianization of the

---

[72] HRUŠOVSKÝ, František: Boleslav Chrabrý a Slovensko. In: Sborník na počesť Jozefa Škultétyho. Turčiansky Svätý Martin, MS 1933, pp. 454-482; MARSINA, Richard: Přemysl Otakar II. a Uhorsko. In: Folia historica Bohemica 1, 1979, pp. 37-65.

[73] BREZOVÁKOVÁ, Blanka: Politický zápas Anjouovcov o uhorskú korunu. In: HČ 39, 1991, pp. 569-587; BREZOVÁKOVÁ, Blanka: Konsolidačné snahy Karola I. v Uhorsku po zvolení za kráľa (1310-1317). In: HČ 41, 1993, pp. 361-378.

[74] BARTL, Július: K poľsko-uhorským vzťahom v prvej tretine 15. storočia. In: Zb FFUK Historica 26, 1975, pp. 77-95; KARTOUS, Peter: Akcie poľských vojsk na území Slovenska v rokoch 1438-1439. In: HČ 21, 1973, pp. 21-36; KARTOUS, Peter: Habsbursko-jagelovské dvojvládie v Uhorsku v rokoch 1440-1444. In: HŠt 24, 1980, pp. 225-263.

[75] DVOŘÁKOVÁ, Daniela: Stiborovci v Uhorsku. In: HČ 41, 1993, pp. 3-22.

[76] VARSIK, Branislav: Otázky vzniku a vývinu slovenského zemianstva. Bratislava, Veda 1988; LUKAČKA, Ján: Majetky a postavenie Ludanickovcov na Slovensku do začiatku 14. storočia. In: HČ 38, 1990, pp. 3-14.

[77] OSLANSKÝ, František: Pozemkové vlastníctvo ostrihomského arcibiskupstva na Slovensku v stredoveku. In: HČ 38, 1990, pp. 364-390; OSLANSKÝ, František: Predialisti Ostrihomského arcibiskupstva na Slovensku do začiatku 16. storočia. In: HČ 34, 1986, pp. 487-508.

Magyars and the Hungarian Kingdom was, from the beginning, caught in the struggle between East and West, Byzantium and Rome. Only around 970 did Prince Gejza definitively turn toward the western church and the influence of clerics from Bavaria increased. With the foundation of the organized Hungarian church at the beginning of the eleventh century, there was no effort to renew the Nitra bishopric, which had been established by Pope John VIII in 880 and which had lapsed at the beginning of the tenth century. The territory held by the Nitra bishopric during the ninth century was granted to the archdiocese of Ostrihom (Esztergom) in the eleventh century.[78] In Bratislava, at the transition of the thirteenth to the fourteenth century, there were already many church institutions (including some abbeys and monasteries), the foundations of which dated back to the second half of the ninth century and which functioned continuously until the end of the tenth century after a presumed interruption at the beginning of the tenth century.[79]

Because they lacked their own self-government, research on Slovaks was devoted to their ethnogenesis and historical consciousness in the Middle Ages. For this, documentation has been sporadically available, mostly in situations where Slovaks in certain regions felt threatened or injured by other ethnic groups.[80]

In Slovakia, relatively few medieval manuscripts have been preserved. Modern research has identified more such manuscripts pertaining to Slovakia abroad (primarily in Budapest, and Alba Iulia in Romania) than remain in Slovakia, where the biggest collection is the medieval library of the Bratislava chapter. The majority of these are stored at two locations, the Slovak National Archive and the Archive of the City of Bratislava. The codices which are or were located or created in Slovakia, were first researched from the perspective of art history and then a systematic catalogue was made. In a like manner, an inventory

---

[78] MARSINA, Richard: Kristianizácia Maďarov a Uhorska medzi Východom a Západom. In: HČ 40, 1992, pp. 409-421; MARSINA, Richard: Nitrianske biskupstvo a jeho biskupi od 9. do polovice 13. storočia. In: HČ 41, 1993, pp. 529-542; MARSINA, Richard: Prečo nebolo obnovené biskupstvo v Nitre hneď začiatkom 11. storočia? In: Szomszédaink között Kelet-Európában. Budapest 1993, pp. 27-32.

[79] OSLANSKÝ, František: Cirkev v stredovekej Bratislave. In: HČ 41, 1993, pp. 113-122.

[80] RATKOŠ, Peter: Otázky vývoja slovenskej národnosti do konca 17. storočia. In: HČ 20, 1972, pp. 19-64; KUČERA, Matúš: O historickom vedomí Slovákov v stredoveku. In: HČ 25, 1977, pp. 217-238; VARSIK, Branislav: O vzniku a rozvoji slovenskej národnosti v stredoveku. In: HČ 32, 1984, pp. 529-554; MARSINA, Richard: Über die Besiedlung der Slowakei vom 11. bis in die Hälfte des 13. Jahrhunderts. In: SHS 16, 1988, pp. 206-219.

of incunabulae was assembled.[81] From the two oldest codices (from the eleventh century) with a relation to Slovakia, only the Nitra Codex is kept here, in the treasury of the Nitra diocese. The other is located in Zagreb. In the Bibliotheca Apostolica Vaticana only one codex by Slovak scribes has been found so far.[82] The dictionary of medieval authors, sources and scribes with Slovak connections was quite extensively carried out but on the other hand research on medieval and also Slovak literature is sketchy.[83] Research on schools and education has been published in the form of individual articles in broader collections and brief reviews. In 1465 the Danubian University (Universitas Istropolitana, Studium Generale) was founded in Bratislava, the only one in the Hungarian Kingdom. It had a short duration, only fifteen years, and from the sixteenth century the incorrect name for it, Academia Istropolitana, has been used.[84]

Great attention has been devoted to medieval arts and architecture in Slovakia. A knowledge of crafts has been gradually enriched by archaeological finds.[85] The Romanesque style has a strong presence in architecture, but Gothic architecture, from the early to late style, predominates. While in older periods wall painting is characteristic, in the fifteenth century Gothic panel painting prevails (on altars). In the fourteenth century, particularly in the second half, wood carving gained an important position.[86] The culmination of

---

[81] SABÓL, Eugen: Z dejín kódexov a miniatúr na Slovensku. Martin, MS 1955; GÜNTHE-ROVÁ, Alžbeta - MIŠIANIK, Ján: Stredoveká knižná maľba na Slovensku. Bratislava, SVKL 1961, 1977; SOPKO, Július: Stredoveké latinské kódexy. I-II. Martin, MS 1981, 1982; KOTVAN, Imrich: Inkunábuly na Slovensku. Martin, MS 1979.

[82] SOPKO, Július: O najstarších kódexoch so vzťahmi k územiu Slovenska. In: SlArchiv 21, 1986, pp. 50-71; SOPKO, Július: Nitriansky kódex. Martin, MS 1987; SOPKO, Július: Kódex slovenských skriptorov v Ríme. In: HČ 40, 1992, pp. 215-225.

[83] KUZMÍK, Jozef: Slovník starovekých a stredovekých autorov, prameňov a knižných skriptorov so slovenskými vzťahmi. Martin, MS 1983; MINÁRIK, Jozef: Stredoveká literatúra. Svetová, česká, slovenská. Bratislava, SPN 1977.

[84] SOPKO, Július: O školstve a vzdelanosti na Slovensku v stredoveku. In: HČ 36, 1988, pp. 175-197; Humanizmus a renesancia na Slovensku v 15. a 16. storočí. Edited by HOLOTÍK, Ľudovít - VANTUCH, Anton. Bratislava, Vydavateľstvo SAV 1967; JANKOVIČ, Vendelín: Stredoveká bratislavská univerzita vo svetle nových prameňov. In: HČ 40, 1992, pp. 145-170.

[85] RUTTKAY, Alexander: Stredoveké umelecké remeslo. Bratislava, Tatran 1979.

[86] Zo starších výtvarných dejín Slovenska. Bratislava, SAV 1965; KAHOUN, Karol: Neskorogotická architektúra na Slovensku a stavitelia východného okruhu. Bratislava, Vydavateľstvo SAV 1973; MENCL, Václav: Stredoveká architektúra na Slovensku. Praha-Prešov, ČSGU 1937; DVO-ŘÁKOVÁ, Vlasta - KRÁSA, Josef - STEJSKAL, Karel: Stredoveká nástenná maľba na Slovensku. Praha-Bratislava, Odeon, Tatran 1978.

Gothic art in Slovakia is the work of Master Pavol of Levoča. His Gothic altar, still standing in the parish church of St. James in Levoča, is the highest medieval altar in central Europe.[87]

---

[87] HOMOLKA, Jaromír - HORVÁTH, Pavol - KOTRBA, František - KOTRBA, Viktor - PAŠTEKA, Július - TILKOVSKÝ, Vojtech: Majster Pavol z Levoče. Tvorca vrcholného diela slovenskej neskorej gotiky. Bratislava, SVKL 1961.

SLOVAK HISTORIOGRAPHY ON THE PERIOD 1526–1800

After the Battle of Mohács in 1526 and the election of Ferdinand I as Hungarian king, Slovakia became a part of the Habsburg monarchy. The Turks occupied the central part of Hungary, along with Buda, which became a part of the Ottoman Empire. The focus of the Hungarian state was transferred to Slovak territory to which moved all central administration and church institutions. For the next 150 years, Slovakia abutted the sphere of Ottoman power and the subsequent events on their borders were constantly a subject of international interest. Also drawing attention was the Reformation, which spread into Slovakia after the defeat at Mohács. Efforts at re-Catholicization and the establishment of absolutism from the Viennese court created anti-Habsburg revolts of the estates through the seventeenth to the beginning of the eighteenth century. Only then did a long period of peace begin in Slovakia.

Among the old Slovak historians, Michal Matunák devoted the greatest attention to issues of *Ottoman expansion* in Slovakia. His numerous studies retain their material value, which is why even in 1983 a selection was published. Among later historians, most attention was paid by the Turkish studies specialist Jozef Blaškovič, and Peter Ratkoš and Jozef Vlachovič, and among contemporary historians Pavel Horváth and Vojtech Kopčan. The last two published the first synthesis of Turkish expansion in Slovakia in 1971. Kopčan, a Turkish studies specialist, besides numerous articles, also published a book on the Turkish occupation of Slovakia in 1986.[1]

---

[1] MATUNÁK, Michal: Život a boje na slovensko-tureckom pohraničí. Edited by KOPČAN, Vojtech. Bratislava, Tatran 1983; VLACHOVIČ, Jozef: Príspevok k problematike prenikania tureckej moci na Slovensko. In: HČ 7, 1959, pp. 234-265; BLAŠKOVIČ, Jozef: K dejinám tureckej expanzie na Slovensku. In: HŠt 8, 1962, pp. 95-116; SUCHÝ, Michal: Das Echo der türkischen Expansion in Ungarn in der ersten Hälfte des 16. Jahrhundert in Deutschland. In: SHS 6, 1969, pp. 63-106; HORVÁTH, Pavel - KOPČAN, Vojtech: Turci na Slovensku. Bratislava, SPN 1971; BLAŠKOVIČ, Jozef: Rimavská Sobota v čase osmansko-tureckého panstva. Bratislava, Obzor 1974; KOPČAN, Vojtech: Die osmanische Expansion und die Slowakei (Ergebnisse und Perspektiven). In: Asian and African Studies 16, 1980, pp. 35-52; KOPČAN, Vojtech - KRAJČOVIČOVÁ, Klára: Slovensko v tieni polmesiaca. Martin, Osveta 1983; HORVÁTH, Pavel: Posledné obdobie

Branislav Varsik devoted himself to the beginnings of the *Reformation* in Slovakia investigating, in his 1932 book, whether there was a connection between the Hussites and the spread of the Reformation into Slovakia. He reached a negative conclusion, based on the fact that the Reformation came to Slovakia from Germany. The well known Comenius scholar Ján Kvačala wrote a brief synthesis on the Reformation in Slovakia, published posthumously in 1935. Counter-Reformation issues were dealt with by the church historians Vojtech Bucko and Ján Oberuč, as well as by the late Anton Špiesz. Though the research of church history stagnated for a considerable period, recently attention has been devoted to the interpretation of various aspects of the Lutheran Reformation and the activities of anti-Reformation orders.[2]

Of the earlier Slovak historians, Július Botto devoted himself to *uprising of the estates against the Habsburgs*. His contributions were overly dependent on Hungarian historical literature and contributed nothing new. An original contribution in this area waited on *The Rákoczi Uprising and the Slavs* (1930) of Anna Gašparíková. This researched the uprising in broader international connections and demonstrated the participation in it of Slavic and Slovak elements. Of a similar tendency is work on the anti-Habsburg uprisings by the historians

tureckej moci na Slovensku. In: HČ 33, 1985, pp. 423-434; KOPČAN, Vojtech: Turecké nebezpečenstvo a Slovensko. Bratislava, Veda 1986; BLAŠKOVIČ, Jozef: The Period of Ottoman-Turkish Reign at Nové Zámky (1663-1685). In: Archiv Orientální 54, 1986, pp. 105-130; KOPČAN, Vojtech: Osmanská výprava na Slovensko v rokoch 1663-1664. In: HČ 40, 1992, pp. 297-325.

[2] VARSIK, Branislav: Husiti a reformácia na Slovensku do žilinskej synody. Bratislava 1932; KVAČALA, Ján: Dejiny reformácie na Slovensku (1517-1711). Liptovský Sv. Mikuláš, Tranoscius 1935; BUCKO, Vojtech: Reformné hnutie v arcibiskupstve ostrihomskom do r. 1564. Bratislava, Unia 1939; ; OBERUČ, Ján: Les persécution de Luthériens en Slovaquie au XVIIe siécle. Strassbourg 1927; ŠPIESZ, Anton: Rekatolizácia na Slovensku v mestách v rokoch 1681-1781. In: HČ 39, 1991, pp. 588-612; ŽUDEL, Juraj: Náboženská štruktúra obyvateľstva v slobodných kráľovských mestách v druhej polovici 18. storočia. In: Geografický časopis 43, 1991, pp. 215-230; DANIEL, David P.: The Historiography of the Reformation in Slovakia. In: Sixteenth Century Bibliography 10, St. Louis Missouri, Center for Reformation Research 1977; DANIEL, David P.: Výskum obdobia reformácie na Slovensku. In: HČ 37, 1989, pp. 572-595; DANIEL, David P.: The Reformation and Eastern Slovakia. In: Human Affairs 1, 1991, pp. 172-186; DANIEL, David P.: Hungary. In: The Early Reformation in Europe. Edited by PETTEGREE, Andrew. Cambridge University Press 1992; VARSIK, Branislav: Vznik a vývoj kalvínov na východnom Slovensku. In: HČ 39, 1991, pp. 129-148; Dejiny Spoločnosti Ježišovej na Slovensku. Cambridge, On., Canada 1990; KAČIC, Ladislav: Missa franciscana der Marianischen Provinz im 17. und 18. Jahrhundert. In: Studia Musicologica Academiae Scientiarum Hungaricae 33, Budapest 1991, pp. 5-107; KOWALSKÁ, Eva: Kláštory františkánov na Slovensku a národnostný problém v 17.-18. storočí. In: Slovenský národopis 34, 1993, pp. 55-76.

Michal Suchý, Anton Špiesz and Jozef Kočiš and the military historian Vojtech Dangl. Contributions by Ľudovít Haraksim and Pavol Horváth deal more specifically with the participation of the ordinary Slovak people in these uprisings. The work of Jozef Vlachovič, Jozef Vozár and Július Slaný pay attention to the negative results of the uprisings on the economies of central Slovak mining towns.[3]

An extensive article by Ján Tibenský covers the political conditions of the period of peace after 1711, while Karol Rebro, Jozef Šimončič, Eva Kowalská and Viliam Čičaj research enlightened despotism, its reforms, the influence of the French Revolution in Slovakia, and the system of power at the end of the eighteenth and the beginning of the nineteenth century.[4]

The Ottoman expansion and the anti-Habsburg uprisings of the estates had an influence also on the economic development of Slovakia after 1526. The Turkish occupation of central Hungary and the presence of a great number of armies concentrated in Slovakia against its expansion created a boom for agriculture, mining and crafts for military needs. This lasted until the beginning of the seventeenth century, after which, as a result of internal disturbances, the

---

[3] SUCHÝ, Michal: Úlohy habsburskej monarchie a protihabsburské stavovské povstania. In: HČ 23, 1975, pp. 73-111; ŠPIESZ, Anton: Absolutistické snahy Habsburgovcov a uhorské stavy na konci 17. a na začiatku 18. storočia. In: HČ 17, 1979, pp. 208-221; DANGL, Vojtech: Slovensko vo víre stavovských povstaní. Bratislava, SPN 1986; SUCHÝ, Michal: Vzťah Poľska k povstaniu Štefana Bočkaja. In: HŠt 18, 1973, pp. 209-234; DANGL, Vojtech: Bethlen proti Habsburgům. In: Slovo k historii 37, Praha, Melantrich 1992; GAŠPARÍKOVÁ, Anna: Povstanie Rákocziho a Slovania. Bratislava, FFUK 1930; KOČIŠ, Jozef: Príspevok k vzťahu Františka Rákocziho II. k Slovensku. In: HČ 26, 1978, pp. 272-282; HARAKSIM, Ľudovít: Slovenská účasť v protihabsburských stavovských povstaniach v druhej polovici 17. a na začiatku 18. storočia. In: Príspevky k dejinám východného Slovenska. Bratislava, SAV 1964, pp. 157-167; HORVÁTH, Pavel: O účasti poddaných v protihabsburských povstaniach. In: HČ 27, 1979, pp. 357-368. VLACHOVIČ, Jozef: Stredoslovenské banské mestá a protihabsburské povstania v prvej tretine 17. storočia. In: HČ 7, 1960, pp. 526-556; VOZÁR, Jozef: Baníctvo na Slovensku v čase protihabsburských stavovských povstaní. In: HČ 33, 1985, pp. 85-98; SLANÝ, Július: Povstanie Štefana Bočkaja a jeho dôsledky na hospodársky život v Banskej Bystrici. In: Stredné Slovensko, Spoločenské vedy 7, 1989, pp. 223-231.

[4] TIBENSKÝ, Ján: Slovensko po szatmárskom mieri a v prvom období osvietenského absolutizmu. In: HČ 4, 1956, pp. 331-396; ŠIMONČIČ, Jozef: Hnutie uhorských jakobínov a Slovensko. In: HČ 24, 1980, pp. 117-145; REBRO, Karol: K niektorým otázkam osvietenských reforiem na Slovensku. In: HČ 10, 1965, pp. 423-439; KOWALSKÁ, Eva: Otázky politickej moci a ich vyjadrenie v procese osvietenského absolutizmu. In: Slovensko v období prechodu od feudalizmu ku kapitalizmu. Compiled by MATULA, Vladimír. Bratislava, Veda 1989, pp. 72-84; ŠIMONČIČ, Jozef: Ohlasy Francúzskej revolúcie na Slovensku. Košice, VV 1982; ČIČAJ, Viliam: Politickospoločenské aspekty prechodu od feudalizmu ku kapitalizmu. In: Slovensko v období prechodu od feudalizmu ku kapitalizmu, pp. 41-61.

economy declined to its nadir in the eighteenth century. This was only reversed by the restoration of wartime destruction.

The first work on the *economic development* of Slovakia between 1526 and 1848 was published in 1932 by Štefan Janšák. Although no comparable work has since been published there have been many articles by later historians on individual areas of economic life in this period. The global economic context was explicated by Ratkoš, Špiesz, Horváth and Vozár. Horváth concentrated on the history of agricultural production, Štefan Kazimír and Jozef Baďurík on the history of viticulture, and Marián Skladaný on pisciculture. Jozef Watzka devoted himself to the development of the allodial economy of the nobility in the sixteenth to the eighteenth centuries.

Although most of the territory of Slovakia was forested in the past, the history of forestry and its economy have been left uninvestigated. Only a publication by the earlier Slovak historian Andrej Kavuljak as well as a few minor articles contributes to an understanding of this area.[5]

Much attention has been devoted to mining in Slovakia in the sixteenth to eighteenth centuries. The connection of the Viennese court to the mining industry in Slovakia was Vozár's specialization. He also wrote an article on the English engineer Isaac Potter, who in the eighteenth century built water pumping machines in the Slovak mines. Potter was also the author of the so-called golden book of mining, which gives a picture of the technical equipment of mining in Slovakia during the same period. Kazimír and Vlachovič wrote about the extraction of precious metals and copper, their trade, and the profits

---

[5] JANŠÁK, Štefan: Slovensko v dobe uhorského feudalizmu. Hospodárske pomery od roku 1514 do roku 1848. Bratislava, Zemedelské múzeum 1932; RATKOŠ, Peter: Vývin feudálnej renty na Slovensku v 16.-18. storočí. In: HŠt 17, 1972, pp. 9-26. ŠPIESZ, Anton: Slovensko v procese refeudalizácie. In: HŠt 17, 1972, pp. 45-61; HORVÁTH, Pavel: Der Charakter des Spätfeudalismus in der Slowakei. In: SHS 7, 1974, pp. 78-101; VOZÁR, Jozef: Narastanie kapitalistických prvkov v ekonomických odvetviach na Slovensku v 18. a v prvej polovici 19. storočia. In: Slovensko na prechode od feudalizmu ku kapitalizmu, pp. 85-120; HORVÁTH, Pavel: K dejinám poľnohospodárskej výroby na Slovensku v prvej polovici 18. storočia. In: HŠt 6, 1960, pp. 215-262; KAZIMÍR, Štefan: Pestovanie viniča a produkcia vína na Slovensku v minulosti. Bratislava, Veda 1985; BAĎURÍK, Jozef: Malokarpatské vinohradníctvo v 16. storočí. Bratislava, UK 1990; SKLADANÝ, Marian: Rybnikárstvo na fuggerovskom panstve Červený Kameň v 16. storočí. In: HŠt 10, 1965, pp. 22-53; WATZKA, Jozef: Vývin majerského hospodárenia na trenčianskom a bánovskom panstve od polovice 16. do konca 18. storočia. In: HŠt 1, 1955, pp. 50-104; HORVÁTH, Pavel: Poľnohospodárstvo na Slovensku v období rozkladu feudalizmu. In: Hospodářské dějiny 7, 1981, pp. 207-226; KAVULJAK, Andrej: Dejiny lesníctva a drevárstva na Slovensku. Turčiansky Sv. Martin, Lesnícka a drevárska komora 1943.

from their production. Štefan Butkovič looked at the extraction of salt in eastern Slovakia.[6]

On the history of crafts, the first work of synthesis was published in 1943 by Ivan Houdek. The next historical synthesis on crafts in the era of the guilds was published only in 1972 by Špiesz. A publication by Viliam Decker concentrated on hand paper manufacture, an article by Ján Gasper on glass production, and a book Ján Horák on the history of the Kremnica mint. Špiesz is the author of an analytic work on the manufacturing period in Slovakia, and two articles on technical advances in this sphere. Kazimír wrote about the conditions and location of the iron industry in Slovakia in an extensive article while Ákoš Paulíny concentrated on the same topic for central Slovakia in a monograph.[7]

The history of trade was also dealt with by these historians. Kazimír focused on the issues of this economic branch, researching as well the role of Slovakia in foreign trade. Horváth wrote articles about the trade contacts of eastern Slovak towns with Poland and Transylvania, and Špiesz wrote an article about the influence of marketplaces on the development of towns. Kazimír also devoted

---

[6] VOZÁR, Jozef: Habsburský panovnícky dvor a slovenské baníctvo v 16.-18. storočí. In: HČ 38, 1990, pp. 8-21.; KAZIMÍR, Štefan: Die Gewinne in der Edelmetallproduktion in der Slowakei in 16. und 17. Jahrhundert. In: Hospodářské dějiny 10, 1989, pp. 111-130; VLACHOVIČ, Jozef: Produktion und Handel mit ungarischen Kupfer in 16. und in ersten Viertel des 17. Jahrhundert. In: Aussenhandel Ostmittel-Europas 1450-1650. Wien-Köln 1971, pp. 600-627; Das goldene Bergbuch (Schemnitz, Kremnitz und Neusohl). Edited by VOZÁR, Jozef. Bratislava, Veda 1983; VLACHOVIČ, Jozef: Slovenská meď v 16. a 17. storočí. Bratislava, SAV 1964; VOZÁR, Jozef: English Mechanic Isaac Potter - Constructor of the First Fire-Engines in Slovakia. In: SHS 7, 1974, pp. 102-140; BUTKOVIČ, Viktor: Dejiny ťažby soli v Solivare. Košice, VV 1978.

[7] HOUDEK, Ivan: Cechovníctvo na Slovensku. Turčiansky Sv. Martin, Muzeálna slovenská spoločnosť 1943; ŠPIESZ, Anton: Remeslo na Slovensku v období existencie cechov. Bratislava, SAV 1972; DECKER, Viliam: Dejiny ručnej výroby papiera na Slovensku. Martin, MS 1983; GASPER, Ján: K dejinám technológie sklárskej výroby na Slovensku do konca 19. storočia. In: Z dejín vied a techniky na Slovensku 5, 1969, pp. 11-44; HORÁK, Ján: Kremnická mincovňa. Banská Bystrica, SV 1965; ŠPIESZ, Anton: Manufaktúrne obdobie na Slovensku (1725-1825). Bratislava, SAV 1961; ŠPIESZ, Anton: Prvé strojové pradiarne bavlny na Slovensku. In: HŠt 2, 1956, pp. 39-53; KAZIMÍR, Štefan: Stav a rozmiestnenie železiarskeho priemyslu na Slovensku v druhej polovici 18. storočia. In: HŠt 4, 1958, pp. 137-160; ŠPIESZ, Anton: K technickému pokroku na Slovensku na prelome 18. a 19. storočia: In: Z dejín vied a techniky na Slovensku 1, 1962, pp. 35-56; PAULÍNYI, Ákoš: Železiarstvo na Pohroní v 18. a v prvej polovici 19. storočia. Bratislava, SAV 1966.

himself to the development of prices and salaries in Slovakia, closely connected with individual branches of economic life.[8]

Of course economic events influenced *social conditions* in Slovakia. They influenced development of demographics and settlement, migration patterns, the life of individual social classes and their legal position. A good overview of village settlement was written by the geographer Štefan Fekete in 1945, and older works on Wallachian (shepherd) colonization were supplemented by a new article by Ratkoš. Mária Kohútová gave a demographic and settlement picture of western Slovakia in the sixteenth and seventeenth centuries on the basis of tax records, and Ján Sirácky researched the creation and development of Slovak settlements in the so-called Lower Lands (Dolná zem) during the eighteenth century (this southern region of the former Kingdom of Hungary is now divided between in Hungary, Romania and Yugoslavia) in the eighteenth century. Horváth, in two articles, looked at the settlement of farmers on newly cleared land and so called dispersed habitation. Juraj Žudel provided information on records of all settlements in Hungary, compiled under Maria Theresa in 1772. Špiesz dealt with the existence of so-called curial villages, where the lower nobility lived, and Ján Svetoň, Pavel Horváth and Mária Kohútová researched the number and social structure of inhabitants at the end of the eighteenth and beginning of the nineteenth century. A bibliography of Slovak historical demography was assembled by Kohútová.[9]

---

[8] KAZIMÍR, Štefan: Problémy dejín obchodu neskorého feudalizmu. In: Zborník prednášok z konferencie K dejinám obchodu. Bratislava 1987; HORVÁTH, Pavel: Obchodné styky Levoče s Poľskom v druhej polovici 16. storočia. In: HŠt 1, 1955, pp. 105-145; KAZIMÍR, Štefan: Der Fernhandel in der Slowakei im 16. Jahrhundert. In: SHS 15, 1986, pp. 47-76; HORVÁTH, Pavel: Príspevok k obchodným stykom východoslovenských miest s Poľskom a Sedmohradskom v 16. a 17. storočí. In: Nové obzory 7, 1965, pp. 131-142; KAZIMÍR, Štefan: Slovensko v medzinárodnom obchode s dobytkom v 16. storočí. In: HŠt 18, 1973, pp. 175-208; ŠPIESZ, Anton: Vplyv trhov na rozvoj miest na Slovensku v období neskorého feudalizmu. In: HČ 25, 1977, pp. 221-231; KAZIMÍR, Štefan: Der Geldumlauf im 16. Jahrhundert und die Slowakei. In: SHS 9, 1979, pp. 115-132; KAZIMÍR, Štefan: Menový vývoj na Slovensku v rokoch 1630-1703. In: Slovenská numizmatika 6, 1980, pp. 145-176; KAZIMÍR, Štefan: Preisbewegung als die Kennziffer der wirtschaftlichen Entwicklung in der Slowakei seit Anfang des 16. Jahrhunderts bis Mitte des 19. Jahrhunderts. In: SHS 7, 1974, pp. 141-160; KAZIMÍR, Štefan: Základné tendencie vývoja peňažných miezd na Slovensku v 16.-18. storočí. In: Slovenská numizmatika 1, 1970, pp. 232-251.

[9] FEKETE, Štefan: Typy vidieckeho osídlenia na Slovensku. Bratislava, 1947; RATKOŠ, Peter: Problémy kolonizácie na valašskom práve na území Slovenska. In: HŠt 24, 1980, pp. 181-224; KOHÚTOVÁ, Mária: Demografický a sídlištný obraz západného Slovenska. Bratislava, Veda 1990; SIRÁCKY, Ján: Ku vzniku a vývoju slovenského osídlenia na Dolnej zemi v 18. storočí. In: HČ 11, 1963, pp. 433-465; HORVÁTH, Pavel: Vývoj kopaníc a kopaničiarskeho osídlenia v oblasti

Pavel Križko wrote about mining towns, and a selection from his articles was published in a new edition in 1964. The overall position of towns in Slovakia was covered in articles and books by Špiesz and Michal Suchý. Vozár looked at mining towns in central Slovakia, and Marta Dobrotková examined the social structure of western Slovak towns. Špiesz also authored an article on the Slovak bourgeoisie in the eighteenth century and Žudel about the inhabitants of free royal towns in Slovakia in the second half of that century.[10]

In contrast to the previous period, we do not have any important articles about the nobility in Slovakia from the sixteenth to the eighteenth century, which during the era had been mostly Magyarized. Slovak historians devoted their attention to it only in works of synthesis on the history of Slovakia. More books and articles were written on the condition of farm serfs and mine workers and their struggle to improve their social position. Monographs on the history of serfs in the eighteenth century were published by Horváth, Špiesz and Watzka. The question of the social differentiation of these people received attention from Emilián Stavrovský, and Horváth looked at their overall role in sixteenth

---

Myjavskej pahorkatiny do konca 18. storočia. In: HŠt 23, 1979, pp. 87-170; HORVÁTH, Pavel: Historický prehľad vzniku a rozvoja chotárnych sídiel v slovenskej oblasti Karpát. In: Slovenský národopis 28, 1980, pp. 8-17; ŽUDEL, Juraj: Tereziánsky lexikón sídiel (Lexicon universorom regni Hungariae locorum populosorum). In: SlArchiv 15, 1980, pp. 74-91; ŠPIESZ, Anton: Kuriálne dediny v časoch urbárskej regulácie Márie Terézie. In: HČ 41, 1993, pp. 171-187; SVETOŇ, Ján: Obyvateľstvo Slovenska v 18. storočí. In: Demografický zborník 1, 1959, pp. 34-44; HORVÁTH, Pavel: Štruktúra spoločnosti v prechodnom období. In: Slovensko v období prechodu od feudalizmu ku kapitalizmu, pp. 131-151; KOHÚTOVÁ, Mária: Prechod od feudalizmu ku kapitalizmu a vývoj obyvateľstva. In: ibidem, pp. 152-165; NADMERNÉ ubúdanie obyvateľstva Slovenska v období r. 1700-1938. Zborník materiálov zo sympózia. Bratislava, Slovenská demografická a štatistická spoločnosť SAV 1987; KOHÚTOVÁ, Mária: Výskum vývoja obyvateľstva na Slovensku v predštatistickom období do roku 1850. In: HČ 31, 1983, pp. 437-445; Bibliografia slovenskej historickej demografie do roku 1988. In: Historická demografie 15, Praha 1991, pp. 193-205.

[10] KRIŽKO, Pavel: Z dejín banských miest. Edited by LEHOTSKÁ, Darina. Bratislava, SAV 1964; SUCHÝ, Michal: Postavenie miest na Slovensku v 16.-18. storočí. In: HŠt 17, 1972, pp. 149-154; ŠPIESZ, Anton: Mestá na Slovensku na prelome 17. a 18. storočia. In: Zb FFUK Historica 26, 1975, pp. 185-198; ŠPIESZ, Anton: Slobodné kráľovské mestá na Slovensku v rokoch 1680-1780. Košice, VV 1983; VOZÁR, Jozef: Banské mestá ako osobitný typ miest na Slovensku. In: HČ 21, 1973, pp. 386-396; DOBROTKOVÁ, Marta: K sociálnej štruktúre západoslovenských miest v 18. storočí. In: Zb FFUK Historica 37, 1987, pp. 107-117; SUCHÝ, Michal: Z politických zápasov miest so šľachtou od 16. do začiatku 18. storočia. In: HŠt 19, 1974, pp. 109-132; VOZÁR, Jozef: Boj stredoslovenských banských miest proti prejavom habsburského absolutizmu v 16. storočí. In: Sborník archívních prací 12, Praha 1962, pp. 87-112; ŠPIESZ, Anton: Slovenské meštianstvo v 18. storočí. In: HČ 14, 1966, pp. 10-36; ŽUDEL, Juraj: Obyvateľstvo slobodných kráľovských miest v druhej polovici 18. storočia. In: Geografický časopis 39, 1987, pp. 148-168.

to eighteenth centuries. The legal historian Karol Rebro published a book on land registration under Maria Theresa and on the regulations concerning serfs under Joseph II. Archivist František Sedlák wrote about views from the second half of the eighteenth and beginning of the nineteenth century on solving the serf question in Slovakia. Serf movements in Slovakia from the sixteenth to eighteenth centuries were dealt with by Horváth and Haraksim, and the role of mine workers and their social struggles in the late eighteenth and early nineteenth century by Vozár and Paulíny.[11]

Žudel published a monograph on districts (counties), and in a further article looked at their territorial reform under Joseph II. Self-administration in free royal towns in the sixteenth to the eighteenth centuries was dealt with by Špiesz and Suchý. Vlachovič wrote about the beginnings of Habsburg administration in mining and Sedlák authored a brief overview on the development of feudal domains in Slovakia. Archivist Marta Melníková published a study on the administration of serf villages and its documents.[12]

In recent times, more attention has been devoted to *national conditions* and national development of the Slovaks. A similar interest was concentrated on the

---

[11] HORVÁTH, Pavel: Poddaný ľud na Slovensku v prvej polovici 18. storočia. Bratislava, SAV 1963; ŠPIESZ, Anton - WATZKA, Jozef: Poddaní v Tekove v 18. storočí. Bratislava, Archívna správa 1966; STAVROVSKÝ, Emilián: K sociálnej diferenciácii poddaných na východnom Slovensku v 16.-17. storočí. In: Zb FFUK Historica 15, 1964, pp. 263-301; HORVÁTH, Pavel: Hospo-dársko-spoločenské a právne pomery poddanského obyvateľstva na Slovensku v 16.-18. storočí. In: HŠt 17, 1972, pp. 27-46; REBRO, Karol: Urbárska regulácia Márie Terézie a poddanské úpravy Jozefa II. Bratislava, SAV 1959; SEDLÁK, František: Názory na poddanskú otázku a jej riešenie v druhej polovici 18. a na začiatku 19. storočia. In: Hospodářské dějiny 7, 1981, pp. 339-363; HORVÁTH, Pavel: K niektorým otázkam poddanských hnutí na Slovensku v období neskorého feudalizmu. In: Acta Universitatis Carolinae, Studia Philosophica et Historica 1, Praha 1974, pp. 55-72; HARAKSIM, Ľudovít: Príspevok k roľníckemu povstaniu na východnom Slovensku v rokoch 1631-1632. In: HČ 2, 1954, pp. 351-374; VOZÁR, Jozef: Postavenie banského robotníctva na Slovensku v období neskorého feudalizmu. In: HŠt 17, 1972, pp. 161-187; PAULÍNYI, Ákoš: Sociálne hnutia baníkov na strednom Slovensku na prelome 18. a 19. storočia. Banská Bystrica, SV 1966.

[12] ŽUDEL, Juraj: Stolice na Slovensku. Bratislava, Obzor 1984; ŽUDEL, Juraj : Jozefínska reforma územnej organizácie Uhorska s osobitným zreteľom na Slovensko. In: Geografický časo-pis 24, 1972, pp. 61-85; ŠPIESZ, Anton: Samospráva slobodných kráľovských miest v rokoch 1681-1750. In: SlArchiv 12, 1977, pp. 50-88; SUCHÝ, Michal: Orgány mestskej samosprávy v Levoči v 16. a 17. storočí. In: Spiš 2, 1969, pp. 125-154; VLACHOVIČ, Jozef: Počiatky habsburskej správy v slovenskom baníctve. In: HČ 5, 1957, pp. 477-483; SEDLÁK, František: Náčrt vývinu správy feudálnych panstiev na Slovensku od polovice 16. do polovice 19. storočia. In: HŠt 10, 1965, pp. 54-87; MELNÍKOVÁ, Marta: Správa poddanských obcí a jej písomnosti v období neskorého feudalizmu. In: SlArchiv 22, 1987, 1, pp. 59-81.

development of a national consciousness and ideology. Concerning national conditions in Slovakia there exist a great number of articles and books among which it is possible to mention only a few. The Slovak living space attracted the attention of Varsik while ethnic changes in Slovakia during the sixteenth to eighteenth centuries were studied by Kveta Kučerová, who also was the author of an article about the migration of Croatians to Slovakia in the sixteenth century. The arrival and settlement of Ruthenians and/or Ukrainians in Slovakia is the subject of a book by Haraksim, and the Czech immigration after the Battle of White Mountain in 1620 is the topic of an article by Horváth. To earlier works on the Habans (descendents of the Anabaptists) in Slovakia František Kalesný contributed new research. Špiesz and Horváth wrote about Slovaks in Hungary in the eighteenth century and Ján Sirácky on their migration to the "Lower Lands" in this period. The problem of Slovak-Magyar ethnic demarcations in the past was treated by Varsik. Jozef Škultéty wrote on the Germans in Slovakia, Soňa Kovačevičová on the migration of Jews, and Emília Horváthová on the history and culture of the Romanies. A new edition of the first book on the Romanies in Hungary from the eighteenth century was published.[13]

The development of the *national life and consciousness* of Slovaks was a topic studied by Daniel Rapant, Tibenský, Ratkoš and Horváth. Vlachovič, Vozár and

---

[13] VARSIK, Branislav: Slovenský etnický priestor v minulosti. In: Slovenská liga 19, 1942, pp. 235-245; KUČEROVÁ, Kveta: Etnické zmeny na Slovensku od polovice 16. do polovice 18. storočia. In: HČ 31, 1983, pp. 523-543; HARAKSIM, Ľudovít: K sociálnym a kultúrnym dejinám Ukrajincov na Slovensku do r. 1867. Bratislava, SAV 1961; KUČEROVÁ, Kveta: Sťahovanie Chorvátov na Slovensko v 16. storočí. In: SlŠt 8, 1966, pp. 5-68; HORVÁTH, Pavel: Česká pobelohorská emigrácia na Slovensku. In: O vzájomných vzťahoch Čechov a Slovákov. Compiled by HOLOTÍK, Ľudovít. Bratislava 1956, pp. 91-96; KALESNÝ, František: Habáni na Slovensku. Bratislava, Tatran 1981; ŠPIESZ, Anton: Slováci a ich hospodárske a sociálne postavenie v Uhorsku v 18. storočí. In: HČ 28, 1980, pp. 381-399; HORVÁTH, Pavel: Slovenská societa v 18. storočí. In: Hugolín Gavlovič v dejinách slovenskej kultúry. Martin, MS 1984, pp. 217-225; SIRÁCKY, Ján: Sťahovanie Slovákov na Dolnú zem v 18. a 19. storočí. Bratislava, SAV 1966; VARSIK, Branislav: Die slowakisch-magyarische Grenze in den letzten zwei Jahrhunderten. Bratislava - Pressburg, Universum 1940; ŠKULTÉTY, Jozef: Nemci na Slovensku. In: O Slovákoch. Martin, MS 1928, pp. 293-316; KOVAČEVIČOVÁ, Soňa: Imigračné a emigračné cesty Židov na Slovensku. In: Slovenský národopis 39, 1991, 3-4, pp. 288-302; BÁRKÁNY, Eugen - DOJČ, Ľudovít: Židovské náboženské obce na Slovensku. Bratislava, Vesna 1991; HORVÁTHOVÁ, Emília: Cigáni na Slovensku. Bratislava, SAV 1964; other titles devoted to Romanies in Slovakia are for example GECELOVSKÝ, Vladimír: Rómovia na Gemeri do roku 1945. Rožňava, Okresné osvetové stredisko 1990; ŠALAMON, Pavol: Cigáni z Abovskej a Turnianskej stolice v období osvietenstva. In: Neznámi Rómovia. Compiled by MANN, Arne B. Bratislava, Ister Science Press 1992, pp.73-77; AUGUSTINI ab Hortis, Samuel: Cigáni v Uhorsku 1775 / Zigeuner in Ungarn 1775. Bratislava, Štúdio -dd- 1995.

Jozef Markov investigated the national struggle of Slovaks in towns. Horváth and Sedlák looked at the contribution of the citizens of small towns towards Slovak national life and the linguist Ján Doruľa at the language of Slovaks in the past.[14]

Concerning the national development of Slovaks during the Slovak national revival, most of the new information has been provided by Mária Vyvíjalová, Anton A. Baník, Ján Tibenský and Ján Považan. Hadrián Radváni and Ján Hučko researched the cultural, organizational and educational activities of the members of the first generation of the national revival, and Vladimír Matula the process of the formation of the modern Slovak nation.[15]

On the creation of the national ideology of Slovaks and their historical traditions, we can find the most information in books and journal articles by Tibenský, Baník, Vyvíjalová, Rapant and Jozef Butvin.[16]

---

[14] RAPANT, Daniel: Vývin slovenského národného povedomia. In: Historický zborník Matice slovenskej 5, 1947, 1, pp.1-16; TIBENSKÝ, Ján: Problémy výskumu, vzniku a vývoja slovenskej feudálnej národnosti. In: HČ 9, 1961, pp. 397-419; RATKOŠ, Peter: Otázky vývoja slovenskej národnosti do začiatku 17. storočia. In: HČ 20, 1972, pp. 19-64; HORVÁTH, Pavel: Slovenská národnosť v 16. a 17. storočí. In: HČ 28, 1980, pp. 361-380; VLACHOVIČ, Jozef: Národnostné boje v mestách na Slovensku v 16. a v 17. storočí. In: Slováci a ich národný vývin. Compiled by MÉSÁROŠ, Július. Bratislava, SAV 1966, pp. 73-91; VOZÁR, Jozef: Národnostné zápasy v stredoslovenských banských mestách a národné povedomie od 16. do polovice 18. storočia. In: HČ 28, 1980, pp. 554-557; MARKOV, Jozef: Odraz politických zápasov v obecnej správe Banskej Bystrice v 16.-19. storoč. Bratislava, SAV 1973; HORVÁTH, Pavel - SEDLÁK, František: Zemepanské mestá a mestečká a ich prínos pre rozvoj slovenskej národnosti v období neskorého feudalizmu. In: HČ 29, 1983, pp. 877-894; DORUĽA, Ján: O jazyku slovenskej feudálnej národnosti v 15.-18. storoč. In: Jazykovedný časopis 27, 1977, pp. 46-57.

[15] K počiatkom slovenského národného obrodenia. Bratislava, SAV 1964; VYVÍJALOVÁ, Mária: Bratislavský generálny seminár a jeho význam pre slovenské národné hnutie. In: Slovenské učené tovarišstvo 1792-1992. Edited by PETRÁŠ, Milan. Trnava, Západoslovenské múzeum 1993, pp. 19-40; BANÍK, Anton A.: Pomocníci Antona Bernoláka v rokoch 1786-1790 pri diele slovenského literárneho obrodenia. In: Kultúra 9, 1937, č. 9-10, pp. 193-203; TIBENSKÝ, Ján: Bernolák's Influence and the Origine of the Slovak Awakening. In: SHS 2, 1962, pp. 140-180; POVAŽAN, Ján: Bernolák a bernolákovci. Martin, Osveta 1990; RADVÁNI, Hadrián: Slovenské učené tovarišstvo. Organizácie a členstvo 1792-1796. Trnava, Spolok Sv. Vojtecha 1992; HUČKO, Ján: Výchovnovzdelávacia činnosť buditeľov ľudu na počiatku slovenského národného obrodenia. In: HŠt 4, 1958, pp. 89-116; MATULA, Vladimír: Prechod od feudalizmu ku kapitalizmu a formovanie slovenského národa. In: HČ 30, 1982, pp. 40-46.

[16] TIBENSKÝ, Ján: Ideológia slovenskej feudálnej národnosti pred národným obrodením. In: Slováci a ich národný vývin. Bratislava 1969, pp. 92-113; TIBENSKÝ, Ján: Slovanství a ideologie slovenské národnosti v 17. a 18. století. In: Slovanství v dějinách našich národů. Brno 1968, pp. 75-95; TIBENSKÝ, Ján: Chvály a obrany slovenského národa. Bratislava, SVKL 1965; BANÍK, Anton A.: Ján Baltazár Magin a jeho politická, národná i kultúrna obrana Slovákov roku 1728. In: Zborník

In the *cultural and educational sphere* from the sixteenth to eighteenth century, different ideological streams developed (Humanism, the Baroque and the Enlightenment), as well as diverse literary and artistic expressions. The beginnings of Slovak historiography are connected with the development of humanistic literature and education in the second half of the sixteenth and the beginning of the seventeenth century. Cultural development in Slovakia covers a broad area which is why not only historians but scholars from other disciplines have contributed to its investigation. About ideological streams in the sixteenth to eighteenth centuries, new understanding has been brought not only by the historians Čičaj, Tibenský and Kowalská, but by literary scholars Ján Ďurovič and Milan Hamada. It is necessary to admit that issues of the Baroque as an ideological movement have not yet been researched in Slovak historiography.[17]

Concerning the history of schools in this period, there are many articles and books from the pens of historians and educational historians. Of these, Peter Vajcík published a monograph on schools, study and school rules in the sixteenth century, and Vladislav Ružička wrote on the history of schools on late feudalism. The historian Anton Vantuch interpreted the school reforms under Maria Theresa, and a reprint of these (*Ratio Educationis*) was brought out. Eva Kowalská published a book on elementary schools in Slovakia at the end of the eighteenth and the beginning of the nineteenth century and added an article on the Royal Academy in Bratislava during the same period. The development of more advanced schools in Slovakia concerned František Bokes, while Vendelín

---

literárnovedeckého odboru Spolku sv. Vojtecha III. 1-2. Trnava 1936; VYVÍJALOVÁ, Mária: Formovanie ideológie rovnoprávnosti Slovákov v 18. storočí. In: HČ 29, 1981, pp. 373-403; RAPANT, Daniel: K počiatkom maďarizácie I.-II. Bratislava, Zemedelské múzeum 1927, 1931; TIBENSKÝ, Ján: Funkcia cyrilometodskej a veľkomoravskej tradície v ideológii slovenskej národnosti. In: HČ 40, 1992, pp. 575-594; BUTVIN, Jozef: Cyrilometodejská a veľkomoravská tradícia v slovenskom národnom obrodení. In: HŠt 16, 1971, pp. 133-148.

[17] ČIČAJ, Viliam: Vývoj vzdelanosti v našich dejinách v období neskorého feudalizmu. In: HČ 34, 1986, pp. 349-361; Humanizmus a renesancia na Slovensku v 15. a 16. storočí. Edited by HOLOTÍK, Ľudovít - VANTUCH, Anton. Bratislava, SAV 1967; ĎUROVIČ, Ján: Slovenský pietizmus. In: Historica Slovaca 3-4, 1945-1946, pp. 95-113; Matej Bel, doba, život a dielo. Edited by TIBENSKÝ, Ján. Bratislava, Veda 1987; ČIČAJ, Viliam: Príspevok ku kultúrnemu obrazu Slovenska v prvej polovici 18. storočia. In: HČ 31, 1983, pp. 711-723; TIBENSKÝ, Ján: Prvé snahy a pokusy o organizovanie vedeckého života v Bratislave. In: Kapitoly z vedeckého života v Bratislave. Compiled by PÖSS, Ondrej. Bratislava, Veda 1991, pp. 9-26; HAMADA, Milan: Zrod osvietenskej kultúry. In: Slovenská literatúra 37, 1990, pp. 393-427; KOWALSKÁ, Eva: Osvietenstvo ako model modernizácie spoločnosti. In: Slovenské učené tovarišstvo 1792-1992 (see note 15), pp. 13-18; TIBENSKÝ, Ján: Príspevok k dejinám osvietenstva a jozefinizmu na Slovensku. In: HŠt 14, 1969, pp. 98-115.

Jankovič and Ondrej R. Halaga researched the history of the universities in Trnava and Košice, and Vlachovič devoted attention to the mining academy in Banská Štiavnica.[18]

The literary creativity of the periods of Humanism and Baroque was researched mostly by literary historians, Eva Tkáčiková, Jozef Minárik, Hamada and Ján Mišianik producing synthetic reviews. Monographs of the works of individual authors were published either as annals or from the pens of Anton Vantuch, Miloslav Okáľ and Gizela Gáfriková. Ján Vilikovský researched the collection of Catholic spiritual songs. Review of bibliographic culture and the development of printing were covered by Čičaj, Valach and Jozef Repčák.[19]

Examining (in books and annals) the development of the visual arts and music were art historians Vladimír Wagner, Jaroslav Dubnický, Ivan Rusina, Alžbeta Güntherová-Mayerová, Anna Petrová-Pleskotová, and musicologists Ladislav

---

[18] VAJCÍK, Peter: Školstvo, študijné a školské poriadky na Slovensku v 16. storočí. Bratislava, SAV 1955; RUŽIČKA, Vladislav: Školstvo na Slovensku v období neskorého feudalizmu. Bratislava, Štátne pedagogické nakladateľstvo 1974; VANTUCH, Anton: Cesta k tereziánskym školským reformám a boje o ich charakter. In: HČ 24, 1980, pp. 141-161; Ratio educationis 1777 a 1806. Prvá jednotná sústava výchovy a vzdelávania v dejinách našej kultúry. Edited by MIKLEŠ, Ján - NOVACKÁ, Mária. Bratislava, SPN 1988; KOWALSKÁ, Eva: Štátne ľudové školstvo na Slovensku na prelome 18. a 19. storočia. Bratislava, Veda 1987; BOKES, František: Rozvoj vyššieho školstva na Slovensku v 17.-19. storočí. In: Prešovské kolégium v slovenských dejinách. Compiled by SEDLÁK, Imrich. Košice, VV 1967, pp. 7-39; JANKOVIČ, Vendelín: Založenie trnavskej univerzity. In: SlArchiv 23, 1988, 2, pp. 60-79; Trnavská univerzita v Slovenských dejinách. Edited by ČIČAJ, Viliam. Bratislava, Veda 1987; HALAGA, Ondrej R.: Z dejín košickej univerzity. In: HČ 4, 1956, pp. 521-535; VLACHOVIČ, Jozef: Die Bergakademie im 18. Jahrhundert. In: SHS 2, 1964, pp. 103-139; KOWALSKÁ, Eva: Kráľovská akadémia v Bratislave na prelome 18. a 19. storočia. In: Kapitoly z vedeckého života v Bratislave (see note 17), pp. 27-38.

[19] TKÁČIKOVÁ, Eva: Podoby slovenskej literatúry obdobia renesancie. In: Litteraria 26, 1988; VANTUCH, Anton: Ján Sambucus, život a dielo renesančného učenca. Bratislava, SAV 1975; OKÁĽ, Miloslav: Život a dielo Martina Rakovského. Martin, MS 1979; Jakub Jakobeus, život, dielo a doba. Compiled by OTČENÁŠ, Michal - KÓNYA, Peter. Prešov, Filozofická fakulta Univerzity P. J. Šafárika 1993; MINÁRIK, Jozef: Baroková literatúra. Svetová, česká, slovenská. Bratislava, SPN 1984; Tranovského sborník. Liptovský Sv. Mikuláš, Tranoscius 1936; VILIKOVSKÝ, Ján: Canthus Catholici. In: Bratislava 9, 1935, pp. 269-306; HAMADA, Milan: Od baroka ku klasicizmu. Bratislava, SAV 1967; MIŠIANIK, Ján: Pohľady do staršej slovenskej literatúry. Bratislava, SAV 1974; ČIČAJ, Viliam: Knižná kultúra na Slovensku v 16.-18. storočí. Bratislava, Veda 1985; VALACH, Július: Staré tlačiarne a tlačiari na Slovensku. Martin, MS 1987; REPČÁK, Jozef: Prehľad dejín kníhtlačiarstva na Slovensku. Bratislava, "Tlač" 1948.

Burlas, Ján Fišer, Antonín Horejší, Richard Rybarič, Darina Múdra and Ladislav Mokrý.[20]

A review of the beginnings of Slovak historiography in the period before the national revival came from Horváth, and, in the period of the national revival, from Tibenský. Books on its individual representatives were written by Vantuch, Marsina and Sopko.[21]

---

[20] WAGNER, Vladimír: Vývin výtvarného umenia na Slovensku. Bratislava, SAVU 1948; Architektúra na Slovensku do 19. storočia. Bratislava, SVKL 1958; DUBNICKÝ, Jaroslav: Ranobarokový univerzitný kostol v Trnave. Bratislava, SAVU 1948; RUSINA, Ivan: Renesančná a baroková plastika v Bratislave. Bratislava, Tatran 1983; Donnerov okruh na Slovensku. Bratislava 1955; GÜNTHEROVÁ-MAYEROVÁ, Alžbeta: Barokové umenie na Slovensku. In: Pamiatky a múzeá 5, 1955, pp. 145-167; PETROVÁ-PLESKOTOVÁ, Anna: Maliarstvo 18. storočia na Slovensku. Bratislava, Veda 1983; Svätci v strednej Európe / Heilige in Zentraleuropa. Edited by RUSINA, Ivan. Bratislava, Slovenská národná galéria 1993; BURLAS, Ladislav - FIŠER, Ján - HOREJŠÍ, Antonín: Hudba na Slovensku v 17. storočí. Bratislava, SAV 1954; RYBARIČ, Richard: Slovenská hudba 17.-18. storočia vo svetle novoobjavených prameňov. In: Sborník prací Filosofické fakulty brněnské university 14, Řada uměnovědná. Brno 1965; MOKRÝ, Ladislav: Počiatky hudobného baroka na Slovensku. In: Hudobnovedné štúdie 7, 1966; RYBARIČ, Richard: Dejiny hudobnej kultúry na Slovensku. I. Stredovek, renesancia, barok. Bratislava, Opus 1984; MÚDRA, Darina: Dejiny hudobnej kultúry na Slovensku II. Klasicizmus. Bratislava, Slovenský hudobný fond 1993.

[21] HORVÁTH, Pavel: Počiatky slovenskej historiografie. In: HČ 30, 1982, pp. 859-877; HORVÁTH, Pavel: Slovenská historiografia v období pred národným obrodením. Part 1. In: HČ 31, 1983, pp. 85-110; Part 2. In: HČ 31, 1983, pp. 231-250; VANTUCH, Anton: Martin Szentiványi - príspevok k jeho životu a dielu. In: HČ 27, 1979, pp. 533-552; MARSINA, Richard: Samuel Timon a jeho predstavy o najstarších dejinách Slovákov. In: HČ 28, 1980, pp. 238-252; SOPKO, Július: Dielo Petra Revu a jeho význam pre slovenskú historiografiu. In: HČ 28, 1980, pp. 400-417; MARSINA, Richard: Osvietenský historik Ján Severíni (1716-1789). In: HČ 29, 1981, pp. 404-414; MARSINA, Richard : Adam František Kollár ako historik. In: Literárnomúzejný letopis 19, 1985, pp. 155-180; TIBENSKÝ, Ján: Slovak Historiography in the Period of the Beginnings of the Slovak National Revival (1780-1830). In: SHS 13, 1984, pp. 107-135.

SLOVAK HISTORIOGRAPHY ON THE PERIOD 1800–1918

We can divide Slovak historiography concerning this period according to our conception of Slovak history and periodization of historical development, that is, to the basic phases of the historical process. The tendency and content of the historical development of Slovakia in these phases, as well as its specific problems, arising from the peculiarities and foreign and domestic conditions of the emancipation process, have been reflected in the goals of historical research and the character of its literature. This was not only the result of the differentiation of a variety of research activities but also a reflection of the improvement of the conceptual and theoretical tools for the interpretation of historical development including those events that are the key elements of the basic concepts. The three phases of historiographical review start with the years 1800-1848, which include the active development of the modern Slovak nation, and ideas concerning the need to change feudal to a modern civil society. This was followed by the 1848–1914 phase when the basic aim of the national emancipation movement was the struggle for political recognition of the independence of the Slovak nation and then by the 1914–1918 phase when, as a result of the interaction of power interests during the war, the idea of ending the Austro-Hungarian monarchy was realized, creating conditions in which the right to national self-determination in independent states was possible.

A complex review of the development of Slovakia in this period can be obtained from the newest synthetic works such as *Dejiny Slovenska II–IV* (Bratislava 1986–1992). These also contain sections of bibliography of published sources and works. Michal Potemra and Michal Otčenáš in particular devoted themselves to the historiography of this period.[1]

1. 1800–1848

Concerning the period before the revolution of 1848-1849, the first works were created by the older Slovak historiography, before 1918. Its interest was

---

[1] OTČENÁŠ, Michal: Slovenská historiografia v rokoch 1848-1918. Prešov, Metodické centrum 1993; POTEMRA, Michal: Slovak Historiography at the Turn of the 19th and 20th Centuries (1880-1918). In: SHS 13, 1984, pp. 217-271.

focused above all upon the problems of the national emancipation process in the political and cultural sphere. This interest came from the need to stress the continuity of nation-building which also resulted in the desire to explain its historical roots. In the same way Slovak historians stressed those tendencies in public and political life that falsely presented the multinational Hungary as a Magyar political state, neglecting the natural rights and interests of non-Magyar nations to development their own national life. In this context they emphasized the "national defense" actions of the Slovaks, which contributed to the concept of Slovak national identity and to the formation of the further program of the national movement. This concentration upon aspects of the national emancipation in historical development was important in explaining the movement's emphasis on national equality in the Hungarian state.

After 1918 works on economic and social problems were created,[2] though central were always questions of the Slovak national movement and its protagonists.[3]

After the creation of the Czechoslovak Republic attention was devoted to the relation between Slovaks and Czechs in the national revival. However, there was confusion on the issue of the Slovak national identity and the role of Štúr's generation in the statutory establishment of the Slovak written language. This depended upon the view of a particular author on whether Slovaks were an independent nation[4] or part of a Czechoslovak nation.[5]

Slovak historiography after 1945 stressed the economic and social issues of society's development. Important for the understanding of these issues are works and editions of documents that deal with the role of serfs and anti-feudal struggles before 1848.[6] Works were published on crafts, manufacturing[7] and

---

[2] JANŠÁK, Štefan: Slovensko v dobe uhorského feudalizmu. Hospodárske pomery od roku 1514 do roku 1848. Bratislava, Zemedelské múzeum 1932.

[3] RAPANT, Daniel: Slovenský prestolný prosbopis z roku 1842. Liptovský Sv. Mikuláš, Tranoscius 1943; BUJNÁK, Pavol: Dr. Karol Kuzmány. Život a dielo. Liptovský Sv. Mikuláš, Tranoscius 1927; PAUČO, Jozef: Ľudovýchova u štúrovcov. Turčiansky Sv. Martin, MS 1943.

[4] ŠKULTÉTY, Jozef: Stodvadsaťpäť rokov zo slovenského života 1790-1914. Turčiansky Sv. Martin, Kníhtlačiarsky účastinársky spolok 1920.

[5] HODŽA, Milan: Československý rozkol. Turčiansky Sv. Martin, published by author 1920;

[6] RAPANT, Daniel: Sedliacke povstanie na východnom Slovensku roku 1831. I. - Dejiny, II. - Dokumenty. Bratislava, Vydavateľstvo SAV 1953; Roľnícke povstanie 1831. Edited by ŠULC, Viliam. Košice, VV 1984; GÁCSOVÁ, Alžbeta (Ed.): Dokumenty k protifeudálnym bojom slovenského ľudu (1113-1848). Bratislava, SAV 1955; HORVÁTH Pavol (Ed.): Listy poddaných z rokov 1538-1848. Bratislava, SAV 1955.

[7] ŠPIESZ, Anton: Manufaktúrne obdobie na Slovensku 1725-1825. Bratislava, SAV 1961; ŠPIESZ, Anton: Remeslá, cechy a manufaktúry na Slovensku. Martin, Osveta 1983; ŠPIESZ, Anton: Remeslo na Slovensku v období existencie cechov. Bratislava, SAV 1972.

ironworks.[8] Attention was also devoted to social issues,[9] migration movements,[10] the beginning of cooperatives,[11] and the structure of the Slovak intelligentsia.[12]

For the research of political, social and cultural activities, it was crucial to publish books of sources, particularly the works and letters of the leaders of the national revival as well as resource materials on additional themes. The edition of national defense documents in Slovak translation gave material on Slovak argumentation in the struggle for linguistic and cultural equality of the peoples in Hungary and against Magyarization tendencies in public life,[13] to the analysis of which a special monograph was devoted.[14]

Historiography after 1945 broadened and deepened research on the national revival.[15] It was mostly expressed through the interpretation of Bernolák's movement in the national emancipation process which created the beginning phases of the revival. Besides the ideological and political profile of the movement, research concentrated on personalities and their understanding of the identity of the Slovak nation, language and culture.[16]

Research of the second phase of national revival had a similar intention,

---

[8] HAPÁK, Pavel: Dejiny železiarskeho priemyslu na Slovensku od konca 18. storočia do roku 1867. Bratislava, SAV 1962; PAULINYI, Ákoš: Železiarstvo na Pohroní v 18. a v prvej polovici 19. storočia. Bratislava, SAV 1966.

[9] PAULINYI, Ákoš: Sociálne hnutie baníkov na strednom Slovensku na prelome 18. a 19. storočia. Banská Bystrica, SV 1966.

[10] SIRÁCKY, Ján: Sťahovanie Slovákov na Dolnú zem v 18.a 19. storočí. Bratislava, SAV 1966.

[11] RUTTKAY, Fraňo: Samuel Jurkovič, priekopník slovenského družstevníctva a jeho doba. Bratislava, Obzor 1965.

[12] HUČKO, Ján: Sociálne zloženie a pôvod slovenskej obrodeneckej inteligencie. Bratislava, Veda 1974.

[13] ORMIS, Ján Vladimír (Ed.): O reč a národ. Slovenské národné obrany z rokov 1832 - 1848. Bratislava, SAV 1973.

[14] RAPANT, Daniel: Ilegálna maďarizácia 1790-1840. Martin, MS 1947.

[15] BUTVIN, Jozef: Slovenské národnozjednocovacie hnutie (1780-1848). Bratislava, SAV 1965; HUČKO, Ján (Ed.): Bratislava a počiatky slovenského národného obrodenia. Dokumenty. Bratislava, Obzor 1992; TIBENSKÝ, Ján (Ed.): K počiatkom slovenského národného obrodenia. Bratislava, SAV 1964; KOTVAN, Imrich: Bernolákovci. Trnava, Spolok sv. Vojtecha 1948; PETRÁŠ, Milan (Ed.): Slovenské učené tovarišstvo 1792-1992. Trnava, Západoslovenské múzeum 1993; POVAŽAN, Ján: Bernolák a bernolákovci. Martin, Osveta 1990; SEDLÁK, Imrich: Strieborný vek I.-II. Košice, VV 1970; ŠIMONČIČ, Jozef: Ohlasy Francúzskej revolúcie na Slovensku. Košice, VV 1982.

[16] BRTÁŇ, Rudolf: Bohuslav Tablic (1769-1832). Bratislava, Veda 1974; CHOVAN, Juraj - MAJTÁN, Milan (Ed.): Pamätnica Antona Bernoláka. Martin, MS 1992.

devoting itself to the problem of the national unification process, which was current in Catholic and Protestant elements of the nationally conscious intelligentsia – for it was the intelligentsia which created the ideology, outlined the aims and directed the activities of the emancipation movement.[17]

The greatest attention of Slovak historiography was devoted to the third phase of the national revival: Štúr's period. Research was concentrated on the organization of the activity of Štúr's movement,[18] the character of its ideological and political orientation,[19] its anti-feudal goals, and the democratic nature of the program of national emancipation efforts,[20] as well as on cooperation with other Slavic nations and the concept of Slavic mutuality.[21] Books and annals on the leading personalities of Štúr's generation witness not only their personal profile but their role in political, social and cultural events, which formed the basis of the national creative process.[22]

According to the degree to which the spiritual side of this process was considered important, the attention of individual researchers naturally was devoted to the revival's philosophy and ideas,[23] as well as to the individual elements of national culture. This is reflected in the scope of literary-historical works that emphasized the connection of the trends and content of literary creativity with the struggles of national emancipation. It also was reflected in the concentration of research on the development of the written Slovak language,[24] particularly on

---

[17] HUČKO, Ján: On the Questions of the Historical Work of Štúr's Generation. In: SHS 13, 1984, pp. 165-199; GOLEMA, Andrej: Pavol Jozeffy. Banská Bystrica, SV 1967; HUČKO, Ján: Gašpar Fejérpataky-Belopotocký. Bratislava, SAV 1965; JANKOVIČ, Vendelín: Ján Čaplovič, Turčiansky Sv. Martin, MS 1945; BOLFÍK, Július (Ed.): Juraj Palkovič. Bratislava, Obzor 1971; VONGREJ, Pavol (Ed.): Karol Kuzmány 1806-1866. Martin, MS 1967; MAŤOVČÍK, Augustín: Martin Hamuljak. Bratislava, SAV 1971; ROSENBAUM, Karol: Pavol Jozef Šafárik. Bratislava, Osveta 1961; VYVÍJALOVÁ, Mária: Juraj Palkovič (1769-1950). Bratislava, SAV 1968.

[18] BÉDER, Ján: Spoločnosť česko-slovenská a Slovanský ústav v Bratislave v rokoch 1835-1840. Bratislava, Vysoká škola pedagogická 1957; RAPANT, Daniel: Tatrín. Martin, MS 1950.

[19] MATUŠKA, Alexander: Štúrovci. Bratislava, Pravda 1948.

[20] MATULA, Vladimír (Ed.): Ľudovít Štúr - život a dielo. Bratislava, SAV 1956.

[21] HARAKSIM, Ľudovít: K sociálnym a kultúrnym dejinám Ukrajincov na východnom Slovensku do roku 1867. Bratislava, SAV 1961; HOLOTÍK, Ľudovít (Ed.): Ľudovít Štúr und die slawische Wechselseitigkeit. Bratislava, SAV 1969.

[22] GOLÁŇ, Karol: Ľudovít Štúr 1856-1956. Bratislava, SPN 1956; HUČKO, Ján: Michal Miloslav Hodža. Bratislava, Epocha 1970; HUČKO, Ján: Život a dielo Ľudovíta Štúra. Martin, Osveta 1984.

[23] VÁROSSOVÁ, Elena: Slovenské obrodenecké myslenie. Bratislava, SAV 1963.

[24] PAULINY, Eugen: Dejiny spisovnej slovenčiny od začiatku po súčasnosť. Bratislava, SPN 1983.

the initiatives of the Štúr generation–for the written language was one of the most important attributes of the identity of the Slovak nation. From the need to explain the whole spiritual climate of the period of the Slovak nation's formation, works were created on schools,[25] culture,[26] societies,[27] journalism,[28] theaters[29] and other branches of cultural activities.

2. 1848–1914

Already in this period, important works about contemporary Slovak history were being written. At that time Slovak historians stressed, above all else, aspects of continuity in the development of the Slovaks and focused mostly upon events characteristic of the struggle for recognition of national rights within the Habsburg monarchy. Research of events in the political and cultural sphere that played an important role in the emancipation process, such as the revolutionary movement of 1848–1849,[30] occupied the foreground. Also emphasized were the actions of important personalities who took part in forming the ideology and program of the political movement and who created the shape of Slovak society.

Historical production on this period reflected the wider social function of Slovak historiography, because it helped to establish the ideas of national identity and equality in the context of the broader intentions of the emancipation movement.

From this period it is necessary to mention not only works of synthesis[31] but

---

[25] BAKOŠ, Ľudovít: Štúrovci a slovenská škola v prvej polovici 19. storočia. Bratislava, SPN 1960.

[26] PASIAR, Štefan: Dejiny knižníc na Slovensku. Bratislava, SPN 1977; PASIAR, Štefan - PAŠKA, Pavol: Osveta na Slovensku. Jej vznik, začiatky a vývoj. Bratislava, Osveta 1964.

[27] PASIAR, Štefan: Spolkový život Slovákov - náčrt jeho začiatkov a vývinu do roku 1918. Bratislava, Osvetový ústav 1968; MANNOVÁ, Elena: Spolky a ich miesto v živote spoločnosti na Slovensku v 19. storočí. Stav a problémy výskumu. In: HČ 38, 1990, 1, pp. 15-27; MANNOVÁ, Elena: Historický prehľad spolkového hnutia na Slovensku z aspektu formovania občianskej spoločnosti. In: Občianska spoločnosť. Problémy a perspektívy v ČSFR. Bratislava, Sociologický ústav SAV, pp. 71-80.

[28] RUTTKAY, Fraňo: Ľudovít Štúr ako publicista a tvorca slovenskej politickej žurnalistiky. Martin, MS 1982; VYVÍJALOVÁ, Mária: Slovenskje národňje novini. Boje o ich povolenie. Martin, Osveta 1972.

[29] ČAVOJSKÝ, Ladislav - ŠTEFKO, Vladimír: Slovenské ochotnícke divadlo 1830-1980. Bratislava, Obzor 1983.

[30] DOHNÁNY, Mikuláš: Historia povstaňja slovenskjeho z r. 1848. Skalica, F.X.Škarnicel 1850; ŠTEFANOVIČ; Samuel: Slovenské povstanie z roku 1848/49. Trnava, published by author 1886.

[31] BOTTO, Július: Krátka história Slovákov. Turčiansky Sv. Martin, Kníhtlačiarsky účastinársky spolok 1914; BOTTO, Július: Slováci, vývin ich národného povedomia I.-II. Turčiansky Sv. Martin, Kníhtlačiarsky účastinársky spolok 1906, 1910.

also monographs[32] that form an organic part of the values of the developing modern Slovak historical science. In the creation of historical consciousness and dissemination of historical knowledge, journalism played an important role, because in the given conditions, it was a substitute for the missing parts of professional historiography. Historical journalism stressed the connection of historiography with other branches of science, culture and education.

After the creation of Czechoslovakia in 1918, the conditions for the development of Slovak historiography were changed, not only in the professional intentions of the research, but also in the broader thematic spectrum of published works. A significant feature was the approach to the research of previous periods from the reality of the new state. The variation in ideological positions of the authors of new works was highlighted in the interpretation and evaluation of personalities and events that had become the subject of professional interest.

Slovak historiography devoted its primary attention to the questions of political development. Witness to this are publications devoted to the revolutionary years of 1848–1849[33] as well as other monographs employing a serious resource basis.[34]

In this period publication of a monumental work by Daniel Rapant concerning the Slovak uprising 1848-1849[35] was begun. The author's interpretation of the issues explicates the continuity of the Slovak national creative process of the first half of the nineteenth century with regard to the political and national conditions in central Europe. An important part of historical production is work on the activities of the leading figures in national life, in which broader

---

[32] HURBAN VAJANSKÝ, Svetozár: Život Štefana Moyzesa. Turčiansky Sv. Martin, Kníhkupecko-nakladateľský spolok 1897; STODOLA, Emil: Štatistika Slovenska. Turčiansky Sv. Martin, published by author 1912; ŠKULTÉTY, Jozef: Slovenské memorandum roku 1861. Turčiansky Sv. Martin, Kníhtlačiarsky účastinársky spolok 1911.

[33] GOLÁŇ, Karol: Revolučné pokolenie. Príspevky k dejinám slovenského povstania v roku 1848-1849 v podbradlanskom kraji. Myjava, Daniel Pažický 1926; GOLÁŇ, Karol: Rok so štúrovcami. Myjava, Daniel Pažický 1944; KOMPIŠ, Peter: Slovenské povstanie roku 1848-1849. Praha, Ministerstvo školství a národní osvěty 1924.

[34] BOKES, František: Pokusy o slovensko-maďarské vyrovnanie v rokoch 1861-1868. Turčiansky Sv. Martin, MS 1941; RAPANT, Daniel: Viedenské memorandum slovenské z roku 1861. Turčiansky Sv. Martin, MS 1943; VOTRUBA, František: Slovensko v politickej aktivite. In: ŠTEFÁNEK, Anton - VOTRUBA, František - SEĎA, František (Ed.): Milan Hodža. Publicista, politik, vedecký pracovník. Praha, Českomoravské podniky tiskařské a vydavatelské 1930.

[35] RAPANT, Daniel: Slovenské povstanie roku 1848-1849. Dejiny a dokumenty I.-IV. Turčiansky Sv. Martin - Bratislava, MS - SAV 1937-1973.

aspects of national, political and cultural development[36] are also reflected. An extensive book on the life of Slovak emigrants to the USA was written.[37]

The general problems of national and political life were dealt with in works of review,[38] but especially in specialized articles and historical journalism. The intention of these was to emphasize the direction of Slovak emancipational efforts, the character of the national question in Hungary, and the pursuit of Hungarian politics and its negative impact on the national life of Slovaks.

The importance of the cultural sphere for the preservation and cultivation of national identity was manifested in the need to explain the history of Matica slovenská,[39] the women's society Živena,[40] and the unfavorable conditions for the education of Slovak youth.[41]

After 1945, the development of Slovak historiography was determined by the political and social conditions resulting from the power position of the Communist Party and the dominance of its ideology. This ran through the whole world of historical production, from the methodological principles to the thematic structure of research. The impact of non-scientific influences was felt especially strongly in the research of modern history, mostly in the interpreta-

---

[36] BOKES, František: Viliam Pauliny-Tóth, slovenský poslanec v rokoch 1869-1872. Turčiansky Sv. Martin, MS 1942; ČULEN, Konštantín: Karol Salva. Život a dielo. Liptovský Sv. Mikuláš, Tranoscius 1943; JANŠÁK, Štefan: Andrej Kmeť. Turčiansky Sv. Martin, Muzeálna slovenská spoločnosť 1941; JANŠÁK, Štefan: Daniel G. Lichard. Bratislava - Skalica, Komitét pre rozširovanie Lichardových spisov 1932; JANŠÁK, Štefan: Život Štefana Fajnora. Bratislava, Bibliotheka 1935; KUČERA, Matúš: F. V. Sasinek - Founder of Slovak Historiography. In: SHS 13, 1984, pp. 201-216; MEDVECKÝ, Karol Anton: Andrej Kmeť, jeho život a dielo I.-II. Bojnice, published by author 1925; MRÁZ, Andrej: Jozef Škultéty. Turčiansky Sv. Martin, MS 1933; MRÁZ, Andrej: Svetozár Hurban Vajanský. Bratislava, Slovenská grafia 1926; SIDOR, Karol: Andrej Hlinka (1864-1926). Bratislava, Andrej 1934; ŠTEFÁNEK, Anton: Milan Hodža. Bratislava, Grafia 1938; ŠTELLER, Ferdinand: Andrej Radlinský I.-II. Trnava, Spolok sv. Vojtecha 1934.

[37] ČULEN, Konštantín: Dejiny Slovákov v Amerike I.-II. Bratislava, Slovenská liga 1942.

[38] BOKES, František: Vývin predstáv o slovenskom území v 19. storočí. Martin, MS 1945; ĎURČANSKÝ, Ferdinand: Pohľad na slovenskú politickú minulosť. Bratislava, published by author 1943; RUPPELDT, Fedor: Koncentračné snahy slovenské do roku 1928. Turčiansky Sv. Martin, Kníhtlačiarsky účastinársky spolok 1928; ŠTEFÁNEK, Anton: Základy sociografie Slovenska. Slovenská vlastiveda. Volume III.: Spoločnosť. Bratislava, Nakladateľstvo SAVU 1945.

[39] BOTTO, Július: Dejiny Matice slovenskej (1863-1875). Turčiansky Sv. Martin, MS 1922; MRÁZ, Andrej: Matica slovenská v rokoch 1863-1875. Turčiansky Sv. Martin, MS 1935.

[40] VOTRUBOVÁ, Štefánia: Živena, jej osudy a práca. Turčiansky Sv. Martin, Živena 1931.

[41] ČULEN, Konštantín: Roky slovenských nádejí a sklamaní 1848-1875. Trnava, Ústredie slovenského katolíckeho študentstva 1932; ČULEN, Konštantín: Slovenské študentské tragédie I.-II. Bratislava, Slovenská liga 1935.

tion of issues involving workers and the socialist movement, churches and religious life, ideology, the national consciousness, and relations with other nations.

At this time, emphasis on the investigation of economic and social development grew. In this area, books on agrarian[42] and industrial[43] issues, transport[44] and the monetary system[45] appeared. Demographical development and habitation patterns[46] also attracted attention. Collected source documents concerning the history of Slovak emigration[47] covered not only the reasons of this significant phenomenon in the development of Slovak society but also the basic aspects of the lives of Slovaks abroad and their fruitful contacts and connections with Slovakia.

In political history basic sources on national political efforts of 1848-1901 were published.[48] The original project for the period till 1914 has yet to be completed. The published works and letters of many leading personalities of national life contained valuable material.[49] In addition to factual data this

[42] MÉSÁROŠ, Július: K problematike feudálnych prežitkov na Slovensku v druhej polovici XIX. storočia. Bratislava, SAV 1955; HOLEC, Roman: Poľnohospodárstvo na Slovensku v poslednej tretine 19. storočia. Bratislava, Veda 1991.

[43] VADKERTYOVÁ, Katarína: Dejiny cukrovarníckeho priemyslu a pestovania cukrovej repy na Slovensku (1800-1918). Bratislava, SAV 1972.

[44] PURGINA, Jozef: Vývoj železníc na Slovensku od roku 1837 so zreteľom na Bratislavu. Bratislava, SAV 1957.

[45] HORVÁTH, Štefan - VALACH, Ján: Peňažníctvo na Slovensku do roku 1918. Bratislava, Alfa 1975.

[46] SVETOŇ, Ján: Obyvateľstvo Slovenska za kapitalizmu. Bratislava, SVPL 1958; KOVÁČ, Dušan: Probleme der sozialhistorischen Forschung zum 19. und 20. Jahrhundert in der slowakischen Historiographie. In: Archiv für Sozialgeschichte 34, 1994, pp. 111-130.

[47] Slovenské vysťahovateľstvo. Dokumenty. Korešpondencia. I.-IV. Edited by BIELIK, František - RÁKOŠ, Elo. Bratislava - Martin, SAV - MS 1969-1985.

[48] Dokumenty k slovenskému národnému hnutiu 1848-1914. I.-III. Edited by BOKES, František. Bratislava, SAV 1962-1972.

[49] AMBRUŠ, Jozef (Ed.): Vzájomné listy Jaroslava Vlčka a Jozefa Škultétyho. Bratislava, SAV 1963; KOCÁK, Michal (Ed.): Listy Jozefa Škultétyho I.-II. Martin, MS 1982, 1983; PETRUS, Pavol (Ed.): Korešpondencia Svetozára Hurbana Vajanského I.-III. Bratislava, SAV 1967, 1972, 1978; SOKOLÍK, Viliam (Ed.): Listy Andreja Kmeťa Ľudovítovi V. Riznerovi. Martin, MS 1984; SOKOLÍK, Viliam (Ed.): Listy Ľudovíta V. Riznera Andrejovi Kmeťovi. Martin, MS 1970; ŠMATLÁK, Stanislav (Ed.): Korešpondencia P. O. Hviezdoslava so Svetozárom Hurbanom Vajanským a Jozefom Škultétym. Bratislava, SAV 1962; DAXNER, Štefan Marko: V službe národa. Bratislava, SVKL 1958; FRANCISCI, Ján: Vlastný životopis. Bratislava, SVKL 1956; PALÁRIK, Ján: Za reč a práva ľudu. Bratislava, SVKL 1956; SMETANA, Ján: Medzi dvoma vekmi. Bratislava, Tatran 1950; ŠROBÁR, Vavro: Z môjho života. Praha, Fr. Borový 1950; VAJANSKÝ, Svetozár Hurban: Listy z Uhorska. Martin, MS 1977.

material also indicates their ideas within the broader context of important questions of social life.

In scholarly activity research on workers and the socialist movement[50] took a primary place, accompanied by the tendency to stress this element of political activity as the most progressive factor of the historical development of the nation. Despite this, work on forming the Slovak national identity with its manifestations in the political and cultural context was able to continue.

This was reflected not only in books[51] and annals,[52] but also in a number of articles, including ones on a broader understanding of the Slovak question in Austria-Hungary.[53]

Great attention was devoted to the events of 1848–1849. (Rapant finished publishing The Slovak Uprising of 1848-1849.)[54] Among the important themes was Slovak political activity in the 1860s, particularly in connection with the Memorandum of 1861 and accompanying events,[55] the result of which was the acceptance of the basic program of the Slovak national emancipation movement, valid until the dissolution of Austria-Hungary. There was special interest in research on Matica slovenská's activity (1863-1875)[56] in terms of its role in

[50] GOSIOROVSKÝ, Miloš: Dejiny slovenského robotníckeho hnutia (1848-1918). Bratislava, SVPL 1956.

[51] MÉSÁROŠ, Július: Roľnícka a národnostná otázka na Slovensku 1848-1900. Bratislava, Osveta 1959.

[52] HOLOTÍK, Ľudovít (Ed.): K slovenskému národnému vývinu na východnom Slovensku (1848-1918). Košice, VV 1970.

[53] BOKES, František: Príspevok k uhorskej školskej politike v rokoch 1848-1918 so zreteľom na Slovákov. In: HČ 3, 1955, pp. 361-409; BUTVIN, Jozef: Česko-slovenské vzťahy koncom 19. a začiatkom 20. storočia (1880-1914). In: Zb FFUK Historica 29-30, 1978-1979, pp. 13-57; DANGL, Vojtech: Národnostná problematika v rakúsko-uhorskej armáde a Slováci. In: ČSČH 24, 1976, pp. 851-884; DANGL, Vojtech: Organizácia rakúsko-uhorskej armády so zvláštnym zreteľom na Slovensko (1868-1914). In: Historie a vojenství, 32, 1983, 4, pp. 78-98; DANGL, Vojtech: Rast militarizmu v Uhorsku v období balkánskych vojen. In: ČSČH 28, 1980, pp. 377-398; HOLOTÍK, Ľudovít: Slováci medzi Pešťou a Viedňou v rokoch 1860-1867. In: HČ 20, 1972, pp. 525-539; MÉSÁROŠ, Július: Kríza dualizmu a slovenské národné hnutie v deväťdesiatych rokoch. In: HČ 14, 1966, pp. 372-411; MÉSÁROŠ, Július: Vnútorné príčiny rozkladu dualistickej monarchie a postavenie Slovákov v Uhorsku. In: HČ 17, 1969, pp. 43-56; POTEMRA, Michal: Prejavy supremácie maďarských vládnucich kruhov v politickom živote Slovenska v rokoch 1901-1914. In: HČ 28, 1980, pp. 41-74; POTEMRA, Michal: Slovenská otázka v európskom kontexte v rokoch 1901-1914. In: HČ 28, 1980, pp. 210-237.

[54] See note 35.

[55] ELIÁŠ, Michal (Ed.): Z prameňov národa. Na pamiatku stodvadsiateho piateho výročia vzniku Memoranda slovenského národa z roku 1861. Martin, MS 1988.

[56] Matica slovenská v našich dejinách. Edited by MÉSÁROŠ, Július - KROPILÁK, Miroslav. Bratislava, SAV 1963.

national life, while its abolition was used to demonstrate the position of the ruling government against attributes of the Slovak national life.

Works on the New Slovak School[57] and the Slovak National Party[58] were devoted to issues in political development and a number of articles concentrated on other important questions of Slovak politics.[59]

Many works dealt with the foreign policies of Austria-Hungary,[60] the relations of Slovaks to other Slavic nations,[61] the idea of Slavic co-operation,[62] and emancipation movements of non-Magyar nations in Hungary.[63] These, among others, contributed to a deeper understanding of the role of Slovakia and Slovaks in the development of power and politics in central and eastern Europe.[64]

[57] KOSTICKÝ, Bohuš: Nová škola slovenská. Bratislava, SAV 1959.

[58] PODRIMAVSKÝ, Milan: Slovenská národná strana v druhej polovici XIX. storočia. Bratislava, Veda 1983.

[59] FABIAN, Juraj: Uhorská verejná správa v koncepciách a politike slovenského národného hnutia (1890-1918). In: SlArchiv 19, 1984, 1, pp. 110-128; HRONSKÝ, Marián: K politickému profilu generácie okolo časopisu Prúdy (prúdistov) 1909-1914. In: HČ 23, 1975, pp. 509-531; POLLA, Belo: Slovenské politické snahy v rokoch 1859-1860. In: HŠt 15, 1970, pp. 7-36; POLLA, Belo: Slovenská politika pred zvolaním memorandového zhromaždenia. In: HŠt 16, 1971, pp. 109-130; POTEMRA, Michal: Rozvoj spoločenského myslenia na začiatku 20. storočia. In: HČ 29, 1981, pp. 329-372; POTEMRA, Michal: K vývinu slovenskej politiky v rokoch 1901-1914. In: HČ 27, 1979, pp. 49-111; POTEMRA, Michal: Uhorské volebné právo a voľby na Slovensku v rokoch 1901-1914. In: HČ 23, 1975, pp. 201-239; TAJTÁK, Ladislav: Vývoj robotníckeho hnutia na Slovensku na začiatku 20. storočia. In: HČ 29, 1981, pp. 820-856; ZUBEREC, Vladimír: Formovanie slovenského agrárneho hnutia v rokoch 1900-1918. In: HČ 20, 1972, pp. 205-246.

[60] KOVÁČ, Dušan: Od Dvojspolku k politike anšlusu. (Nemecký imperializmus a Rakúsko do roku 1922). Bratislava, Veda 1979.

[61] BORODOVČÁK, Viktor: Ohlas poľského povstania roku 1863 na Slovensku. Bratislava, SAV 1960; BORODOVČÁK, Viktor: Poliaci a slovenský národný zápas v rokoch dualizmu. Bratislava, SAV 1969. TKADLEČKOVÁ - VANTUCHOVÁ, Jarmila: Česi a Slováci v národnooslobodzovacom boji do rakúsko-uhorského vyrovnania roku 1867. Bratislava, SAV 1970.

[62] IVANTYŠYNOVÁ, Tatiana: Česi a Slováci v ideológii ruských slavianofilov. Bratislava, Veda 1987; ŠŤASTNÝ, Vladislav (Ed.): Slovanství v národním životě Čechů a Slováků. Praha, Melantrich 1968.

[63] KRAJČOVIČ, Milan: Slovenská politika v strednej Európe 1890-1901. Bratislava, SAV 1971; KRAJČOVIČ, Milan: Slovenská spoločnosť v Uhorsku. Slováci a Juhoslovania v národnodemokratizačnom zápase v 30. až 70. rokoch 19. storočia. Bratislava, Veda 1986.

[64] HOLOTÍK, Ľudovít (Ed.): Der österreichisch-ungarische Ausgleich 1867. Bratislava, SAV 1971; CHROMEKOVÁ, Valéria: Politické strany Uhorska. I. Vznik a vývin politických strán Uhorska do roku 1890. Bratislava, SPN 1979; KOVÁČ, Dušan: Nemecko a nemecká menšina na Slovensku (1871-1945). Bratislava, Veda 1991; PÍSCH, Mikuláš: Ohlas ruskej buržoáznodemokratickej revolúcie na Slovensku (1905-1907). Bratislava, VPL 1966.

The roles of important figures in national life were introduced in books,[65] articles and essay collections[66] from a variety of perspectives, in their contributions to politics and culture. We can learn from these about the atmosphere of the Slovak intelligentsia of the day, as well as the moments of differentiation in Slovak public life, and the formation of different streams in politics through the actions of their protagonists.

Portrayals of the broad scale of cultural activity give concise views of individual branches of culture, mostly literature,[67] theater,[68] education,[69] journalism,[70] science,[71] extra-curricular education [72] and libraries. Works from this area document the fact that the phenomenon of the cultural identity of Slovaks had an exceptional impact in the emancipation process. To a large extent, culture supplemented the role of politics, which, as a result of the existing constitutional conditions and system of the government in Hungary, was unabled to be openly or fully expressed.

---

[65] GAŠPARÍK, Mikuláš: Ján Palárik a jeho boj o demokratizáciu slovenského národného života. Bratislava, SAVU 1952; GOMBALA, Eduard: Viliam Pauliny - Tóth. Martin, MS 1976; JANŠÁK, Štefan: Život dr. Pavla Blahu I.-II. Trnava, Spolok sv. Vojtecha 1947; RUTTKAY, Fraňo: Daniel G. Lichard a slovenské novinárstvo jeho doby. Martin, MS 1961; SROGOŇ, Tomáš: Samuel Ormis. Život a dielo. Bratislava, SPN 1976; ŠTILLA, Miloš: Martin Čulen - pedagóg a národný buditeľ. Bratislava, SPN 1983; VAVROVIČ, Jozef: Ján Palárik, jeho ekumenizmus a panslavizmus. Martin, MS 1993.

[66] KOCÁK, Michal (Ed.): Jozef Škultéty (1853-1948). Martin, MS 1970; VONGREJ, Pavol (Ed.): Karol Kuzmány (1806-1866). Martin, MS 1967; WINKLER, Tomáš (Ed.): Štefan Moyzes 1869-1969. Martin, MS 1971.

[67] PIŠÚT, Milan - ROSENBAUM, Karol - KOCHOL, Viktor: Dejiny slovenskej literatúry II. Bratislava, SAV 1960; ČEPAN, Oskar - KUSÝ, Ivan - ŠMATLÁK, Stanislav - NOGE, Július: Dejiny slovenskej literatúry III. Bratislava, SAV 1965; KUSÝ, Ivan - ŠMATLÁK, Stanislav: Dejiny slovenskej literatúry IV. Bratislava, Veda 1975; CHMEL, Rudolf: Literárne vzťahy slovensko-maďarské. Martin, Osveta 1973.

[68] TURZO, Ivan: Maják v tme. Slovenský spevokol v Martine. Martin, Osveta 1974.

[69] GALLO, Ján: Revúcke gymnázium 1862-1874. Bratislava, Obzor 1969; ŠTILLA, Miloš: Znievske gymnázium. Banská Bystrica, SV 1966.

[70] RUTTKAY, Fraňo: Prehľad dejín slovenského novinárstva do roku 1918. Bratislava, UK 1972; RUTTKAY, Fraňo: Robotnícka žurnalistika v sociálnom a národnom hnutí Slovákov (1897-1918). Martin, MS 1980; CHMEL, Rudolf: Dejiny v dejinách. K storočnici Slovenských pohľadov. Bratislava, Slovenský spisovateľ 1981.

[71] RYBECKÝ, Milan: Muzeálna slovenská spoločnosť a jej miesto v národnej kultúre. Martin, Osveta 1983; TIBENSKÝ, Ján: Dejiny vedy a techniky na Slovensku. Martin, Osveta 1979; TIBENSKÝ, Ján and team: Priekopníci vedy a techniky na Slovensku II. Bratislava, Obzor 1988.

[72] SOKOLÍK, Viliam: Z bojov o pokladnicu slovenskej kultúry. Martin, MS 1966; TKADLEČKOVÁ - VANTUCHOVÁ, Jarmila: Živena - spolok slovenských žien. Bratislava, Epocha 1969.

3. World War I 1914–1918

Issues concerning the conditions in Slovakia during the First World War, and questions connected to the process of the founding of the Czecho-Slovak state in 1918, were already being dealt with in the early post-war years by a number of authors who were among the active personalities of the pre-war and wartime period.[73] They emphasized their participation in these political events and from their own points of view they interpreted the solution of the Slovak question and the connection of Czech and Slovak lands in a common state. They stressed above all the participation of Slovaks in the realization of the Czecho-Slovak state and their role in the military, diplomatic and political activities of resistance domestic and abroad. Among these works, chiefly memoirs, Karol Anton Medvecký's[74] holds an important place, containing historical interpretation and rich documentation on the preparation and integration of Slovakia into the joint state. In addition to scholarly historical works, these themes were dealt with in extensive historical journalism which in the spirit of the official state ideology stressed the roots of Czecho-Slovak mutuality and cooperation, the reasons for a common state as the most convenient for the realization of the right of self-determination and the needs of the Czechs and Slovaks.

After 1945, the approach of Slovak historiography to the question of the development of Slovakia in the years of the First World War was basically determined by Marxist interpretation of history. Social change in Slovakia, the disintegration of the Austro-Hungarian Empire, and the formation of the Czecho-Slovak state were attributed to the influence of workers and the socialist movement, including, in its international context, the revolutionary events in Russia.[75] This was a misinterpretation of the situation, and these works can be

---

[73] DÉRER, Ivan: Slovensko v prevrate a po ňom. Bratislava - Praha, Grafické, kníhařské a nakladatelské družstvo 1924; GETTING, Milan: Americkí Slováci a vývin československej štátnej myšlienky v rokoch 1914-1918. Pittsburgh, STJ Sokol 1933; MARKOVIČ, Ivan: Slováci v zahraničnej revolúcií. Praha, Památník odboje 1923; MARKOVIČ, Ivan: Slovensko pred prevratom. Bratislava - Praha, Grafické, kníhařské a nakladatelské družstvo 1924; STODOLA, Kornel: Válečné roky s Milanom Hodžom. Bratislava, published by author 1938; ŠROBÁR, Vavro: Pamäti z vojny a väzenia (1914-1918). Praha, G. Dubský 1922; ŠTEFÁNEK, Anton: Masaryk a Slovensko. Bratislava, Vatra 1920; ŠTEFÁNEK, Anton: Slovensko pred prevratom a počas prevratu. Praha, Památník odboje 1923.

[74] MEDVECKÝ, Karol Anton: Slovenský prevrat I.-IV. Trnava, Spolok sv. Vojtecha 1930-1931.

[75] HOLOTÍK, Ľudovít: Októbrová revolúcia a národnooslobodzovacie hnutie na Slovensku v rokoch 1917-1918. Bratislava, SAV 1958; HOLOTÍK, Ľudovít: Štefánikovská legenda a vznik ČSR. Bratislava, SAV 1958; KVASNIČKA, Ján: Československé légie v Rusku 1917-1920. Bratislava, SAV 1963.

differentiated according to their degree of objectivity. Towards later years, however,[76] scholarship became less ideological as was shown by documents finally made available on the years 1917–1918.[77]

It is not possible to accurately portray Slovak historiography on the years 1800–1918 by mentioning monographs alone. For thematic, content and methodological information we must look also at specialized articles included in historical bibliographies. Much of the historiography on Slovaks and Slovakia is the work of Czechs and Hungarians and belongs here as well.

[76] GOSIOROVSKÝ, Miloš: Z histórie česko-slovenských vzťahov. Bratislava, Pravda 1978; HRONSKÝ, Marián: Slovensko pri zrode Československa. Bratislava, Pravda 1987; HRONSKÝ, Marián: Vzbura slovenských vojakov v Kragujevci roku 1918. Martin, Osveta 1982; KOVÁČ, Dušan and team: Muži Deklarácie. Martin, Osveta 1991; ŠTVRTECKÝ, Štefan: Náš Milan Rastislav Štefánik. Bratislava, Smena 1990; TAJTÁK, Ladislav: Národnodemokratická revolúcia na východnom Slovensku v roku 1918. Bratislava, SPN 1972.

[77] Sociálne a národné hnutie na Slovensku od Októbrovej revolúcie do vzniku československého štátu. Dokumenty. Edited by HOLOTÍK, Ľudovít. Bratislava, Veda 1979.

SLOVAK HISTORIOGRAPHY ON THE PERIOD 1918–1938

The re-establishment of the Czechoslovak Republic after 1945 enabled more public personalities, most of them not professional historians, to publish their memoirs, largely focused on politics.[1] With older memoirs, they are the basic source to the history of Slovakia between the wars.[2] In particular it is necessary to mention the historical work *The Martin Declaration,* which is the source for the objective evaluation of the state act for the entrance of Slovakia into the Czechoslovak Republic.[3]

The seizing of political power by the communists in 1948, resulted not only in a change of political system and social conditions, but also the establishment of a specific role for historiography: to re-evaluate history from an political ideological stance and from the viewpoint of a specific class. The history of the workers' movement and class struggle, thus far unresearched, was brought to the foreground. The first resulting articles and monographs appeared in the early 1950s.[4] This research trend, broadened with investigation into the social

---

[1] DÉRER, Ivan: Slovenský vývoj a ľudácka zrada. Praha, Kvasnička a Hampl 1946; ŠROBÁR, Vavro: Z môjho života. Praha, Fr. Borovský 1946.

[2] JURIGA, Ferdinand: Blahozvesť kriesenia slovenského národa a slovenskej krajiny. Trnava, Urbánek a spol. 1937; HODŽA, Milan: Slovenský rozchod s Maďarmi roku 1918. Bratislava, Redakcia Slovenského denníka 1929; HODŽA, Milan: Články, reči, štúdie. Volume II.: Československá súčinnosť 1898-1919. Praha, Novina 1930; Volume V.: Slovenské roľnícke organizácie 1912-1933. Praha, Novina 1933; Volume VII.: Slovensko a republika. Bratislava, Linografia K. Jaroň a spol. 1934; HOUDEK, Fedor: Vznik hraníc Slovenska. Bratislava, Prúdy 1931; MEDVECKÝ, Karol A.: Slovenský prevrat I.-IV. Trnava, Spolok sv. Vojtecha 1930; STODOLA, Emil: Prelom. Spomienky, úvahy, štúdie. Praha, L. Mazáč 1933; SIDOR, Karol: Andrej Hlinka (1864-1926). Bratislava, Kníhtlačiareň sv. Andreja 1934; SIDOR, Karol: Slovenská politika na pôde pražského snemu (1918-1938). I.-II. Bratislava, without publisher 1943; ŠROBÁR, Vavro: Osvobozené Slovensko. Pamäti z rokov 1918-1920. Praha, Čin 1928.

[3] GREČO, Martin: Martinská deklarácia. Martin, MS 1947. The first edition was published in 1939, and for its pro-Czechoslovak orientation, the Ministry of Education and National Enlightenment put it on the index.

[4] GOSIOROVSKÝ, Miloš: Dejiny slovenského robotníckeho hnutia 1848-1918. Bratislava, SVPL 1956; HOLOTÍKOVÁ, Zdenka: Klement Gottwald na Slovensku v rokoch 1921-1924. Bratislava, SAV 1953; PRECHTL, Ivan: Za prácu, chlieb a slobodu. (Zápisky odborárskeho priekopníka.) II.-III. Bratislava, Práca 1954; MOTOŠKA, Vladimír: Revolučné tradície prvých májov na Slovensku. Bratislava, SVPL 1957.

struggles of peasants and the unemployed, continued into the following years.[5]

Despite stress upon the importance of economic determinism in history, research on political development was given priority. Politically immediate themes were chosen, not respecting the demands of historiography, which became dependent for its existence on totalitarian political reality. The struggle against "bourgeois nationalism" and against the residue of nationalistic ideology in the public, represented by the former Hlinka's Slovak People's Party (or "Ľudák" movement), was in the early 1950s the axis of the ideological struggle of the Communist Party. This movement got to the center of Slovak historiography presented as a reactionary, bourgeois nationalistic, separatist and last but not least a clerico-fascist political movement.[6]

In addition to tendentious and non-scholarly works, the first serious research based on analysis of original sources and the contemporary press appeared. This includes research for the only monograph to date concerning the "Ľudák" movement which still reflects the main criteria of those days.[7] The next important theme was the foundation and character of Czechoslovakia. The interpretation of this process was shaped by the attempt to stress the role and significance of the Great October Socialist Revolution and to marginalize other factors: the victory of the Allies, the role of Czechoslovak foreign resistance and activity of legions, but mostly the role of personalities like Tomáš Garrique Masaryk, Milan Rastislav Štefánik, and Eduard Beneš. At the same time deeper research on the domestic situation and the interior disintegration of the Austro-Hungarian Empire began.[8]

---

[5] FILO, Milan: Udalosti v Rumanovej r. 1920. In: HČ 1, 1953, 1, pp. 106-117.; MLYNÁRIK, Ján: Triedne boje horehronského ľudu v rokoch svetovej hospodárskej krízy 1930-1933. Bratislava, SVPL 1956; MLYNÁRIK, Ján: Štrajkové boje na Slovensku. Volume I.: Priemyslové robotníctvo v období 1921-1924. Bratislava, Práca 1959; Volume II.: Zemerobotníci v rokoch 1919-1929. Bratislava, Práca 1962; Volume III. Bratislava, Práca 1965; HOLOTÍKOVÁ, Zdenka: Štrajk poľnohospodárskych robotníkov na Slovensku 1929. Bratislava, SVPL 1960; JABLONICKÝ, Jozef: Robotnícke hnutie na Trnavsku za kapitalistickej ČSR. Martin, Osveta 1961; PLEVZA, Viliam: Revolučné hnutie zemerobotníkov na Slovensku v rokoch 1929-1938. Volume I.: Triedne boje zemerobotníkov v rokoch svetovej hospodárskej krízy 1929-1933. Volume II.: (1933-1938). Bratislava, Práca 1960 and 1963.

[6] PROTI prežitkom ľudáctva. Zborník prejavov z ideologickej konferencie Filozofickej fakulty Slovenskej univerzity v dňoch 28. a 29. januára 1954. Preface by HRUŠOVSKÝ, Igor. Bratislava, SVPL 1954; VIETOR, Martin: Príspevok k objasneniu fašistického charakteru tzv. slovenského štátu. In: HČ, 8, 1960, 4, pp. 482-508.

[7] KRAMER, Juraj: Iredenta a separatizmus v slovenskej politike. Bratislava, SVPL 1957; KRAMER, Juraj: Slovenské autonomistické hnutie v rokoch 1918-1929. Bratislava, SAV 1962.

[8] DZVONÍK, Michal: Ohlas Veľkej októbrovej revolúcie na Slovensku (1918-1919). Bratislava,

Connected with the question of the foundation of the Czechoslovak Republic and the integration of Slovakia within the new state, was the Slovak Soviet Republic and its interpretation. It was understood as an attempt to create the first republic of the proletariat on the territory of Slovakia, and not as an attempt to trespass upon the sovereignty and integrity of Czechoslovakia, nor as an attempt by Hungary to join Slovakia or any of its parts to the Hungarian state. This understanding survives although it went into remission at the end of the 1960s and also in the 1980s.[9]

After the rejection of bourgeois nationalism, but with the rehabilitation of its representatives, the interest of Slovak historiography concentrated on the Slovak question. As an issue of the quality of Czech and Slovak co-existence in a common state, this question became ever-present in the broad context of research themes on the inter-war period. Its emergence and elaboration in Slovak historiography had, in 1968, a positive impact upon social practice and contributed to the systematic solution of the governmental status of Slovakia.[10]

In the framework of research on political developments in the period between the wars, the main stress was upon the history of the Communist Party which was understood as the crucial factor. To the political hegemony of the Czechoslovak Communist Party and its consolidation was subordinated the research and interpretation of all social activity during the first Czechoslovak Republic. This approach limited not only the choice of theme and interpretation but already deformed the basic selection of facts and the whole process of their analysis. It favored the contemporary position of the Communist Party towards the political, economic, social and cultural issues of the period between the wars, without taking into account whether the position of the Communist Party was historically significant and well-founded. With the deepening of knowledge of the

SVPL 1957; O VZÁJOMNÝCH vzťahoch Čechov a Slovákov. Compiled by HOLOTÍK, Ľudovít. Bratislava, SAV 1956; HOLOTÍK, Ľudovít: Októbrová revolúcia a národnooslobodzovacie hnutie na Slovensku v rokoch 1917-1918. Bratislava, SAV 1958; HOLOTÍK, Ľudovít: Štefánikovská legenda a vznik ČSR. Bratislava, VSAV 1958; second supplemented edition Bratislava, SAV 1960.

[9] VIETOR, Martin: Slovenská sovietska republika v roku 1919. Bratislava, SVPL 1955; SLOVENSKÁ republika rád. Dokumenty. Compiled by SMUTNÝ, Anton. Bratislava, Epocha 1970; SLOVENSKÁ republika rád. Materiály z ideologickej konferencie k 60. výročiu SRR konanej v Prešove 17.-18. mája 1979. Compiled by KANIS, Pavol. Bratislava, Pravda 1980.

[10] SLOVÁCI a ich národný vývin. Compiled by MÉSÁROŠ, Július. Bratislava, SAV 1966; FALŤAN, Samo: Slovenská otázka v Československu. Bratislava, VPL 1968; GOSIOROVSKÝ, Miloš: K niektorým otázkam vzťahu Čechov a Slovákov v politike KSČ. In: HČ 16, 1968, 3, pp. 354-407; KULÍŠEK, Vladimír: Úloha čechoslovakizmu ve vztazích Čechů a Slováků (1918-1938). In: HČ 12, 1964, 1, pp. 50-74.

history of the communist movement, occasional mistakes were acknowledged in the understanding of the national question, of the issues of the allies of the party, of the evaluation of social democracy and the political system of parliamentary democracy, and in attitudes towards the trade unions, women and youth but without admitting integral errors in the basic interpretative position prescribed.[11]

The preparation of a synthesis of the history of Slovakia stimulated in the 1960s an evaluation of the condition of research of the inter-war period, while drawing attention to some unsolved questions: the development of the political system and its parts, of political parties, and political administration. The issues of agrarian and industrial development, as well as those of class and social struggles, were also raised. In addition to the analysis of ideology, politics and social classes, stress was also placed upon the historical development of government as well as upon legislative and economic analysis.[12]

Many of the issues raised were dealt with in books which advanced the knowledge of the history of the inter-war period in Slovakia and primarily its political and economic role.[13] A more liberal approach in work on a broader spectrum of historical issues respecting the needs of the scholarly development of Slovak historiography was forcefully interrupted by the process of "normalization" after 1968.

For the next two decades, Slovak historiography concentrated on the most recent history of Slovakia. Again it preferred the history of the Communist Party and class struggles. Documents from the history of the party and re-prints of the results of party congresses were published. Ideological political criteria became the significant ones for research and publication.[14] No book was pub-

---

[11] FILO, Milan: Boj KSČ za obranu republiky v rokoch 1937-1938. Bratislava, SVPL 1960; PLEVZA, Viliam - VEBR, Lubomír - CAMBEL, Samuel: KSČ a roľnícka otázka na Slovensku (1921-1960). Bratislava, SVPL 1961; PLEVA, Ján: Príspevok k dejinám boľševizácie KSČ na Slovensku. Bratislava, VPL 1962; HOLOTÍK, Ľudovít: Sjazd sociálnodemokratickej strany (ľavice) v Ľubochni v januári 1921. In: HČ 11, 1963, 3, pp. 337-366; PLEVZA, Viliam: KSČ a revolučné hnutie na Slovensku 1929-1938. Bratislava, SAV 1965; HUBENÁK, Ladislav: Vznik a založenie KSČ na západnom Slovensku. Bratislava, Slavín 1969.

[12] KONFERENCIA o vývoji Slovenska počas I. ČSR. In: HČ 9, 1961, 2, pp. 177-324.

[13] LIPSCHER, Ladislav: K vývinu politickej správy na Slovensku v rokoch 1918-1938. Bratislava, SAV 1966; LIPTÁK, Ľubomír: Slovensko v 20. storočí. Bratislava, SAV 1968; STRHAN, Milan: Kríza priemyslu na Slovensku 1921-1923. Počiatky odbúravania slovenského priemyslu. Bratislava, VSAV 1960.

[14] KREMPA, Ivan: Za internacionálnu jednotu revolučného hnutia v Československu. Podiel slovenského a zakarpatského hnutia na utvorení KSČ (1919–1921). Bratislava, Pravda 1975;

lished about any other political parties although at the end of the sixties much work was being done on these subjects.[15] Many works on the Czechoslovak statehood were published, broadening the range of perspectives on this issue. Historians devoted attention to the political system of the first Czechoslovak Republic, evaluating it positively for the democratic opportunities of developing the Slovak social organism, though again the Communist Party between the wars dominates their portrayal.[16] The defense of the Czechoslovak Republic against fascism and events that led to Munich form an important chapter.[17] A very small circle of researchers devoted themselves to issues of foreign relations. Besides Czechoslovak-Soviet relations, they were also occupied with questions of security, the Little Entente, and the development of relations with neighboring states.[18]

ČADA, Václav: Vznik a vývoj marxistickej ľavice (1917-1921). Bratislava, Pravda 1980; DOKU-MENTY k dejinám KSČ na Slovensku 1929-1938. Compiled by FILO, Milan. Bratislava, Pravda 1980; DOKUMENTY k dejinám KSČ na Slovensku (1917-1928). Compiled by HAUTOVÁ, Júlia. Bratislava, Pravda 1981; PLEVZA, Viliam: Trvalé hodnoty. I. Proti kapitálu. Bratislava, Pravda 1976.

[15] ZUBEREC, Vladimír: Čechoslovakizmus agrárnej strany na Slovensku v rokoch 1919-1938. In: HČ 27, 1979, pp. 515-532; ŠAVEL, Róbert: Vznik a činnosť maďarských buržoáznych strán na Slovensku do podpísania Trianonskej mierovej zmluvy. In: ZbÚML UK 4, 1973, Dejiny robotníc-keho hnutia, pp. 19-39; KRAJČOVIČOVÁ, Natália: Slovenská otázka v programoch Slovenskej národnej strany (1919-1925). In: Kmetianum II. Martin, Osveta 1971, pp. 133-143; BARTLOVÁ, Alena: Spolupráca buržoáznych politických strán na Slovensku v rokoch 1930-1935. In: ČSČH 22, 1974, pp. 329-360.

[16] PLEVZA, Viliam: Československá štátnosť a slovenská otázka v politike KSČ. Bratislava, Práca 1971; GOSIOROVSKÝ, Miloš: Z histórie česko-slovenských vzťahov. Bratislava, Pravda 1978; PLEVZA, Viliam: Národnostná politika KSČ a česko-slovenské vzťahy. Bratislava, Práca 1979.

[17] DEÁK, Ladislav: Pakt štyroch veľmocí - predohra k Mníchovu. In: HČ 20, 1972, pp. 333-362; HUBENÁK, Ladislav: Mníchovská dohoda r. 1938. In: Právny obzor 56, 1973, pp. 557-579; BYSTRICKÝ, Valerián: Postoj štátov juhovýchodnej Európy k Československu roku 1938. In: SlŠt 23, 1982, 2, pp. 43-71; TKADLEČKOVÁ, Herta: Slovensko a Mníchov. In: Minchenskiot dogovor i jugoslovenskite i čechoslovackite narodi. Skopje, INI 1980, pp. 305-326.

[18] BYSTRICKÝ, Valerián - DEÁK, Ladislav: Európa na prelome. Diplomatické a politické vzťahy v rokoch 1932-1933. Bratislava, Pravda 1974; BYSTRICKÝ, Valerián: Kolektívna bezpeč-nosť alebo neutralita. Balkánske štáty a vytváranie záruk bezpečnosti v 30. rokoch. Bratislava, Veda 1981; KOVÁČ, Dušan: Československá zahraničná politika a otázka Rakúska v rokoch 1918-1922. In: SlŠt 23, 1982, 2, pp. 17-41; BYSTRICKÝ, Valerián - DEÁK, Ladislav: The Security of the States of Central and South-Eastern Europe in the Thirties. In: Problems of Continuity and Discontinuity in History. Praha, ÚČSSD ČSAV 1980, pp. 223-242; FERENČUHOVÁ, Bohuslava: Briandov plán európskej federálnej únie a Československo: vláda, paneurópske hnutie, verejná mienka. In: HČ 41, 1993, 2, pp. 123-142; FERENČUHOVÁ, Bohuslava: Sovietske Rusko a Malá dohoda.

Progress was also made in the research of economic history. Works on the economic development of Slovakia and related issues were published.[19] Within work on social development historians devoted attention to emigration and migrational movements of the inhabitants of Slovakia.[20] The relaxation of the social atmosphere in the late 1980s was reflected in research on a broad spectrum of themes in the history of culture, science and the activities of organizations.[21] Works which proceeded from narrow political themes and judgements appeared also in the area of political history.[22]

(K problematike medzinárodných vzťahov v strednej Európe v rokoch 1917-1924). In: SlŠt 28, 1988, 2; V BOJI za mier a povojnovú spoluprácu (1917-1945). Edited by BORODOVČÁK, Viktor. In: SlŠt 1989; KRAJČOVIČ, Milan: Bezprostredný vplyv Veľkej októbrovej socialistickej revolúcie na Slovákov a Juhoslovanov a ich vzájomné vzťahy za prvej svetovej vojny. In: SlŠt 24, 1983, 1, pp. 10-29; FERENČUHOVÁ, Bohuslava: Sovietska zahraničná politika voči víťazným stredoeurópskym štátom v rokoch 1920-1922. In: SlŠt 24, 1983, 1, pp. 43-55; FANO, Štefan: Internacionálna pomoc československého proletariátu mladému sovietskemu štátu pri obnove národného hospodárstva. In: SlŠt 24, 1983, 1, pp. 56-70; POLÁČKOVÁ, Zuzana: Politická emigrácia z Rakúska do ČSR roku 1934 a transporty do ZSSR. In: HČ 40, 1992, 5, pp. 565-578; KOVÁČ, Dušan: Nemecko a nemecká menšina na Slovensku (1871-1945). Bratislava, Veda 1991.

[19] PRŮCHA, Václav and team: Hospodárske dejiny Československa v 19. a 20. storočí. Bratislava, Pravda 1974; HORVÁTH, Štefan - VALACH, Ján: Peňažníctvo na Slovensku 1918-1945. Bratislava, Alfa 1978; MURÍN, Pavol: Vývoj uhoľného baníctva na Slovensku po roku 1918. In: Zborník Slovenského banského múzea 7, 1971, pp. 293-302; HOLOTÍKOVÁ, Zdenka: Mestá na Slovensku v medzivojnovom období. In: HČ 21, 1973, pp. 189-204.

[20] BIELIK, František - RÁKOŠ, Elo: Slovenské vysťahovalectvo. Dokumenty II.-III. Martin, MS 1975, 1976; JAKEŠOVÁ, Elena: Vysťahovalectvo Slovákov do Kanady. Bratislava, Veda 1981.

[21] HARNA, Josef - KAMENEC, Ivan: Na společné cestě. Česká a slovenská kultura mezi dvěma válkami. Praha, Horizont 1988; MAGDOLENOVÁ, Anna: The Development of Slovak Culture Between the Two Wars (1918-1939). In: SHS 17, 1989, pp. 172-241; HAVIAR, Štefan - KUČMA, Ivan: V pamäti národa. Kniha o Matici slovenskej. Martin, MS 1988; PRIEKOPNÍCI vedy a techniky na Slovensku I.-II. Compiled by TIBENSKÝ, Ján. Bratislava, Obzor 1986, 1988; MINÁR, Imrich: Americkí Slováci a Slovensko. Formovanie a vznik slovenskej komunity v spoločenskej štruktúre Spojených štátov severoamerických 1880-1985. Martin, MS 1988; KRÁSNA, Věra - SLÁDEK, Zdeněk: Korespondence Karla Čapka a Milana Hodži na přelomu let 1928-1929. In: HČ 34, 1986, pp. 424-429; BOBRÍK, Miroslav: Nemecké telovýchovné organizácie a spolky na Slovensku v rokoch 1918-1928. In: HČ 36, 1988, pp. 537-560; LIPTÁK, Ľubomír: Múzeá a historiografia na Slovensku v rokoch 1918-1945. In: Zb SNM História 20, 1989, pp. 209-225.

[22] HRONSKÝ, Marián: Slovensko pri zrode Československa. Bratislava, Pravda 1987; KOVÁČ, Dušan: Myšlienka československej štátnosti. Jej vznik a realizácia. In: HČ 36, 1988, pp. 341-352; DEÁK, Ladislav: Československo-maďarské vzťahy v čase nebezpečenstva nacistickej agresie v strednej Európe (1933-1938). In: Nepokojná desetiletí 1918-1945. Studie a dokumenty z dějin československo-maďarských vztahů mezi dvěma světovými válkami. Edited by IRMANOVÁ, Eva. Praha, ČSI 1988, pp. 94-127; LIPTÁK, Ľubomír: Materiálna kultúra a politický systém v medzivojnovom období. In: HČ 36, 1988, pp. 443-447.

New opportunities for Slovak historiography arrived with democratic changes after 1989. These changes created room for a plurality of opinions. Historians of the inter-war period took advantage of this in their scholarly and popular work. They immediately responded to the interest of teachers and the public in the relations and personalities of political life of the period in the form of lectures, articles, radio and television programs, schoolbooks and other educational materials.

Gradually new scholarly works coming from the inner needs of historiography were created, though they also reflect social demand. This is why it is significant that this latest period of Slovak historiography prefers the themes of political development. It concentrates on the character of the political system of the first Czechoslovak Republic, the role of Slovakia within the state struc-

[23] POLITICKÉ strany na Slovensku 1860-1989. Compiled by LIPTÁK, Ľubomír. Bratislava, Archa 1992; SLOVENSKO v politickom systéme Československa. Compiled by BYSTRICKÝ, Valerián. Bratislava, Slovenská národná rada - HÚ SAV 1992; BYSTRICKÝ, Valerián: Národnostný štatút a štátoprávne programy na Slovensku roku 1938. In: HČ 40, 1992, 1, pp. 52-68; BYSTRICKÝ, Valerián: Politické rozvrstvenie spoločnosti na Slovensku vo svetle obecných volieb v roku 1938. In: HČ 40, 1992, 4, pp. 438-466; ŠUCHOVÁ, Xénia: Administratívna samospráva v koncepciách slovenských centralistov Milana Hodžu a Ivana Dérera. In: HČ, 42, 1994, pp. 226-245; KÁZMEROVÁ, Ľubica: Integračné pôsobenie národných socialistov na Slovensku r.1919-1929. In: Češi a Slováci ve střední Evropě ve 20. století. Brno, Vojenská akademie 1993, pp. 143-149; KRAJČOVIČOVÁ, Natália: Príchod českých inžinierov a technikov na Slovensko a ich aktivity v 20. rokoch. In: Češi a Slováci a východní Evropa ve 20. století. Edited by VODIČKA, Stanislav - GONĚC, Vladimír. Brno, Vojenská akademie 1994, pp. 215-220; FERENČUHOVÁ, Bohuslava: Česi, Slováci a Malá dohoda v 20. rokoch. In: Češi a Slováci a východní Evropa, pp. 113-118; ŠOLC, Jaroslav: Slovensko v českej politike. Banská Bystrica, M. O. Enterprise 1993; DEÁK, Ladislav: Slovensko v politike Poľska v rokoch 1933-1938 (od anexie Rakúska). In: HČ 38, 1990, pp. 342-363; Viedenská arbitráž (2. novembra 1938). Mníchov pre Slovensko. Compiled by DEÁK, Ladislav. Bratislava 1994; DEÁK, Ladislav: The Slovaks in the Hungarian Statistics. In: History & Politics. III. Bratislava Symposium held on November 12-15, 1992. Bratislava, Czecho-Slovak Committee of the European Cultural Foundation 1993, pp. 93-104; DEÁK, Ladislav: Slovaks in Hungarian Statistics Before and After 1918. In: Human Affairs 3, 1993, 2, pp. 142-154; Národnosti na Slovensku. Compiled by HARAKSIM, Ľudovít. Bratislava, Veda 1993; Slováci v Maďarsku. Edited by BALÁŽOVÁ, Eva - GRÁCOVÁ, Genovéva. Martin, MS 1994.

[24] KOVÁČ, Dušan and team: Muži deklarácie. Martin, Osveta 1991; BARTLOVÁ, Alena: Andrej Hlinka. Bratislava, Obzor 1991; MILAN Hodža: štátnik a politik. Compiled by MATHÉ, Svätoslav. Bratislava, Politologický kabinet SAV 1992; FERDIŠ Juriga. Compiled by JURKOVIČ, Ján. Bratislava, SNM 1992; MAGDOLENOVÁ, Anna: Národná a štátna idea v diele Františka Hrušovského. In: HČ 41, 1993, pp. 684-691; JURÍČEK, Ján: Martin Rázus, básnik a politik. Bratislava, Stimul 1993;

ture, ethnic relations[23], and profiles of personalities.[24] Economic history and the history of culture and of social issues are less represented until now.[25]

---

[25] FABRICIUS, Miroslav: Vývoj názorov na postavenie ekonomiky Slovenska v predmníchovskej republike. Bratislava, Ekonomický ústav SAV 1990; BARTLOVÁ, Alena: Integrácia slovenského a českého hospodárstva do jednotnej československej ekonomiky. In: Češi a Slováci a východní Evropa, pp. 207-214; KRAJČOVIČOVÁ, Natália: Predpoklady realizácie pozemkovej reformy na Slovensku v medzivojnovom období. In: Československá pozemková reforma 1919-1935 a její mezinárodní souvislosti. Compiled by RAŠTICOVÁ, Blanka. Uherské Hradište, Slovácké muzeum 1994; Z dejín pivovarníctva, sladovníctva a chmeliarstva na Slovensku. Compiled by PETRÁŠ, Milan. Trnava, Západoslovenské múzeum 1993; KRESÁK, Fedor: Nástup modernej architektúry v Bratislave a prínos českých architektov. In: Kontexty českého a slovenského umenia. Edited by STRAKA, Pavol. Bratislava, Správa kultúrnych zariadení Ministerstva kultúry SR 1990, pp. 378-384; HALLON, Ľudovít: Energetika a jej miesto vo vývoji hospodárstva na Slovensku v rokoch 1918-1938. In: HČ 40, 1992, 2, pp. 198-214; FALTUS, Jozef: Vznik a kapitálový vývoj slovenskej všeobecnej úvernej banky v Bratislave. In: HČ 41, 1993, 3, pp. 275-285; KAPITOLY z vedeckého života v Bratislave. Compiled by PÖSS, Ondrej. Bratislava, Veda 1991; LAJCHA, Ladislav: Zrod a formovanie slovenskej činohry. In: Kontexty českého a slovenského umenia, pp. 391-402; BENIAK, Milan - TICHÝ, Miloslav: Dejiny Lekárskej fakulty Univerzity Komenského v Bratislave. Part 1. Bratislava, UK 1992.

SLOVAK HISTORIOGRAPHY
ON THE PERIOD 1938–1945

Dramatic developments from 1938 to 1945, including many important political, national and social changes in central Europe, found their place in Slovak historiography. Attention was concentrated, on the one hand, on the so-called second Czecho-Slovak Republic (October 1938 to March 1939) and the first Slovak Republic and, on the other hand, on the anti-fascist resistance during the Second World War. The interpretation of this period was distorted by the influence of political considerations that were the logical result of the ruling totalitarian power in Czechoslovakia from 1948 to 1989. Efforts to inform the interpretation of the period with ideology still persist even after the fall of the communist system.

The Slovak anti-fascist resistance in all its forms at home and abroad became the most common interest of Slovak historiography. The problems of the First Slovak Republic, its political system and society, at first was researched only sporadically in the background of research on the Slovak anti-fascist resistance. It took quite a long time to overcome the simplistic, even demonized view of the first Slovak state.

The first historical works on 1938-1945, which had more of the character of memoirs and popular and regional work, are found shortly after the end of the War. They tended more towards documentary than analytical value.[1] At the end of 1947 the Institute of the Slovak National Uprising was founded, whose task was to research modern Slovak history, with special emphasis on anti-fascist resistance and other revolutionary and emancipation processes in Slovak society. The first, not very professional results of the research activities of this institute were published in the first two volumes of its annals *Sborník Ústavu SNP* in 1949 and 1950. In the fifties, research of the period of the War had only a very narrow resource basis, and its results were misshapen by the political aims and needs of the ruling party. This was mostly manifested in the elaboration of

---

[1] NAD TATROU sa blýska. Edited by OKTAVEC, František. Praha-Bratislava, Naše vojsko 1946; DEMOKRACIA v ilegalite a povstaní. Bratislava, Ústredný sekretariát DS 1945; NOSKO, Július: Vojaci v Slovenskom národnom povstaní. Bratislava, Povereníctvo informácií 1947.

the history of the Slovak National Uprising.[2] In the flood of hagiographic historical works about the resistance and uprising many works appeared that were influenced by the period's ideological pressures. However, they made a contribution in factual data out of the study of archival material.[3] On this archival basis the first works appeared reconstructing the development of Slovakia in the so-called second Czecho-Slovak Republic,[4] and touched on some, mostly economic problems of the wartime Slovak state.[5]

In the sixties, during the period of liberalization and thanks to the professional growth of Slovak historiography it visibly achieved a higher qualitative level concerning the period 1938-1945. Slovak historiography tried to revise its own mistakes and malformations, quite successfully, mostly in the area of the anti-fascist resistance. It started to intensively research the political system of the Slovak state, including its foreign and domestic politics. An important initiator and co-ordinator of this research was the Slovak Committee for the History of the Anti-Fascist Resistance, founded in 1964. It co-ordinated its research of the war with Czech and other European historians. The result of this cooperation was a number of joint works[6] as well as the publication of two basic resource editions.[7] Historians took advantage of these favorable conditions, including the removal of taboos and the opening of some archival materials. In this period more monographs,[8] syntheses,[9] memoirs,[10] dictionaries,[11]

---

[2] GOSIOROVSKÝ, Miloš: Ilegálny boj KSS a Slovenské národné povstanie. Bratislava, Pravda 1949; GOSIOROVSKÝ, Miloš: Slovenské národné povstanie. Bratislava, SVPL 1954; 15. VÝRO-ČIE Slovenského národného povstania. Edited by GRACA, Bohuslav. Bratislava, SVPL 1959; SLOVENSKÉ národné povstanie. Edited by GRACA, Bohuslav. Bratislava, SAV 1954.

[3] KROPILÁK, Miroslav: Účasť vojakov v Slovenskom národnom povstaní. Bratislava, SAV 1960; FALŤAN, Samo: Partizánska vojna na Slovensku. Bratislava, Osveta 1957.

[4] GRACA, Bohuslav: 14. marec 1939. Bratislava, SVPL 1959; LIPSCHER, Ladislav: Ľudácka autonómia - ilúzie a skutočnosť. Bratislava, SVPL 1957.

[5] LIPTÁK, Ľubomír: Ovládnutie slovenského priemyslu nemeckým kapitálom (1939-1945). Bratislava, SAV 1960; BAUCH, Vlastimil: Poľnohospodárstvo za slovenského štátu. Bratislava, SVPL 1958; KOVÁČIK, Ľudovít: Slovensko v sieti nemeckého finančného kapitálu. Bratislava, SVPL 1955.

[6] SLOVENSKÉ národné povstanie 1944. Edited by HOLOTÍK, Ľudovít. Bratislava, SAV 1965; ODBOJ a revoluce 1938-1945. Compiled by JANEČEK, Oldřich. Praha, Naše vojsko 1965; BEER, Ferdinand and team: DEJINNÁ križovatka. Bratislava, VPL 1964.

[7] SLOVENSKÉ národné povstanie. Dokumenty. Compiled by PREČAN, Vilém. Bratislava, VPL 1965; SLOVENSKÉ národné povstanie. Nemci a Slovensko. Dokumenty. Compiled by PREČAN, Vilém. Bratislava, Epocha 1971.

[8] JABLONICKÝ, Jozef: Slovensko na prelome. Bratislava, VPL 1965; JABLONICKÝ, Jozef:

periodicals and proceedings of a state-wide or regional character were published. In monographs and dozens of articles distributed through specialized journals a serious analysis of the regime of the wartime Slovak Republic[12] was made, including its foreign political activities, especially in relation to Hungary[13], and its economic and social politics[14]. Some issues of its cultural life were analyzed and research of the Holocaust began. The project of historical biographies was started, which also touched on this period.[15] Some attention was devoted to the southern parts of Slovakia, which on the basis of the First Vienna arbitration had from November 1938 to 1945 been occupied by Horthy's Hungary.[16]

This promising start of new historiography on the war years was halted in the seventies by the so-called process of normalization, the beginning of the neo-Stalinist political system in Czechoslovakia. The more important historians who had researched this period (such as Jozef Jablonický, Ľubomír Lipták, Martin Vietor, Samuel Falťan, Ladislav Lipscher, Miroslav Ličko and others) were silenced or emigrated. Their works underwent detailed and unprofessional criticism motivated by ideology. Historiography of the modern period of Slova-

Z ilegality do povstania. Bratislava, Epocha 1969; FALŤAN, Samo: O slovenskom národnom povstaní. Bratislava, Osveta 1964.

[9] LIPTÁK, Ľubomír: Slovensko v 20. storočí. Bratislava, Epocha 1968; FRIŠ, Edo: Myšlienka a čin. Bratislava, VPL 1968; KONFRONTÁCIA. Zostavili KRNO, Miloš a ŠTEVČEK, Pavol. Bratislava, Smena 1968.

[10] HUSÁK, Gustáv: Svedectvo o slovenskom národnom povstaní. Bratislava, VPL 1964; FRIŠ, Edo: Povstanie zďaleka a zblízka. Bratislava, VPL 1964; RAŠLA, Anton: Civilista v armáde. Bratislava, VPL 1967.

[11] CHREŇO, Jozef: Malý slovník slovenského štátu 1938-1945. Bratislava, Slovenská archívna správa 1965; KROPILÁK, Miroslav - JABLONICKÝ, Jozef: Malý slovník slovenského národného povstania. Bratislava, VPL 1964.

[12] See articles by Ľ. Lipták, J. Sopko and F. Bielik in miscellany "Slovenské národné povstanie 1944" (see note 6) and articles by Ľ. Lipták in HČ 13, 1965, 3 and in HČ 14, 1966, 2.

[13] FABIAN, Juraj: Svätoštefanské tiene. Bratislava, SVPL 1966; PRÍSPEVKY k dejinám fašizmu v Československu a Maďarsku. Compiled by HOLOTÍK, Ľudovít. Bratislava, SAV 1969.

[14] KOCISKÁ, Anna: Robotnícka trieda v boji proti fašizmu na Slovensku (1938-1945). Bratislava, SAV 1964; FALTUS, Jozef - PRŮCHA, Václav: Prehľad hospodárskeho vývoja na Slovensku v rokoch 1918-1945. Bratislava, VPL 1969; PLEVA, Ján - TICHÝ, Miloš: Kresťanské odbory na Slovensku. Bratislava, Práca 1967.

[15] HOLOTÍKOVÁ, Zdena - PLEVZA, Viliam: Vladimír Clementis. Bratislava, VPL 1968; ŠTVRTECKÁ, Anna: Ján Osoha. Bratislava 1970.

[16] VIETOR, Martin: Dejiny okupácie južného Slovenska. Bratislava, SAV 1968; PURGAT, Juraj: Od Trianonu po Košice. Bratislava, Epocha 1970.

kia stagnated, undergoing a deep crisis from both the conceptual and research aspects, most serious in the seventies. Most of the monographs and syntheses of those days gave a simplified explanation of the war period, not reaching the professional quality of the previous decade. More source editions[17] and factual works[18], as well as partial studies of some aspects of the Slovak anti-fascist resistance, and about Slovak-German economic, political and military relations during the war, were contributed. Some works of a regional character, dealing with political and social-economic development in different parts of Slovakia, also deserve attention.[19] Some passages in a number of historical biographies also made a contribution.[20]

In the eighties, a revival came about in the research of Slovak history during the war, in professional and thematic concerns. Synthetic works, in spite of their persistant ideological bias, presented new factual data.[21] Research of the armed movement of anti-fascist resistance moved perceptibly forward.[22] Historiography began to return systematically to the research of the foreign and domestic politics of the wartime Slovak regime.[23] In 1976, the miscellany of the Museum (formerly the Institute) of the Slovak National Uprising resumed publication,

---

[17] RÁKOŠ, Elo: Slovenské národné orgány v dokumentoch I. Bratislava, Archívna správa MV 1977; SUŠKO, Ladislav: A národ povstal. Dokumenty. Praha, Horizont 1974.

[18] RÁKOŠ, Elo - RUDOHRADSKÝ, Štefan: Slovenské národné orgány 1943-1948. Bratislava, Archívna správa MV 1972; DEJINY štátu a práva na území Československa v období kapitalizmu, II. 1918-1945. Edited by BIANCHI, Leonard. Bratislava, SAV 1973; CHREŇOVÁ, Júlia: Štruktúra ústredných orgánov na Slovensku v rokoch 1939-1945. Bratislava, Archívna správa MV 1977.

[19] PAŽUR, Štefan: Protifašistický odboj na východnom Slovensku. Košice, VV 1974.

[20] LAVOVÁ, Mária: Marek Čulen. Bratislava, Pravda 1971; KOVÁČIKOVÁ, Terézia: Karol Šmidke. Bratislava, Pravda 1978; HOLOTÍKOVÁ, Zdena: Ladislav Novomeský. Bratislava, Pravda 1980.

[21] ZA NÁRODNÉ oslobodenie. Za novú republiku (1938-1945). Edited by BOUČEK, Miroslav - KLIMEŠ, Miloš - VARTÍKOVÁ, Marta. Bratislava, Pravda 1988; DEJINY Slovenského národného povstania 1944 I.-V. Edited by PLEVZA, Viliam. Bratislava, Pravda 1984. The first two volumes contain specialized texts, and the third and fourth volume contain contemporary archival and press documents, respectively commemorative materials. The fifth volume is in the form of an encyclopedic dictionary; DOKUMENTY k dejinám komunistickej strany na Slovensku (1938-1944) I.-II. Compiled by CHREŇOVÁ, Júlia. Bratislava, Ústav marxizmu leninizmu 1988.

[22] ŠTEFANSKÝ, Václav: Armáda v Slovenskom národnom povstaní. Bratislava, Pravda 1984; BOSÁK, Pavol: Z bojových operácií na fronte Slovenského národného povstania. Bratislava, Pravda 1979; GEBHART, Jan - ŠIMOVČEK, Ján: Partizáni v Československu 1941-1945. Praha-Bratislava, Naše vojsko-Pravda 1984.

[23] KLIMKO, Jozef: Tretia ríša a ľudácky režim na Slovensku. Bratislava, Obzor 1986; HRNKO, Anton: Politický vývin a protifašistický odboj na Slovensku (1939-1941). Bratislava, Veda 1988; FAŠISTICKÉ represálie na Slovensku. Edited by HALAJ, Dušan. Bratislava, Obzor 1990.

and in the subsequent fifteen volumes contained dozens of scholarly studies of not only the resistance but other historical themes of the war period in Slovakia. Attention was also directed to the process of the liberation of Slovakia from Nazi occupation and social and political changes within Slovak society.[24] Also innovative were the studies dealing with the fate of Slovak citizens abroad and the role of national minorities in Slovakia during the war.[25]

Fundamental political changes connected with the fall of the totalitarian political system in Czechoslovakia in 1989 removed traditional ideological barriers from the development of Slovak historiography of modern Slovak history. From the qualitative and also the quantitative point of view this was also reflected in work on the years 1938-1945. These issues have, even from a perspective of fifty years later, not only a historical but a current political dimension. Some Slovak historians and journalists, who were influenced by the works and conceptual attitudes of historiography written by one group in exile, but also by the contemporary ethnic and national tensions that led in 1993 to the foundation of the Slovak Republic, consider the First Slovak Republic as the predecessor of the current one. In these works originating from exile, the regime and leading personalities of 1938-1945 are idealized. From this aspect, even the anti-fascist resistance of Slovakia is not seen as an organic part of the pan-European struggle against Nazi and Fascist totalitarianism but as a tragically mistaken fight of people against their own state.

This ideology has not influenced most Slovak professional historians on the period 1938-1945. After 1989, more articles about the war period of the Slovak state[26] were published, as well as a new collection of documents;[27] works concerning the role of Slovakia after the Munich dictatorship,[28] reconstructing its

[24] PAULIAK, Ervín: Od Povstania k oslobodeniu. Bratislava, Pravda 1985; BARNOVSKÝ, Michal: Sociálne triedy a revolučné premeny na Slovensku v rokoch 1944-1948. Bratislava, Veda 1978.

[25] Articles are published mostly in the annals *Slováci v zahraničí,* which since 1975 has been published in Bratislava by Matica slovenská. Edited by BIELIK, František - BALÁŽ, Claude; devoted to discrimination against the Romanies was an article by NEČAS, Ctibor: Pronásledování Cikánů v období slovenského státu. In: Slovenský národopis 36, 1988, 1, pp. 126-136.

[26] SLOVENSKO v rokoch druhej svetovej vojny. Compiled by BYSTRICKÝ, Valerián. Bratislava, HÚ SAV 1991; KAMENEC, Ivan: Slovenský stát. Praha, Anomal 1992; the relevant chapters from the book POLITICKÉ strany na Slovensku 1860-1989. Edited by LIPTÁK, Ľubomír. Bratislava, Archa 1992.

[27] VATIKÁN a Slovenská republika (1939-1945). Dokumenty. Edited by KAMENEC, Ivan - PREČAN, Vilém - ŠKORVÁNEK, Stanislav. Bratislava, SAP 1992.

[28] DEÁK, Ladislav: Hra o Slovensko. Bratislava, Veda 1991.

war politics,[29] and mapping the roles of the German and Hungarian minorities in Slovakia;[30] articles concerning minority politics and national questions in central Europe;[31] and so on. In professional literature, the gap was filled on "the solution of the Jewish question," that is, the Holocaust in Slovakia.[32] Great attention is still devoted to the issues of anti-fascist resistance. The most fruitful author in this area has been Jozef Jablonický,[33] who during the previous twenty years had only been able to publish unofficially or abroad.[34] More monographs and biographies were written which deal with previously unknown or unmentioned personalities from the history of the anti-fascist resistance in Slovakia.[35] Many histories and memoirs from the pens of domestic and exiled authors[36] also were published of which many are handicapped by their authors' limited knowl-

[29] MALÁ vojna. Edited by DEÁK, Ladislav. Bratislava, SAP 1993; VÝCHODOSLOVENSKÁ armáda a odboj. Edited by ŠTEFANSKÝ, Václav. Banská Bystrica, Múzeum SNP 1992; ŠTEFANSKÝ, Václav - ŠIMUNIČ, Pavel - VIMMER, Pavel: Prvá československá armáda na Slovensku. Bratislava, Zväz protifašistických bojovníkov 1991.

[30] KOVÁČ, Dušan: Nemecko a nemecká menšina na Slovensku (1871-1945). Bratislava, Veda 1991; ČIERNA-LANTAYOVÁ, Dagmar: Podoby česko-slovensko-maďarských vzťahov 1938-1949. Bratislava, Veda 1992.

[31] STREDNÁ a juhovýchodná Európa. Sondy do vývoja v štyridsiatych rokoch. Edited by PETRUF, Pavol. Bratislava, HÚ SAV 1992.

[32] KAMENEC, Ivan: Po stopách tragédie. Bratislava, Archa 1991; TRAGÉDIA slovenských židov. Edited by TÓTH, Dezider. Banská Bystrica, Datei 1992. The miscellany was published also in an English-language edition: The Tragedy of Slovak Jews; LIPSCHER, Ladislav: Židia v slovenskom štáte 1939-1945. Bratislava, Print servis 1992. The work was originally published in the German language: Die Juden im Slowakischen Staat 1939-1945. München, Oldenburg Verlag 1979; Riešenie židovskej otázky na Slovensku (1939-1945). Dokumenty 1.-3. Judaica Slovaca. Compiled by HUBENÁK, Ladislav. Bratislava, Slovenské národné múzeum 1994.

[33] JABLONICKÝ, Jozef: Povstanie bez legiend. Bratislava, Obzor 1990; JABLONICKÝ, Jozef: Glosy o historiografii SNP. Bratislava, NVK International 1994.

[34] In Toronto, in the years 1976, 1980 and 1983, three numbers of the miscellany "Zborník o Slovenskom národnom povstaní" were published, on the one hand specialized articles by exiled Slovak historians, and on the other memoir reflections of members of the anti-fascist resistance in Slovakia.

[35] TAKÁČ, Ladislav: Poslanie. Banská Bystrica, Enterprise 1992; ZABUDNUTÍ velitelia. Edited by TAKÁČ, Ladislav. Bratislava, Pramene, without date; SPOJENECKÉ misie. Edited by ZUDOVÁ, Zlatica. Banská Bystrica, Múzeum SNP 1990; HALAJ, Dušan: Viliam Žingor. Banská Bystrica, Múzeum SNP 1990; TAKÁČ, Ladislav: Nezabudnite na Telgárt. Banská Bystrica, Admini 1992; HALAJ, Dušan: Milan Polák. Banská Bystrica, Agency Royal 1993; SNP v pamäti národa. Zostavovateľ LIPTÁK, Július. Bratislava-Banská Bystrica, NVK International 1994.

[36] LETTRICH, Jozef: Dejiny novodobého Slovenska. Bratislava, Archa 1993. The book was originally published in London in 1955 in the English language, under the title "History of Modern Slovakia"; VNUK, František: Mať svoj štát znamená život. Bratislava, Odkaz 1991; MEDRICKÝ,

edge of domestic archival material or by ideological prejudice. Historians domestic and in exile tried to give an historical picture of one of the most controversial figures of the period, the president of the wartime republic, Josef Tiso,[37] the evaluation of whom is discussed in Slovakia with sharp polemics.

Interestingly, the period of 1938-1945 is of the greatest concern to foreign historiography dealing with Slovak history. A number of articles and the more extensive monographs[38] study the history of the war period of the Slovak state, the anti-fascist struggle, and issues of the Holocaust in Slovakia.

Gejza: Minister spomína. Bratislava, Litera 1993; URSÍNY, Ján: Spomienky na Slovenské národné povstanie. Liptovský Mikuláš, Tranoscius 1994; ČARNOGURSKÝ, Pavol: 14. marec 1939. Bratislava, Veda 1992; KARVAŠ, Imrich: Moje pamäti. V pazúroch gestapa. Bratislava-Banská Bystrica, Múzeum SNP 1994.

[37] POKUS o politický a osobný profil Jozefa Tisu. Edited by BYSTRICKÝ, Valerián - FANO, Štefan. Bratislava, SAP 1992.

[38] KAISER, Johann: Die Politik des Dritten Reiches gegenüber der Slowakei 1939-1945. Bochum 1969; JELINEK, Yeshayahu: The Parish Republic: Hlinka's Slovak People's Party 1939-1945. New York-London, East European Monographes; DRESS, Hans: Slowakei und faschistische Neuordnung Europas 1939-1945. Berlin 1971; HOENSCH, Jörg K.: Die Slowakei und Hitlers Ost Politik. Köln-Graz 1965; ROTKIRCHEN, Livia: The Destruction of Slovak Jewry. Jerusalem, Yad Vashem 1961; VENOHR, Wolfgang: Aufstand in der Tatra. Der Kampf um die Slowakei 1939-1944. Königstein, Athenäum 1979.

SLOVAK HISTORIOGRAPHY ON THE PERIOD AFTER 1945

The low standard of historical works about post-World War II Slovakia was due primarily to realities such as political and ideological pressure. The communist monopoly on power was clearly expressed in historical work. The powerful elite preferred research on contemporary history but even this was strictly directed and controlled from on high, determining not only the direction of research but also its conclusions. What historians had to prove, contradict, glorify and pillory was given to them ahead of time. They were required to justify not only the ruling role of the party, but every change in politics. The professional capabilities of historians were also bent to this role. Research of contemporary history was taken over by young historians, graduating from universities in the fifties, who did not have the opportunity to rely on the works of historians from earlier generations. Not needing to re-evaluate anything, for a long time they did not meet with other conceptions of historical explanation. Part of this group gradually improved in the historical craft, but many stopped growing, failed to cast off dogmatism or felt no need to cast it off since it was enough to repeat the "eternal truths" in order to serve the ruling power. Finally, the quality historiography was influenced by the narrow material basis, the short distance from the researched object, and change in the character of published and archival sources, the value of which had been diminished.

Despite all of the shortcomings of Slovak historiography from the onset of the communist regime, it would not be just to dismiss its results all together. In some areas it assembled a core of knowledge that, after a critical evaluation, could serve as a starting point for further research. Even the totalitarian system was not able to stop the growth of knowledge. In addition, alternating with periods of control, regimentation and regression were ones of loosening the bit, partial tolerance, and liberalization.

The first works on the history of Slovakia after 1945 appeared in the fifties.[1]

---

[1] Príspevok k dejinám ľudovej demokracie v ČSR. Preface: GRACA, Bohuslav. Bratislava, SVPL 1955; FALŤAN, Michal: Cesta slovenského roľníctva k socializmu. Bratislava, SVPL 1954; CAMBEL, Samuel: Agrárna otázka na Slovensku a naša revolúcia (1945-1948). Bratislava, SVPL 1958; INOVECKÝ, Jozef: Slovenská dedina včera a dnes. Bratislava, SNPL 1956; ZAJAC, Ladislav: Slovenské robotníctvo v boji za víťazný február 1948. Bratislava, SVPL 1958; KOVÁČIK, Ľudovít: Boj o banky. Bratislava, Práca 1950.

They were faulty concerning factual material and on a low level in their evaluations marked by the political climate of the Cold War. The most fruitful period was the 1960s. De-Stalinization, which in Czechoslovakia led to the 1968 effort to reform communism and the rehabilitation of illegally sentenced functionaries, provided a freedom for the more objective evaluation of historical events. In those days, the first at least partial efforts to disconnect historiography from the exercise of political power appeared. This favorable trend was halted by normalization. A number of historians were excluded from research activity, the explication of contemporary history was once again influenced by political needs, and many topics were made taboo. Of course in this unfavorable period of the seventies and eighties, some works were produced that made a contribution to factual knowledge. Despite the ideological ballast we can find some new information and ideas. However, they were few.

The bibliography of historical works for these most recent decades shows the best research of the period of 1945-1948. The greater perspective on the dramatic transition of this period from one dictatorship to another played its role, but not less important was the fact that not only the victors but the victims of February 1948 had an interest in giving their version of the historical facts. Interestingly, research of the post-war years seems to have begun from the end and worked backwards. The first works didn't concentrate on the research of the particular social and political situation, but meditated on the character of the revolution: whether it was a bourgeois-democratic, a people's democratic or a socialist revolution.[2] Slovak historians only seldom took part in these unfruitful discussions.

Roughly, from the mid-sixties, the question of the specific road to socialism came to the fore and in this connection appeared many new ideas. The thesis of two levels of revolution in Czechoslovakia (in the Czech lands and in Slovakia) was born which became the main thesis of historians writing on various themes. Before the discussion of "Czechoslovak" or a "special road to socialism" reached a conclusion it was interrupted by normalization. The new party leadership under Gustáv Husák saw in this discussion the manifestation of revisionism. Projects for publication of more sources were not completed;[3] rather, the pub-

---

[2] Vznik a vývoj lidově demokratického Československa. Edited by KRÁL, Václav. Praha, ČSAV 1961; Základní teoretické otázky výstavby socializmu a komunizmu ve světle výsledků společenských věd. Compiled by HOUŠKA, Josef. Praha, Nakladatelství ČSAV 1962.

[3] At the beginning of the sixties, the idea of publishing a six-volume resource edition "Československo na ceste k socializmu" was born. "Normalization" derailed realization of this project. Only the first part, in two volumes, was published, in which are also included documents of Slovak

lication of conformist memoirs, mostly of communist functionaries, was preferred.[4]

In research, most attention was given to the activity of the Communist Party. The Communist Party of Slovakia was idealized along with its politics. Among other political topics, the attention of historians was first dedicated to political Catholicism and the Democratic Party. In some small essays, the positions of the Party of Freedom and the Party of Work were analyzed from a communist perspective.[5] Among the investigation of community and voluntary organizations, the best work was the research of the history of trade unions. The activities

provenance: Cesta ke Květnu I.-II. Edited by KLIMEŠ, Miloš - LESJUK, Petr - MALÁ, Irena - PREČAN, Vilém. Praha, V ČSAV 1965; In Slovakia, in 1970-1971, they managed to publish these documents: KSS. Dokumenty z konferencií a plén 1944-1948. Edited by VARTÍKOVÁ, Marta. Bratislava, Pravda 1971; Z dejín odborového hnutia na Slovensku (1944-1946). Dokumenty. Edited by ŠKURLO, Ivan. Bratislava, Práca 1970; Z dejín odborového hnutia na Slovensku (1946-1948). Dokumenty. Edited by TOMEK, František. Bratislava, Práca 1971.

[4] Víťazný február 1948. Edited by KUBÍN, Václav - MILLEROVÁ, Viera. Praha, SNPL 1959; Spomienky na slávne dni. Edited by SVORÉŇOVÁ-KIRÁLYOVÁ, Blanka. Bratislava, Pravda 1972; Ľudia vo Februári. Edited by KIRÁLYOVÁ, Blanka. Bratislava, Pravda 1977.

[5] Prehľad dejín KSČ na Slovensku. Edited by HAPÁK, Pavol. Bratislava, Pravda 1971; KSČ a vývoj revolučného procesu na Slovensku. I. (1848-1948) Edited by HOLOTÍKOVÁ, Zdena - VARTÍKOVÁ, Marta. Bratislava, Pravda 1987; LIPTÁK, Ľubomír: Slovensko v 20. storočí. Bratislava, VPL 1968; CAMBEL, Samuel: Revolučný rok 1945. Oslobodenie a prvé kroky ľudovej moci na strednom Slovensku. Banská Bystrica, SV 1965; JABLONICKÝ, Jozef: Slovensko na prelome. Zápas o víťazstvo národnej a demokratickej revolúcie na Slovensku. Bratislava, VPL 1965; PREČAN, Vilém: Slovenský katolicizmus pred februárom 1948. Bratislava, Osveta 1961; JAROŠ, Oldřich - JAROŠOVÁ, Viera: Slovenské robotníctvo v boji o moc. Bratislava, Pravda 1965; FALŤAN, Samuel: K problémom národnej a demokratickej revolúcie na Slovensku. Bratislava, VPL 1965; FRIŠ, Edo: Myšlienka a čin. Bratislava, VPL 1968; Prvé kroky po oslobodení. Edited by KRAJČÍKOVÁ, Ružena. Bratislava, Epocha 1970; PLEVZA, Viliam - ŘEHŮŘEK, Miloš: Revolúcia v nástupe. Bratislava, Obzor 1975; PLEVZA, Viliam - ŘEHŮŘEK, Miloš: Víťazná revolúcia. Bratislava, Obzor 1977; Cestou socialistického vývinu. Štúdie o niektorých otázkach Februára a pofebruárového obdobia. Edited by KIRÁLYOVÁ, Blanka. Bratislava, Pravda 1973; Za nové Československo. Materiály z celoštátnej vedeckej konferencie k 25. výročiu oslobodenia Československa. Zborník Ústavu marxizmu-leninizmu ÚV KSS, 12, 1, Bratislava, Pravda 1972; BOUČEK, Miroslav - KLIMEŠ, Miloš - VARTÍKOVÁ, Marta: Program revolúcie. K vzniku Košického vládneho programu. Bratislava, Pravda 1975; BRIŠKÁR, Juraj: DS na východnom Slovensku pred februárom 1948. In: Východné Slovensko pred Februárom. Košice, VV 1968, pp. 167-175. ŠKURLO, Ivan: Celoslovenská konferencia KSS v Žiline roku 1945 a čo jej predchádzalo. In: HČ 19, 1971, 2, pp. 145-175; BOBKOVÁ, Anna: K vzniku tzv. Strany práce - sociálnej demokracie na Slovensku. In: Zb SNM 56, História 2, 1962, pp. 3-19; LACKO, Ján: Vývin v Strane práce od jej vzniku až do rozplynutia. In: Cestou socialistického vývinu, op. cit., pp. 34-60; ŠUTAJ, Štefan: Vznik Strany slobody a formovanie jej programu v prvých rokoch po oslobodení. In: HČ 36, 1988, 1, pp. 59-77.

˙of the Union of Slovak Partisans, of the Union of Slovak Farmers, and of student and youth organizations were examined.[6] Concerning the people's democratic political system, of central interest to historians were the problems of the National Front, national committees, retributional judicial affairs, and the activities of Slovak national offices. Among military organizations most attention was given to the formation of the people's militias and the army.[7]

The question of the constitutional status of Slovakia within the Czechoslovak Republic, of Czecho-Slovak relations and the problems of national minorities came to the fore of historical research in the second half of the sixties in preparation for a federative organization of the state. Even in later years, these themes didn't lose their importance.[8] Many publications deal with the events of

---

[6] JAROŠOVÁ, Viera - ŠKURLO, Ivan - VARTÍKOVÁ, Marta: Odbory na ceste k Februáru (1944-1948). Bratislava, Práca 1967; VARTÍKOVÁ, Marta: Zjazd závodných a zamestnaneckých rád (1947). Bratislava, Práca 1967; FIRDOVÁ, Mária: Vznik a činnosť JZSR na východnom Slovensku. In: Východné Slovensko pred Februárom. Košice, VV 1968. pp. 127-167; STRAKA, Jaroslav: Študentské hnutie na Slovensku v období národnej a demokratickej revolúcie. Bratislava, Smena 1978; SÝKORA, Ernest: Keď sa začala budúcnosť. Dejiny Zväzu slovenskej mládeže v rokoch 1945-1949. Bratislava, Smena 1982; VRANOVÁ, Elena: Spolky na Slovensku v rokoch 1945-1949. In: SlArchiv 15, 1980, 1, s. 63-95; MANNOVÁ, Elena: Spolky v období sociálno-politických zmien na Slovensku 1938-1951. Analýza spolkových stanov. In: Občianska spoločnosť na prahu znovuzrodenia. Compiled by STENA, Ján. Bratislava, Sociologický ústav SAV 1992, pp. 21-30.

[7] VARTÍKOVÁ, Marta: Od Košíc po Február. Bratislava, Obzor 1968; RÁKOŠ, Edo - RUDOHRADSKÝ, Štefan: Slovenské národné orgány 1943-1968. Bratislava, Slovenská archívna správa 1973; RAŠLA, Anton: Ľudové súdy v Československu po II. svetovej vojne ako forma mimoriadneho súdnictva. Bratislava, Vydavateľstvo SAV 1969; DAXNER, Igor: Ľudáctvo pred Národným súdom. Bratislava, Vydavateľstvo SAV 1961; LUBY, Štefan: Národná a demokratická revolúcia a prerušenie formálnej kontinuity s predrevolučným právom. In: Právny obzor 58, 1975, pp. 507-521. RUDOHRADSKÝ, Štefan: Revolučné národné výbory na Slovensku od oslobodenia do celoslovenského zjazdu 1945. In: SlArchiv 12, 1977, 1, pp. 3-49; ŠKURLO, Ivan: Február a ľudové milície. Bratislava, VPL 1968; VARTÍKOVÁ, Marta: Strážime socializmus. Bratislava, Pravda 1973; PAULIAK, Ervín: Zástoj slovenských komunistov v zápase KSČ o ľudovú armádu v rokoch 1945-1948 na Slovensku. In: Cestou socialistického vývinu, op. cit., pp. 125-166.

[8] BARTO, Jaroslav: Riešenie vzťahu Čechov a Slovákov. Bratislava, Epocha 1968; FALŤAN, Samuel: Slovenská otázka v Československu. Bratislava, VPL 1968; BAJCURA, Ivan: Ukrajinská otázka v ČSSR. Košice, VV 1967; ZVARA, Juraj: Maďarská menšina na Slovensku po roku 1945. Bratislava, Epocha 1969; VANAT, Ivan: Narysy novitňoji istoriji Ukrajinciv Schidnoji Slovaččyny. II. 1938-1948. Bratislava-Prešov, SPN 1985; JABLONICKÝ, Jozef: Slovenská otázka v období národnej a demokratickej revolúcie. In: Slováci a ich národný vývin. Edited by MÉSÁROŠ, Július. Bratislava, Vydavateľstvo SAV 1966, pp. 269-290; PURGAT, Juraj: Čo predchádzalo dohode o výmene obyvateľstva medzi Československom a Maďarskom? In: Revue dějin socialismu 8, 1969, 4, pp. 507-527.

February, 1948 although their interpretations are naturally shaped by communist ideology.[9] From economic and social history, the attention of historians was concentrated on agrarian politics of the Communist Party, the agrarian question and land reform, and 1945-1948. They also dealt with the theme of nationalization, the two-year plan, and the material position of different social strata,[10] as well as with the foreign politics of Czechoslovakia and the cultural politics of the Communist Party.[11]

As for the analysis of the pre-February period (from the liberation of Slovakia in 1945 to the imposition of the communist monopoly of power), historiography concentrated on political events. But, in analysis of the post-February period, it preferred socio-economic questions: the economic politics of the Communist Party; changes of ownership; the process of agricultural collectivization; the industrialization and economic development of Slovakia; and also the liquidation of small private businesses.[12] More attention was paid to the quantitative

---

[9] VARTÍKOVÁ, Marta - LANTAY, Andrej: Február rozhodol. Bratislava, VPL 1963; PAULIAK, Ervín: Február a my. Bratislava, SPN 1973; Február a dnešok. Edited by CHRISTO-VOVÁ, Draga. Bratislava, Pravda 1974; PLEVZA, Viliam: Februárová história. Bratislava, Smena - Mladá fronta 1988; PETRUF, Pavol: Februárové udalosti a ich odraz v publikovaných dokumentoch americkej zahraničnej politiky. In: SlŠt 24, 1983, 2, pp. 94-101; LALUHA, Ivan: Február 1948 a stredné Slovensko. Banská Bystrica, SV 1967; ŠKURLO, Ivan: Február 1948 na východnom Slovensku. In: Východné Slovensko pred Februárom. Edited by FIRDOVÁ, Mária. Košice, VV 1968, pp. 197-247.

[10] CAMBEL, Samuel: Slovenská agrárna otázka 1944-1948. O dvoch polohách agrárnej revolúcie na Slovensku a v českých krajinách. Bratislava, Pravda 1972; BARNOVSKÝ, Michal: Sociálne triedy a revolučné premeny na Slovensku v rokoch 1944-1948. Bratislava, Veda 1978; VRABLIC, Emil: Revolúcia a znárodnenie na Slovensku. Bratislava, Práca 1975; VANKO, Augustín: Slovenské a československé poľnohospodárstvo v rokoch dvojročnice. In: HŠt 21, 1976, pp. 165-187.

[11] ČIERNY, Ján: Nová orientácia zahraničnej politiky Československa (1941-1948). Bratislava, Pravda 1979; GREŠÍK, Ladislav: Slovenská kultúra v revolúcii. (1944-1948). Bratislava, Pravda 1977.

[12] TURČAN, Pavol: Socialistická industrializácia Slovenska. Bratislava, Osveta 1960; BARNOVSKÝ, Michal: Problematika industrializácie Slovenska 1945-1950. In: HČ 16, 1968, 2, pp. 169-194; BARNOVSKÝ, Michal: Druhý päťročný plán a hospodársky rozvoj Slovenska. In: Slovensko v období dobudovania základov socializmu (1956-1960). Edited by HOLOTÍKOVÁ, Zdena. Bratislava, Pravda 1978, pp. 44-97; JAURA, Zdeno: Východiská a základné predpoklady socialistickej industrializácie Slovenska. Bratislava, Veda 1988; JAURA, Zdeno: K periodizácii socialistickej industrializácie Slovenska. In: HČ 32, 1984, pp. 126-137; Tridsať budovateľských rokov. Compiled by KOLLÁR, Jozef. Bratislava, Pravda 1975; Generálna línia výstavby socializmu. Edited by VARTÍKOVÁ, Marta. Bratislava, Pravda 1975; VOJÁČEK, Alois: Vývoj socialistického poľnohospodárstva na Slovensku. Bratislava, Príroda 1973; CAMBEL, Samuel - SKRIP, Vasil - VANKO, Augustín: Roľnícka politika KSČ v období výstavby socializmu na Slovensku.

than the qualitative side of these processes. No doubt was expressed about the need of collectivization. When critical opinions were expressed, these concerned only its pace and methods, without analysis of the reasons or consequences.

While historians turned their attention to collectivization, economists took the industrialization and economic development of Slovakia as their topic of concern. The thematic concerns were the result of accepting research tasks from above and historiography's inability to escape from the confines of the political system. Works from political, pedagogical, cultural and legal history had an even more apologetic character. They did not step outside their prescribed role of justifying the legitimacy of the power of the Communist Party and its leading task, and the advantages of the communist regime. Often they were only descriptions of party congress resolutions or of meetings of the Central Committees of Slovakia and Czechoslovakia.[13]

Several efforts to synthesize the view of Slovak and Czechoslovak history since 1945 did not produce the expected results.[14] The scholarly contribution of

Bratislava, Pravda 1978; Kapitoly z dejín socialistického poľnohospodárstva v Československu. Edited by CAMBEL, Samuel. Bratislava, Pravda 1982; Formovanie triedy družstevného roľníctva. Edited by CAMBEL, Samuel. Bratislava, Pravda 1984; Skúsenosti KSČ A KSSZ z riešenia roľníckej otázky. Edited by CAMBEL, Samuel. Bratislava, Pravda 1985; Rozvíjanie socializmu na Slovensku v prvej polovici šesťdesiatych rokov. Ústav marxizmu-leninizmu ÚV KSS, 19, 1, Bratislava, Pravda 1979; Rozvoj Slovenska v politike a programe KSČ. Edited by BAŠŤOVANSKÁ, Magdaléna - ONDRUŠOVÁ, Alžbeta. Bratislava, Vydavateľstvo SAV 1973; ZELENÁK, Peter: Socializácia živnosti na Slovensku. In: HŠt, Bratislava, Veda 1988.

[13] Rozvoj socialistického štátu a práva v oslobodenom Československu. Edited by HUTTA, Vladimír. Bratislava, Veda 1977; ŘEHŮŘEK, Miloš: Výstavba socialistického politického systému. Bratislava, Veda 1985; ŘEHŮŘEK, Miloš: Spoločenské organizácie v socialistickom politickom systéme. Bratislava, Veda 1982; GABAĽ, Andrej: Na rozhraní etáp. Bratislava, Pravda 1981; ŽATKULIAK, Jozef: Vývoj národných výborov na Slovensku v prvých rokoch výstavby socializmu (1948-1954). HŠt, Bratislava, Veda 1986; SIKORA, Stanislav: KSČ a národné výbory na Slovensku v začiatkoch socialistickej výstavby. Bratislava, Pravda 1989; GREŠÍK, Ladislav Slovenská kultúra v začiatkoch budovania socializmu (1948-1955). Bratislava, Pravda 1980; GREŠÍK, Ladislav: Kultúrna politika KSS v období dobudovania základov socializmu (1956-1960). Bratislava, Pravda 1986; PAVLOVIČ, Gustáv: K histórii socialistickej školy. Bratislava, SPN 1977; Národnostné vzťahy v socialistickom Československu. Edited by PŘIKRYL, František. Bratislava, Pravda 1976; PLEVZA, Viliam: Československá štátnosť a slovenská otázka v politike KSČ. Bratislava, Práca 1971.

[14] PLEVZA, Viliam: Trvalé hodnoty II. Bratislava 1977; PLEVZA, Viliam: Socialistické premeny Československa. Bratislava, Pravda 1983; Socialistické Slovensko. Edited by CIRBES, Vladimír - BAUCH, Vlastimil. Bratislava, Pravda 1978; Dejiny Slovenska VI. (1945-1960) Edited by BARNOVSKÝ, Michal. Bratislava, Veda 1988.

these publications was minimal, lower even than individual studies and monographs. The reason for this was that conditions were not ripe for synthesis, since a sufficient number of good analytic studies was missing. In addition, this sort of historical work was under the close supervision of the party apparatus, which anxiously guarded the party principle of historical science.

We can conclude that while domestic historiography collected a certain amount of factual data, this was compromised by its service to the official ideology, narrow conceptual focus, and politically influenced thematic orientation. Even if the orientation sometimes varied, the research revolved around the same problems, whether real or fictitious. All the themes were dealt with from the perspective of the ruling class and, as far as the contents are concerned, they were directed towards the history of the party rather than of society. Only the fall of communism created the conditions for overcoming the received concept of history, a task which will be neither a simple nor quick one, for the historical sources conform to the view of history through the eyes of the ruling power.

The destruction of the totalitarian system and the opening of new collections of historical documents have allowed historians to approach closer to the essence of historical processes and the multi-faceted historical picture. The earliest results show that the concerns of historians are traditional but their content is richer, including themes previously taboo (such as 1968), and treatment of events up to the early seventies.[15] The barriers that internationally isolated Slovak historiography have been removed.

---

[15] MIKLOŠKO, František: Nebudete ich môcť rozvrátiť. Z osudov katolíckej cirkvi na Slovensku. Bratislava, Archa 1991; FEDOR, Michal: Z dejín gréckokatolíckej cirkvi v Československu 1945 - máj 1950. Košice, Byzant 1993; HLINKA, Anton: Sila slabých, slabosť silných. Cirkev na Slovensku v rokoch 1948-1989. Trnava, Spolok sv. Vojtecha 1990; ŠUTAJ, Štefan: Maďarská menšina na Slovensku v rokoch 1945-1948. Východiská a prax politiky k maďarskej menšine na Slovensku. Bratislava, Veda 1993; GAJDOŠ, Marián - KONEČNÝ, Stanislav: K politickému a sociálnemu postaveniu Rusínov-Ukrajincov na Slovensku v povojnových rokoch. Košice, Spoločenskovedný ústav SAV 1991; ŠUTAJ, Štefan: Reslovakizácia. Zmena národnosti časti obyvateľstva na Slovensku po II. svetovej vojne. Košice, Spoločenskovedný ústav SAV 1991; PLEVZA, Viliam: Vzostupy a pády. Gustáv Husák prehovoril. Bratislava, Tatrapress 1991; LALUHA, Ivan - UHER, Ján - KOČTUCH, Hvezdoň: Dubček. Profily vzdoru. Bratislava, Smena 1991; GABZDILOVÁ, Soňa: Školy s maďarským vyučovacím jazykom na Slovensku po druhej svetovej vojne. Košice, Spoločenskovedný ústav SAV 1991; JUROVÁ, Anna: Vývoj rómskej problematiky na Slovensku po roku 1945. Košice, Spoločenskovedný ústav SAV, Goldpress 1993; BARNOVSKÝ, Michal: Na ceste k monopolu moci. Mocenskopolitické zápasy na Slovensku v rokoch 1945-1948. Bratislava, Archa 1993; LETZ, Róbert: Slovensko v rokoch 1945-1948. Na ceste ku komunistickej totalite. Bratislava, Ústredie slovenskej kresťanskej inteligencie 1994; Osem mesiacov pražskej jari. 21. august 1968. Edited by BENČÍK, Antonín. Martin, Osveta 1990; ČOMAJ, Ján - VEREŠ, Juraj: Čo nebolo

The multiplicity of ideas has been renewed. But unfortunately also the effort of new political parties to subordinate historical analysis to their own needs has grown. The future of Slovak historiography depends on how it succeeds in overcoming the old sickness and avoiding the new politicization and service to ideology.

The research of general history after 1945 suffered not only from "outside" pressure but also from certain pressure from within Slovak historiography supported by the conviction that the research of general history can only be an adjunct to Slovak history.[16] Thus this research was much less holistic, less conceptual and quantitatively less well represented than research of the history of Slovakia.

Before 1989 the main stress was placed on the questions of the foundation of the so-called world socialist bloc, and its political, economic and military co-operation. On these issues several works of synthesis were created,[17] as well as

---

v novinách. August 1968. Bratislava, Mladá fronta 1990; Slovenská spoločnosť v krízových rokoch 1967-1970. Zborníky štúdií I-III. Edited by Komisia vlády SR pre analýzu udalostí 1967-1970. Bratislava, Politologický kabinet SAV 1992; **Memoirs and documents:** Proces s dr. J. Tisom. Spomienky obžalobcu Antona Rašlu, obhajcu Ernesta Žabkayho. Bratislava, Tatrapress 1990; Naděje umírá poslední. Vlastní životopis Alexandra Dubčeka. Praha, Svoboda 1993; MURÍN, Karol: Spomienky a svedectvo. Partizánske, Garmond 1992; KOREC, Ján Chryzostom: Od barbarskej noci. Pokračovanie druhej časti Listy z väzenia. Bratislava, Lúč 1991; Dva retribučni procesy. Komentované dokumenty (1946-1947). Edited by KAPLAN, Karel. Praha, ÚSD ČSAV 1992; Pražské dohody 1945-1947. Sborník dokumentů. Edited by KAPLAN, Karel. Praha, ÚSD ČSAV 1992; Slovensko v rokoch 1967-1970. Výber dokumentov. Edited by Komisia vlády pre analýzu historických udalostí z rokov 1967-1970. Bratislava, Politologický kabinet SAV 1992; Charta 77. 1977-1989. Od morální k demokratické revoluci. Dokumentace. Edited by PREČAN, Vilém. Bratislava, Pravda 1990.

[16] The unambiguous orientation of Slovak historiography on the research of its own national history can be illustrated with a few numbers. From 1980-1989 approximately 200 specialized articles and books were published in Slovakia in the area of general history. When we take into account that during this period approximately 2,200 historical articles and books were published, the proportion devoted to general history does not make up even ten percent. (These statistics are supported by data in these publications: Historiografie v Československu 1980-1985. Výběrová bibliografie. Praha, ÚČSSD ČSAV 1985; Historiografie v Československu 1985-1989. Výběrová bibliografie. Praha, HÚ ČSAV 1990). To the research of older general history compare: KOPČAN, Vojtech: Stav a perspektívy bádania starších všeobecných dejín na Slovensku. In: HČ 39, 1991, 4-5, pp. 403-404.

[17] For example: Svetová socialistická sústava. Vznik a rozvoj do šesťdesiatych rokov. Compiled by CAMBEL, Samuel. Bratislava, Obzor 1981; Dejiny svetovej socialistickej sústavy. Formovanie a rozvoj svetového socialistického spoločenstva do začiatku 60. rokov. Compiled by CAMBEL, Samuel. Bratislava, SPN 1987.

a great number of articles published mostly in the periodical *Slovanské štúdie*.[18] The most obvious shortcoming of these works was their schematic view of historical processes and their interpretation in the spirit of the ideology of the Communist Party. Sporadic attention in the research of general history was devoted to so called critiques of the bourgeois interpretation of the history of communist countries.[19] The themes of books published before November 1989 were diverse, but with only few exceptions they did not reach beyond the geographic framework and issues of the relations of communist countries.[20] Articles from this period sometimes touched developments in non-European parts of the communist bloc,[21] questions of national defensive movements and colonialism,[22] and in some cases authors devoted themselves to issues that in Slovak historiography were mostly neglected.[23]

After November 1989, some authors attempted a more critical view of the

---

[18] Compare these numbers of the journal Slovanské štúdie: SlŠt 22, 1981; Medzinárodný význam februára 1948. Niektoré aspekty. Edited by KRAJČOVIČ, Milan. In: SlŠt 24, 1983, 2 ; Veľká októbrová socialistická revolúcia a formovanie svetovej socialistickej sústavy. Edited by KRAJ-ČOVIČ, Milan. In: SlŠt 25, 1985, 1; ČSSR a svetová socialistická sústava. Edited by KRAJČOVIČ, Milan. In:SlŠt 25, 1985, 2; Medzinárodné aspekty vývinu svetovej socialistickej sústavy v päťdesiatych rokoch. Edited by IVANIČKOVÁ, Edita. In: SlŠt 27, 1987, 2; ZSSR a krajiny ľudovej demokracie v zápase za udržanie mieru 1945-1949. Edited by BORODOVČÁK, Viktor. In: SlŠt 1989.

[19] Ku kritike buržoáznych interpretácií dejín socialistických krajín. Edited by KOVÁČ, Dušan. In: SlŠt 23, 1982, 1; Predstavy o dezintegrácii socialistického spoločenstva na Západe (1975-1985). Edited by BORODOVČÁK, Viktor. In: SlŠt 1989.

[20] For example: ČIERNA-LANTAYOVÁ, Dagmar: O nové Maďarsko. Korene, vznik a vývoj maďarskej ľudovej demokracie 1941-1948. Bratislava, Veda 1979; HLIVKA, Ivan: Komunisti a Európa. Bratislava, Pravda 1980; ZELENÁK, Štefan: Bulharsko na prahu socializmu 1944-1948. Bratislava, Pravda 1980; BORODOVČÁK, Viktor: Poľský národ a národy Československa na dejinnej križovatke (1939-1948). Bratislava, Veda 1982; HUBENÁK, Ladislav: Jaltská a Postupimská konferencia a povojnové usporiadanie Európy. Bratislava, Smena 1985; PETRUF, Pavol: USA a studená vojna. Politika amerického imperializmu v Európe 1945-1949. Bratislava, Pravda 1985; ČIERNY, Ján: Ho Či Min. Bratislava, Pravda 1985; VODERADSKÝ, Ján: Nigérijské križovatky. Cesty africkej nezávislosti. Bratislava, Veda 1989.

[21] VIŠVÁDER, František: Batistova diktatúra a kubánska revolúcia (Od Moncady po Granmu). In: Zborník ÚML a FFUK Historica 32-33, 1981-1982, published 1986, pp. 291-310.

[22] PAWLIKOVÁ-VILHANOVÁ, Viera: Problémy kolonializmu a antikolonializmu v Afrike v marxistickej historickej vede. In: HČ, 34, 1986, 1, pp. 83-102; SORBY, Karol: Národnooslobodzovacie hnutie po 2. svetovej vojne v Ázii a Afrike. In: HČ, 34, 1986, 2, pp. 217-231.

[23] KUŤKA, Karol: The Question of Japanese Reparations after World War II and its Development up to the Year 1949. In: Asian and African Studies, 16, 1980, pp. 91-116; KUŤKA, Karol: Preparation and Conclusion of a Separate Peace Treaty with Japan and the Related Question of Reparations. In: Asian and African Studies, 17, 1981, pp. 95-119.

inception and development of the Soviet bloc.[24] In this period, thematic concerns were broadened, and some publications with a more "objective" evaluation of historical themes of research.[25] Finally it is necessary to stress that research up till now has concentrated itself to a large extent on the so called issues of relations, that is, on the research of relations of Slovakia mostly with neighboring states, and then on some questions touching the development of the former communist bloc. Important themes from general history after 1945 have been left outside the attention of Slovak historians. It is necessary to recognize that overcoming these deficits will take a very long time.

---

[24] ČIERNA-LANTAYOVÁ, Dagmar: Vznik, formovanie a kríza politického systému v európskych krajinách sovietskeho bloku. Náčrt vývojových etáp 1944-1986. Bratislava, Vysoká vojenská pedagogická škola 1992.

[25] ČIERNA-LANTAYOVÁ, Dagmar: Podoby česko-slovensko-maďarského vzťahu 1938-1949. Východiská, problémy a medzinárodné súvislosti. Bratislava, Veda 1992; PETRUF, Pavol: Marshallov plán. Bratislava, Slovac Academic Press 1993; Stredná a juhovýchodná Európa. Sondy do vývoja v štyridsiatych rokoch. Edited by PETRUF, Pavol. Bratislava, HÚ SAV 1992; Stredná a juhovýchodná Európa v politike veľmocí. Sondy do vývoja II. Edited by PETRUF, Pavol. Bratislava, HÚ SAV 1994; MULÍK, Peter: Cirkev v tieni totality. Súbor štúdií. Trnava, Dobrá kniha 1994.

Organization
of Historical Work

HISTORICAL INSTITUTIONS

One of the possible views concerning historical scholarship in and especially about Slovakia, is the currently popular bemoaning of its "youth and lack of development." However, a tracing of the development of the institutional and organizational bases of historiography in Slovakia offers another, less tragic view. Despite ideological limitations and other obstacles and changes in the nineteenth and twentieth centuries which hindered the complex, systematic and proportional development of this discipline, there is clear evidence of the continuity of serious historical research in the territory of Slovakia. Although very few names of historians are remembered by the general public today, during the second half of the nineteenth century approximately three hundred people devoted themselves to researching, evaluating and raising the profile the past.[1]

The members of the historical community functioned in Hungarian universities and gymnasiums, in learned societies and regional organizations, published in scholarly journals and annuals. Scholars from both Slovak cultural circles, Catholic and Protestant, sporadically organized in scholarly societies which took as one of their tasks the investigation of the past, for example Bernolák's *Slovenské učené tovarišstvo,* founded in 1792 in Trnava, and Juraj Rybay's project *Societas bohemo-slavica inter Slavos in Hungaria* (1793). Learned societies in Banská Štiavnica and Malohont published historical articles in their *Annales* and *Sollennia* while self-educational student societies at lyceums eagerly devoted themselves to literature, history and linguistics. In many towns (Bratislava, Košice, Rimavská Sobota, Levoča, etc.) regional historical, archaeological and museum societies with German, Hungarian and Slovak members existed since 1860-1880s. The role of a central scholarly institution of Slovaks was temporarily played by the cultural organization *Matica slovenská* (1863 till its dissolution in 1875). In the 1890s, under the direction of Andrej Kmeť, the *Slovak Museum Society* organized all Slovak historians and researchers of the homeland. When it was not possible to rely on national universities and gymnasiums, a great part of

---

[1]OTČENÁŠ, Michal: Historická spisba a otázka budúcnosti. In: HČ 39, 1991, 4 - 5, p. 540.

the organizational and methodological work was taken over by Slovak publishing societies and journalists with periodicals.

The development of Slovak schools and professional scholarship after the foundation of Czechoslovakia influenced for the better the development of the institutional basis of the dicipline of history in Slovakia. The work of historians in the Slovak section of the country was organized between the wars by the *History Department of the Faculty of Philosophy of Comenius University,* the *Learned Society of Šafárik,* a reestablished *Matica slovenská,* and the *Protestant Society of Štúr,* as well as the *Czechoslovak Hungarian Scholarly Literature and Arts Society.* During the Slovak Republic was newly established the primary scholarly institution, the *Slovak Academy of Sciences and Arts,* and the *Slovak Learned Society* as the successor of the Learned Society of Šafárik. Research of regional and church history was carried out in museums, archives, homeland societies and religious institutions.

In 1946, the *Slovak Historical Society* was founded on the initiative of Professor Daniel Rapant. However, with the abolition of voluntary societies at the beginning of the 1950s even the regional homeland societies had to be disbanded and the Slovak Historical Society ceased to exist. It was reestablished in 1957 as part of the Czechoslovak Historical Society.

It is a paradox that the conditions for the intensive growth of Slovak historiography ripened in the period following the inauguration of communist totalitarianism in 1948. The building of a system of historical institutions was completed, the number of periodicals grew, the systematic publication of historical sources began, and a number of monographs and syntheses were made available to the public. The *Institute of Historical Studies of the Slovak Academy of Sciences,* founded in 1953, became the central scholarly institution, the successor to the History Institute of the Slovak Academy of Sciences and Arts. From its beginning, it concentrated on the systematic research of the history of Slovakia and the publishing of sources and of retrospective and continuous bibliography of Slovak historiography. Other academic institutions are also devoted to historical research: the *Asian Studies Institute,* the *Institute for the History of European Socialist Countries,* the *Archaeological Institute,* the *Institute of Social Sciences, State and Legal Institute, Institute of Economics* and the Institutes of *Ethnology* and *Sociology,* etc. In 1948, the *Institute of the Slovak National Uprising* was founded, later changed to the *Institute of the History of the Communist Party in Slovakia* (1954), and later renamed the *Institute of Marxism-Leninism* of the Central Committee of the Communist Party of Slovakia (1970-1989). Party political historiography was created and taught at the *Political University* of the Central Committee of the Communist Party of Czechoslovakia, and at the *Klement Gottwald Military and Political Academy.* To the network of historical institutions, the *Military History Institute,* and the *History Institute of the Slovak National Museum,* were added. The majority of these organizations were situated in Bratislava.

CURRENT HISTORICAL INSTITUTIONS IN SLOVAKIA

1. Scholarly Research Institutions

INSTITUTE OF HISTORICAL STUDIES
SLOVAK ACADEMY OF SCIENCES
Historický ústav Slovenskej akadémie vied
Klemensova 19, 813 64 Bratislava
Tel.: /07/ 325 753, 326 321
Fax: /07/ 361 645
Director: PhDr. Dušan Kováč, DrSc.

The task of the institute is the systematic investigation of Slovak history from ancient times through the present and research into key questions of world history. Its main focal points are the development of settlements in Slovakia and the economic, social, national, political and cultural history of Slovaks and ethnic minorities in Slovakia.

The institute publishes overviews on Slovak history, series of documents (Codex diplomaticus, Regesta diplomatica nec noc epistolaria Slovaciae), monographs and the following periodicals:
– *Historický časopis* (Historical Journal)
– *Studia historica Slovaca*
– *Historické štúdie* (Historical Studies)
– *Slovanské štúdie* (Slavic Studies)
– *Z dejín vied a techniky* (Studies on the History of Science and Technology)
– *Human Affairs*
– *Slavica Slovaca.*

The Institute of Historical Studies is currently pursuing its scientific and research activities in conjunction with the following projects:
1. Publishing of sources for Slovak medieval history
   Project leader: PhDr. Ján Lukačka, CSc.
2. Ethnogenesis of the Slovaks and the Slavs
   Project leader: PhDr. Vincent Sedlák, CSc.
3. Christianity in Slovakia to the eighteenth century

Project leader: PhDr. Alexander Avenarius, CSc.
4. Cultural history of central European regions (the modern history of culture in Slovakia within the framework of an specialized international dictionary)
Project leader: PhDr. Eva Kowalská, CSc.
5. Slovaks and national minorities in the historical development of Slovakia
Project leader: PhDr. Ľudovít Haraksim, CSc.
6. Economic history of Slovakia
Project leader: PhDr. Jozef Vozár, DrSc.
7. Personalities and the elite of public life in Slovakia in the twentieth century
Project leader: PhDr. Ľubomír Lipták, DrSc.
8. Other European states in Slovak political thought and concepts in the first half of the twentieth century
Project leader: PhDr. Pavol Petruf, CSc.
9. The Slovak Republic 1939-1945
Project leader: PhDr. Valerián Bystrický, DrSc.
10. Slovak society in its formation and the first crisis of the totalitarian system (1948-1957)
Project leader: PhDr. Michal Barnovský, DrSc.
11. History of science and technology in Slovakia in the global context
Project leader: RNDr. Miroslav Morovics, CSc.

Located at the institute is the headquarters for the **Foundation Pro historia,** as well. The foundation's main activities are supporting historical research in Slovakia and publishing the results of such work and historical sources.

Bank information: Investičná a rozvojová banka, a.s. Bratislava, SWIFT code INRBSKBX, account number 829783/5200.

ARCHAEOLOGICAL INSTITUTE
SLOVAK ACADEMY OF SCIENCES
Archeologický ústav Slovenskej akadémie vied
Akademická 2, 949 21 Nitra
Tel.: /087/ 356 17, 356 93, 356 13
Fax: /087/ 356 18
Director: Doc. PhDr. Alexander Ruttkay, DrSc.

The main Slovak center of basic research in archaeology, founded in 1953, concentrates on the reconstruction of the life of man and socio-economic relations in the primeval age, the early historical period and the Middle Ages. The

Institute solves theoretical archaeological problems, focusing mostly on the territory of Slovakia and central Europe. It oversees archaeological preservation in Slovakia, and develops and administers the central register of archaeological sites.

The most important scientific results have been attained studying:
- questions of Paleolithic culture in Slovakia
- the origin and evolution of agricultural societies of the prehistoric and early historical ages in central Europe
- the rise and development of the Great Moravian state
- the ethnogenesis of the Slavs
- the evolution of settlements and formation of cultural land.

Completed grant projects:
- Fortified settlements from the Bronze and Iron Ages in Slovakia
- Slovakia in the Early and High Middle Ages
- Ethnic relations in Slovakia in the light of cemeteries from the sixth to eleventh centuries
- Archaeological studies on the history of the first ethnic structures in central Europe (Celts, Romans, and Germans)
- System of central evidence of archaeological sites - a database for the archaeological topography of Slovakia
- Settlement evolution of Western Slovakia in the period of the urnfield cultures
- Culture, society and economy of the Late Bronze Age in Slovakia (cemeteries and settlements)
- Fortifications and proto-urban settlement systems in the fourth century B. C.
- Late Paleolithic cultures with obsidian industry in central and eastern Europe.

The institute publishes its journal *Slovenská archeológia* (Slovak Archaeology) and these periodicals: *AVANS, Študijné zvesti, Acta Interdisciplinaria Archaeologica, Materialia Archaeologica Slovaca, Bibliografia slovenskej archeológie.*

INSTITUTE OF SOCIAL SCIENCES
SLOVAK ACADEMY OF SCIENCES
Spoločenskovedný ústav Slovenskej akadémie vied
Karpatská 5, 040 01 Košice
Tel.: /095/ 558 56, 519 86, 519 87
Fax: /095/ 558 56
E-mail: SvÚ SAV @ CCSUN. tuke. sk.
Director: PaedDr. Štefan Šutaj, CSc.

The institute, founded in 1975, is multidisciplinary and focuses on these main areas:
- The study of social-psychological problematics with emphasis on interpersonal interaction, the regulation of social behaviour, and social cognition and small groups (social psychology),
- The study of macrosocial events, problematics of ethnic minorities, investigation of problematics of the modern history of Slovakia with focus in the period after the Second World War (history and sociology).

Current grant project:
The development of ethnic minorities after the Second World War and inter-ethnic relations in Slovakia
Project leader: PaedDr. Marián Gajdoš, CSc.

INSTITUTE OF ORIENTAL AND AFRICAN STUDIES
SLOVAK ACADEMY OF SCIENCES
Kabinet orientalistiky Slovenskej akadémie vied
Klemensova 19, 813 64 Bratislava
Tel.: /07/ 326 326, 326 321
Fax: /07/ 326 326
Director: PhDr. Viktor Krupa, DrSc.

The scholarly research of the institute concentrates on these territories: the Far East (China and Japan), Southeast Asia and Oceania, India, the Arab-Islamic World and Sub-Saharan Africa. Attention is devoted to these themes:
- The Ottoman expansion in central Europe
- Historiography of Sub-Saharan Africa
- History of the impact and consequences of Western ideas in the East

Current grant project:
- Questions of intercultural contacts and communication between the Orient and the West
Project leader: Dr. Viktor Krupa, DrSc.
The institute publishes two journals: *Asian and African Studies* and *Human Affairs.*

CABINET OF POLITICAL SCIENCE
SLOVAK ACADEMY OF SCIENCES
Politologický kabinet Slovenskej akadémie vied
Grösslingová 6 - 8, 813 64 Bratislava
Tel.: (07) 364 815, 364 618
Fax: (07) 364 614
E-Mail: KABINET @ pk. SAVBA. SK
Director: PhDr. Jozef Jablonický, DrSc.

This interdisciplinary research institution was founded in 1990. Its activity is devoted to problems of the recent history of Slovakia, to the research of the political system, of a civil society, political interests and political thought, to the general theoretical questions of political science, the geopolitical position of Slovakia, and to international relationship and foreign policy.

Within the framework of the activity of the *Slovak Government Commission of the Slovak Republic for Analysis of the Historical Events of the Years 1967-1970,* a great number of documents and materials have been collected, which form today a concentrated archive administered by the Cabinet of Political Science.

At present, research is oriented towards the following themes:
- Power monopoly and repression in Slovakia 1948-1989
  Project leader: PhDr. Jozef Jablonický, DrSc.
- Issues of the geopolitical situation of Slovakia
  Project leader: Juraj Fabián, CSc.
- Parliamentary democracy in Czecho-Slovakia since 1918
  Project leader: Doc. PhDr. Peter Kulašik, CSc.

MILITARY HISTORY INSTITUTE
Vojenský historický ústav
Kutuzovova 8, 830 00 Bratislava, P. O. Box 59, Pošta 3
Tel.: /07/ 252 207
Director: Pplk. Doc. PhDr. Jozef Bystrický, CSc.

The institute is divided into three parts:
1. **The Department of Military Historical Research**
   Odbor vojenskohistorických výskumov
   address as above
   Director: PhDr. Vojtech Dangl, CSc.

139

2. The Military History Archive, Trnava
Vojenský historický archív
Univerzitné námestie 2, 917 00 Trnava, P. 0. Box 71
Tel. /0805/ 255 71
Director: Pplk. PhDr. Pavol Vimmer, CSc.

3. The Military Museum, Trenčín

The main directions of research are:
- Slovak society and the army in the continuity of historical development (the relation of the army and society);
- Organizational development of the military administration, of the army and other armed forces in the territory of Slovakia;
- Military production and industry in Slovakia;
- Military aspects of the geopolitical role of Slovakia;
- Slovakia and Slovaks in armed movements.

Among recent publications of institute staff:
- DANGL, Vojtech: Bethlen proti Habsburkům. Slovo k historii 37. Praha, Melantrich 1992.
- Vojenskopolitické a geopolitické súvislosti vývoja Slovenska v rokoch 1918-1945. Trenčín, Oddelenie sociálneho riadenia VVV 1992.
- KLEIN, Bohuš - RUTTKAY, Alexander - MARSINA, Richard: Vojenské dejiny Slovenska I. Stručný náčrt do roku 1526. Bratislava, Ministerstvo obrany SR 1993.
- Armáda v dejinách Slovenska I.-II. Edited by ŠTEFANSKÝ, Václav. Bratislava, Slovenský zväz protifašistických bojovníkov 1993.
- Z vojenskej histórie Slovenska 1918-1948. Zborník vedeckých štúdií. Edited by Ján Korček. Trenčín, Veliteľstvo Armády 1994.

MATICA SLOVENSKÁ
L. Novomeského 32, 036 52 Martin
Tel.: /0842/ 313 71, 314 92
Fax: /0842/ 331 60

This cultural society, founded in 1863, was the most important national institution of Slovaks in the nineteenth century. Currently it is divided into two parts:
I. The voluntary association which organizes members in local and interest groups (including historical, linguistic, ethnological and musicological);
II. National scientific and cultural institutions:

1. The Slovak National Library
Slovenská národná knižnica[2] with these departments:
The Institute of Library Collections, the National Bibliographical Institute,
the Library Coordination Center, the Database Center.

2. The Archive of Literature and Arts
Archív literatúry a umenia[3]

3. The Slovak National Literary Museum
Slovenské národné literárne múzeum
In addition to permanent exhibitions, it is responsible to maintain the National
Cemetery in Martin, and the Puškin Museum in Partizánske - Brodzany.

4. The Biographical Institute
Biografický ústav
A center for the research, documentation and processing of biographies,
genealogies and sociography of the representatives of the Slovak nation in
the past and present.

5. Institute for Slovaks Abroad
Ústav pre zahraničných Slovákov
Situated in Bratislava, the central department for the development of contacts with Slovaks living abroad, and carrying out research, museological and
documentary work. Museum of Slovaks Abroad on Štefánikova 25.

Among current projects of Matica slovenská:
- History of Matica slovenská;
- Research of the history of bibliographic culture in Slovakia;
- History of Slovak literary museums;
- Personal bibliography of Pavel Jozef Šafárik;
- History of Slovak exiles after 1945;
- Assimilation and anti-assimilation factors in the denationalization of ethnic
  Slovaks in Hungary during World War II;
- National activities of Slovaks living in Poland after 1945;
- Slovaks in Bohemia, Germany, Switzerland, Italy, Romania, Uruguay, etc.

---

[2]See page 183.
[3]See page 174.

2. Universities

BANSKÁ BYSTRICA:
DEPARTMENT OF HISTORY AND ETHNOLOGY
FACULTY OF HUMAN AND NATURAL SCIENCES
MATEJ BEL UNIVERSITY
Katedra histórie a etnológie
Fakulta humanitných a prírodných vied Univerzity Mateja Bela
Tajovského 40, 974 00 Banská Bystrica
Tel.: /088/ 345 55, 345 41
Chair: Doc. PhDr. Stanislav Matejkin, CSc.

Over forty years of activity, the department has taught hundreds of elementary school and gymnasium teachers and staff in the sphere of culture, education, museums, historical sciences and archival science. Scholarly activity concentrates mostly on regional history of central Slovakia and general Slovak issues. The department cooperates with the university's Regional Studies Institute in addition to others.

Current project:
– Politico-social, socio-cultural and economic development in central Slovakia in the nineteenth and twentieth centuries
  Project leader: Doc. PhDr. Karol Fremal, CSc.

Among publications:
– Zborník k 50. výročiu Slovenského národného povstania. Edited by Karol Fremal. Banská Bystrica, Univerzita Mateja Bela 1994.

BRATISLAVA:
DEPARTMENT OF SLOVAK HISTORY AND ARCHIVAL SCIENCE
FACULTY OF PHILOSOPHY OF COMENIUS UNIVERSITY
Katedra slovenských dejín a archívnictva
Filozofická fakulta Univerzity Komenského
Gondova 2, 818 01 Bratislava (deanery)
Tel.: /07/ 361 055, 304 111 ex. 314
Fax: /07/ 366 016
Seat: Šafárikovo námestie 6, 4th floor
Chair: Doc. PhDr. Jozef Baďurík, CSc.

The department educates historians, history teachers, archivists and specialists in related disciplines. In addition to teaching Slovak and Czech history and individual related disciplines (heraldry, genealogy, diplomatic studies, paleography and so on), archive science and the history of administration, the department cooperates in creating textbooks on Slovak history. In scholarly activity, the members of the department concentrate on the key questions of the development of Slovak history, for example, the ethnogenesis of Slovaks, national emancipation, agrarian history and political history of the twentieth century.

Current projects and research themes:
- Genealogy of families in Slovakia (Prof. PhDr. Jozef Novák, DrSc.)
- The Habsburgs and their relation to Slovakia in the sixteenth century (Doc. PhDr. Jozef Baďurík, CSc.)
- The politics of trade and customs in central Europe in the nineteenth century (PhDr. Roman Holec, CSc.)
- Biographies of the personalities of the Slovak national revival (Prof. PhDr. Ján Hučko, DrSc.)
- Slovakia in the World War I (PhDr. Alžbeta Sopušková)
- The crisis of the political system in Czechoslovakia 1966-1968 (PhDr. Ľubomír Gašpierik)
- History of administration in Slovakia (PhDr. Leon Sokolovský, CSc.)

The department has now published the forty-first volume of the *Zborník Filozofickej fakulty Univerzity Komenského - Historica.*

BRATISLAVA:
DEPARTMENT OF GENERAL HISTORY
FACULTY OF PHILOSOPHY OF COMENIUS UNIVERSITY
Katedra všeobecných dejín
Filozofická fakulta Univerzity Komenského
Gondova 2, 818 01 Bratislava
Tel.: /07/ 304 111, ex. 314
Fax: /07/ 366 016
Seat: Šafárikovo námestie 6, 4th floor
Chair: PhDr. Pavol Valachovič, CSc.

The department instructs future historians and teachers of history. In scholarship, it devotes itself mostly to these key themes:

- Roman hegemony and the development of the state administration of the Roman Empire during the fourth and fifth centuries (PhDr. Pavol Valachovič, CSc.)
- Byzantium and the Slavs: Art and architecture on the borderland of the Eastern and Western rites in the ninth to thirteenth centuries (Doc. PhDr. Zuzana Ševčíková, CSc.)
- Church reform movement in the eleventh and twelfth centuries in Western Europe (PhDr. Vincent Mucska)
- Economic history of the fifteenth and sixteenth centuries, and the history of the mining and trade in copper (Doc. PhDr. Marián Skladaný, CSc.)
- Fascist dictatorships in the European context (Doc. PhDr. Herta Tkadlečková, CSc.)
- Creation and development of history textbooks, communication problems of teaching history, and didactics of games in history teaching (PhDr. Viliam Kratochvíl)
- Comparative analysis of Latin American dictatorial regimes (Doc. PhDr. František Višváder, CSc.)

BRATISLAVA
DEPARTMENT OF ARCHAEOLOGY
FACULTY OF PHILOSOPHY OF COMENIUS UNIVERSITY
Katedra archeológie
Filozofická fakulta Univerzity Komenského
Gondova 2, 818 01 Bratislava
Tel.: /07/ 300 111
Fax: /07/ 366 016
Chair: Prof. PhDr. Tatiana Štefanovičová, CSc.

The department provides the study of archaeology with focus on the prehistoric and protohistoric ages in central Europe. The scholarly orientation of the institution:
- Settlement structures in the Neolithic age (PhDr. Viera Pavúková, CSc.)
- Beginnings of metallurgy (Prof. PhDr. Mária Novotná, DrSc.)
- Relations of the territory of Slovakia to the Roman Empire (PhDr. Eduard Krekovič, CSc.)
- Byzantine influences and Great Moravia (Prof. PhDr. Tatiana Štefanovičová, CSc.)
- Medieval towns (PhDr. Jozef Hoššo, CSc.)

BRATISLAVA
DEPARTMENT OF SLOVAK AND GENERAL HISTORY
FACULTY OF EDUCATION OF COMENIUS UNIVERSITY
Katedra slovenských a všeobecných dejín Pedagogickej fakulty Univerzity Komenského
Račianska 59, 813 34 Bratislava
Tel.: /07/ 522 11 24, 522 40 34 ex. 221, 222
Location: Mlynské Luhy 4
Chair: PhDr. Július Bartl, CSc.

Founded in 1992, the department educates history teachers for elementary and high schools. Graduates of this study may also be employed as specialized staff in museums, archives, educational and cultural organizations, and so on.

Current grant work:
– The position of Slovakia in the integration and disintegration processes of central Europe

The faculty of the department devotes themselves to these themes:
– Development of towns in the Middle Ages: political history in the fifteenth century (PhDr. Július Bartl, CSc.)
– Modernization of society: formation of the modern Slovak nation. The Revolution of 1848-1849 (PhDr. Dušan Škvarna)
– History of the Slovak Republic 1939-1945 (PhDr. Róbert Letz)
– History of the Balkans and their Sovietization in the twentieth century (PhDr. Mária Tonková, CSc).

BRATISLAVA
DEPARTMENT OF HISTORY AND CANON LAW
CYRIL AND METHODIUS ROMAN CATHOLIC THEOLOGICAL
FACULTY OF COMENIUS UNIVERSITY
Katedra dejín a kanonického práva, Rímsko-katolícka cyrilometodská bohoslovecká fakulta Univerzity Komenského
Kapitulská 26, 814 58 Bratislava
Tel.: /07/ 330 266, 332 396, 335 109
Fax: /07/ 330 266
Lecturer: Doc. ThDr. Viliam Judák

The department offers study of church history with special attention to Slovakia as well as the study of the legal structure of the Roman Catholic Church as outlined by the Code of Canon Law of 1983. Subjects taught in the department: church history, canon law, Christian archaeology, patrology, church art.

BRATISLAVA
HISTORY DEPARTMENT
FACULTY OF PROTESTANT THEOLOGY, COMENIUS UNIVERSITY
Historická katedra Evanjelickej bohosloveckej fakulty Univerzity Komenského
Svoradova 1, 811 03 Bratislava
Tel.: /07/ 315 707, 316 139, 313 721
Fax: /07/ 311 140
Chair: Doc. ThDr. Igor Kišš

In the department general church history, the history of doctrine, and the history of Protestantism in the territory of Slovakia from the sixteenth to twentieth centuries is taught.

NITRA
DEPARTMENT OF HISTORY AND ARCHAEOLOGY
FACULTY OF HUMANITIES, COLLEGE OF EDUCATION
Katedra dejín archeológie Fakulty humanitných vied Vysokej školy pedagogickej
Hodžova 1, 949 74 Nitra
Tel.: /087/ 413 770
Fax: /087/ 511 243
Chair: PhDr. Jana Hečková, CSc.

The Department of History began its activity in 1961. In 1973 it was merged with the Department of Geography. Since 1991 the Department of History has been autonomous. It trains teachers for elementary and high schools with specialization in history and archaeology. The department is currently divided in two parts: history and archaeology.

A common project with Pädagogische Hochschule in Karlsruhe (Germany):
– Political systems in the history of European states (institutions, political parties, ideology, terminology and historiography)
The project leader: PhDr. Eduard Nižňanský, CSc.

Primary project in archaeology:
- Archaeology on the boundaries of history and the natural sciences
  Project leader: PhDr. Peter Romsauer, CSc.

The department is a collective member of the Allgemeine Geschichts-forschende Gesellschaft der Schweiz.

The department publishes the journal *Studia Historica Nitriensia.*

PREŠOV
DEPARTMENT OF HISTORY AND ARCHIVES
FACULTY OF PHILOSOPHY OF P. J. ŠAFÁRIK UNIVERSITY
Katedra dejín a archívnictva Filozofickej fakulty Univerzity P. J. Šafárika
Ul. 17. novembra 1, 081 16 Prešov
Tel.: /091/ 722 051 ex. 61, 733 231, 733 232
Fax: /091/ 733 268
Chair: PhDr. Michal Otčenáš, CSc.

The department trains future teachers of history in secondary schools, historians and archivists. The study of history is combined with one other subject: Slovak, English, Russian, Ukrainian or German, philosophy or, for non-teachers, studies in archival preservation. The department is also responsible for training research degree candidates from other local and foreign research centres.

Research activity is primarily focused on the history of Slovakia from the prehistoric period to the modern era with special interest devoted to the area of eastern Slovakia, the history of the Slavs, and Slovak historiography.

Current projects:
- History of the Reformation in Eastern Slovakia
  Project leader: Prof. PhDr. Ferdinand Uličný, DrSc.
- Work of Pavel Jozef Šafárik and the literary process in the nineteenth and twentieth centuries
  Project leader: Prof. PhDr. Pavol Petrus, DrSc.
- Selected issues from the history of eastern Slovakia
  Project leader: PhDr. Libuša Franková, CSc.

Recently the department has published these proceedings:
- Jakub Jakobeus - život, dielo a doba. Proceedings of the 400th Anniversary Conference of Jakub Jakobeus, held at Prešov on 5 December 1991. Compiled by Michal Otčenáš and Peter Kónya. Prešov, Filozofická fakulta Univerzity P. J. Šafárika 1993.

- MUDr. Ľudovít Markušovský a jeho doba. Proceedings of the international conference. Compiled by Peter Švorc. Prešov - Bratislava - Viedeň, Universum 1993.
- ULIČNÝ, Ferdinand: Dejiny osídlenia Užskej župy. Prešov 1994.
- História III. Spoločenskovedný zborník. Prešov, Univerzita P.J. Šafárika 1994.

PREŠOV
DEPARTMENT OF HISTORY
FACULTY OF EDUCATION
P. J. ŠAFÁRIK UNIVERSITY
Katedra dejín
Pedagogická fakulta Univerzity P. J. Šafárika
Ul. 17. novembra 1, 081 16 Prešov
Tel.: /091/ 733 234, 733 232
Chair: PhDr. Zdenka Malagová, CSc.

The department prepares history teachers for elementary schools.

PREŠOV
DEPARTMENT OF HISTORY
FACULTY OF GREEK CATHOLIC THEOLOGY
P. J. ŠAFÁRIK UNIVERSITY
Historická katedra
Gréckokatolícka bohoslovecká fakulta Univerzity P. J. Šafárika
Ulica biskupa Pavla Gojdiča 2, 081 16 Prešov
Tel.: /091/ 725 157, 725 166
Chair: Doc. ThDr. František Janhuba

PREŠOV
DEPARTMENT OF HISTORY
FACULTY OF ORTHODOX THEOLOGY
P. J. ŠAFÁRIK UNIVERSITY
Katedra histórie
Pravoslávna bohoslovecká fakulta Univerzity P. J. Šafárika
Masarykova 15, 080 01 Prešov
Tel.: /091/ 724 729
Chair: Prof. ThDr. Pavel Aleš

TRNAVA
DEPARTMENT OF PHILOSOPHY AND HISTORY
FACULTY OF HUMANITIES OF TRNAVA UNIVERSITY
Filozoficko-historická katedra
Fakulta humanistiky Trnavskej univerzity
Hornopotočná 23, 917 43 Trnava
Tel.: /0805/ 214 82, 267 55
Fax: /0805/ 214 83
Chair of the Sub-Department of History: Prof. PhDr. Richard Marsina, DrSc.

The Philosophical-Historical Department, founded in 1992, consists of three sub-departments: Philosophy, History, and the History of Arts and Culture. The historical part provides a specialized study of history with emphasis on languages and those branches of historiography neglected in the past (mostly church and religious history).

Current project:
– The history and culture of the communities of orders in Slovakia
  Project leader: Doc. PhDr. Jozef Šimončič, CSc.

3. Historical Societies

SLOVAK NATIONAL COMMITTEE OF HISTORIANS
Slovenský národný komitét historikov
Klemensova 19, 813 64 Bratislava
Tel.: /07/ 326 321
President: PhDr. Dušan Kováč, DrSc.

The committee originally operated within the National Committee of Czech and Slovak Historians. Since 1993 it has been an independent member of Comité International des Sciences historiques (CISH). Its work concentrates on:
– Preparation of participation of Slovak historians in international congresses of the historical sciences
– Ensuring Slovak participation in affiliated international organizations and internal commissions of the CISH

- Creation of bilateral commissions of historians
- Organization of mutual enterprises with partner national committees of CISH.

Members of the Committee are elected by the Central Committee of the Slovak Historical Society.

SLOVAK HISTORICAL SOCIETY
AT THE SLOVAK ACADEMY OF SCIENCES
Slovenská historická spoločnosť pri Slovenskej akadémii vied
Klemensova 19, 813 64 Bratislava
Tel.: /07/ 326 321
President: Prof. PhDr. Richard Marsina, DrSc.

This scholarly and professional organization of historians in Slovakia includes at present over five hundred members.[4]

Currently these sections of the society are active:
- History of Towns
- Related Disciplines and Archival Science
- Military History of Slovakia
- Current History
- History of Thought
- Economic and Social History
- Teaching of History

Of regional societies of historians, the Trenčín Club of Historians is especially active, as well as the societies in Prešov and Skalica. Independent organizations in cooperation with the Society include the Gemer Homeland Society in Rimavská Sobota and the Spiš Historical Society in Levoča.

---

[4]Further details: KAMENCOVÁ, Lýdia: Vznik Slovenskej historickej spoločnosti a prvá etapa jej činnosti (1946 - 1950). In: HČ 39, 1991, 2, pp. 183 - 193; LAŠÁN, Ľudovít: Z činnosti Slovenskej historickej spoločnosti pri SAV a jej zložiek - Krúžok historikov v Trnave 1963-1973. In: Zborník Pedagogickej fakulty UK v Trnave Spoločenské vedy - História 5, 1976, pp. 5 - 59; Materiály X. zjazdu Slovenskej historickej spoločnosti. In: HČ 39, 1991, 4-5.

THE SLOVAK SOCIETY FOR THE HISTORY OF SCIENCE
AND TECHNOLOGY AT THE SLOVAK ACADEMY OF SCIENCES
Slovenská spoločnosť pre dejiny vedy a techniky pri Slovenskej akadémii vied
Klemensova 19, 813 64 Bratislava
Tel. Fax: /07/ 361 645
President: RNDr. Ondrej Pöss, CSc.

The society organizes institutions and individuals devoted to research of and education in the natural sciences, technology and medicine or who are interested in the history of these disciplines.[5] It is coordinated by the Department of the History of Science and Technology of the Institute of Historical Studies of the Slovak Academy of Sciences. Currently its sections for the history of these areas are active:

Natural Sciences, Mathematical and Physical Sciences, Geography and Cartography, Technology, Mining and Metallurgy, Agriculture, Forestry and Wood Technology, Transport, Medicine, Pharmaceutics, Health Services, and Balneology.

In addition to specialized institutions of universities and colleges, the society cooperates with these museums:

The Slovak Museum of Technology,
Slovenské technické múzeum, Hlavná 88, 043 82 Košice, tel. /095/ 62 259 65, 62 236 65

The Slovak Mining Museum,
Slovenské banské múzeum, Kammerhofská 2, 969 42 Banská Štiavnica, tel. / 0859/ 227 64, 215 44

The Slovak Museum of Agriculture,
Slovenské poľnohospodárske múzeum, Dlhá 94, 950 50 Nitra, tel. /087/ 366 47, 364 93, 532 743

The Museum of Balneology,
Balneologické múzeum, Beethovenova 5, 921 01 Piešťany, tel. /0838/ 228 75

---

[5] TIBENSKÝ, Ján: 20 rokov Slovenskej spoločnosti pre dejiny vied a techniky pri SAV v slovenskej vede a kultúre. In: Veda a technika v dejinách Slovenska 2, Bratislava 1985, pp. 5-23.

The Museum of Forestry, Wood Technology and Hunting,
Lesnícke, drevárske a poľovnícke múzeum, Štátny kaštieľ, 969 72 Antol,
tel. /0859/ 329 32.

THE SLOVAK COMMITTEE FOR THE HISTORY OF SCIENCE
Slovenský komitét pre dejiny vedy
Klemensova 19, 813 64 Bratislava
Tel. Fax: /07/ 361 645
President: Doc. RNDr. Juraj Šebesta, CSc.

The committee is a member of the International Union for the History and Philosophy of Science. It ensures contacts of Slovak research institutions in the area of history of science with those abroad.

INTERNATIONAL COMMITTEE
FOR THE HISTORY OF TECHNOLOGY
Medzinárodný komitét pre dejiny techniky
Klemensova 19, 813 64 Bratislava
Tel. Fax: /07/ 361 645

The committee is a member of the International Committee for the History of Technology. It is oriented towards the cooperation of Slovak institutions and foreign partners in the history of technology.

SOCIETY FOR THE HISTORY AND CULTURE
OF CENTRAL AND EASTERN EUROPE
Spoločnosť pre dejiny a kultúru strednej a východnej Európy
Klemensova 19, 813 64 Bratislava
Tel.: /07/ 326 321 ext. 303
Fax: /07/ 361 645
President: PhDr. Tatiana Ivantyšynová, CSc.

The society supports scholarly interdisciplinary research of the history and culture of central and eastern Europe and intensification of international scholarly contacts.

ARCHIVES

Archives in Slovakia have a long tradition and in the cities date back to the thirteenth century. Modern public archives were created in the nineteenth and twentieth centuries and the state administration of archives was codified after the Second World War. The first legislative regulation occurred in 1954 when the state archives became part of the institutions of culture, science and government. At present, the state archives are under the administration of the Ministry of the Interior, and the leading institution of archives and archival science is the **Department of Archives and Document Service in Bratislava**
Odbor archívnictva a spisovej služby
Ministerstvo vnútra SR
811 04 Bratislava, Križkova 7
Tel.: /07/ 496 051, 497 629
Fax: /07/ 494 530

This department guides the state archives in the Slovak Republic in methodology, represents the archives in the International Council of Archives, and is also the publishing and editing arm of the archives. Since 1966 it has published semi-annually the professional and scientific archival periodical *Slovenská archivistika* (Slovak Archival Science) and it publishes a series of archival aids, guides to archival collections, inventories and catalogues in rotaprint editions, editions of archival documents, other archival publications, and publications from the historical sciences.*

---

*Some of the publications are: Archívy v Slovenskej socialistickej republike (Archives in the Slovak Socialist Republic). Bratislava AS MV SSR, 1976; ŠPIESZ, Anton - WATZKA, Jozef: Poddaní v Tekove v 18. storočí (Villeins in Tekov in the 18th century). Bratislava, SAS, 1967; RÁKOŠ, Elemír - RUDOHRADSKÝ, Štefan: Slovenské národné orgány 1943-1968 (Slovak national authorities 1943 - 1968). Bratislava, SAS MV SSR, 1974; FOJTÍK, Jozef: Mestské a obecné pečate Trenčianskej župy (Town and regional seals of Trenčín County). Bratislava, SAS 1974; KARTOUS, Peter- NOVÁK, Jozef - VRTEĽ, Ladislav: Erby a vlajky miest v Slovenskej republike (Coats-of-arms and flags of towns in Slovak Republic.) Bratislava, MV SR 1991; CHREŇOVÁ, Júlia: Štruktúra ústredných orgánov na Slovensku v rokoch 1939-1945. Prehľad.(Structure of the central authorities in Slovakia 1939 - 1945. Review). Bratislava, SAS MV SSR 1977; RÁKOŠ,

In the state archives all archival documents older than thirty years are available for study. The Department of Archival Administration also provides information concerning church archives. Many significant collections of ecclesiastical provenance are in state archives.

THE SLOVAK NATIONAL ARCHIVE
Slovenský národný archív
817 01 Bratislava, Drotárska cesta 42
Tel.: /07/ 311 300, 311 321, 311 362
Fax: /07/ 312 533

The Slovak National Archive was founded in 1954 under the name State Slovak Central Archive. Its predecessors were the Regional Archive in Bratislava (1928-1939), the Archive of the Ministry of the Interior (1940-1945), and the Archive of the Mandate of the Interior (1945-1954). From the passing of the Act on Archives in 1975 it bore the name of the State Central Archive of the Slovak Socialist Republic which in 1992 was changed to the Slovak National Archive.

The task of the Slovak National Archive is to collect, professionally and scientifically elaborate, and make available archival collections of central Slovak provenance. The Slovak National Archive is the biggest and most important public archive in Slovakia and, since January 1, 1993 has also been the archive of the state. It preserves and manages approximately thirty kilometers of archival material dating from the thirteenth century to 1989.

Archival material is processed through two archival departments and the Department of Pre-Archival Care, the Department of Archival Protection and the Department of Archival Informatics. The Slovak National Archives also has the task of research projects in archival science. In the Office of Archival Science and Research the staff is concerned with archival theory and methodology.

The Department of Early Collections manages the archives of the leading noble families which contain the sources of the economic and cultural history of Slovakia, and in part also of the history of Hungary, Austria, Romania, countries of the former Yugoslavia, Germany, the Trans-Carpathian Ukraine and Poland.

Elemír: Slovenské národné orgány v dokumentoch I. Obdobie Slovenského národného povstania. (Slovak national authorities in documents, I. The Period of the Slovak National Uprising.) Bratislava, AS MV SSR 1977.

Among the large archives of the noble families are those of the Pálffy, Erdödy, Esterházy, Kubíni, Kostoláni, Révay and Zay. There are collections of other families as well as the archives of the imperial estates of the Habsburgs in Slovakia.

For the research of early Slovak history, the archive of trustworthy locations (loca credibilia) have a great importance. It contains two collections from cathedral chapters (Bratislava and Spiš) and three collections from convents (Jasov, Leles, Hronský Svätý Beňadik). The Repository of Documents of the Middle Ages (to 1526) contains 23,000 charters and the oldest document is from 1208.

We can also find valuable historical documents of public foundations from the eighteenth to the twentieth century and of the personal collections of famous figures of Slovakia. The department also processes archival collections of religious institutes, and the Genealogical and Topographical Collections, other collections of different provenance, and collections of stamps and seals since the sixteenth century. It is possible to study documents with the help of recent information aids as well as with original aids.

The Department of Later Collections preserves and administers the archival collections of central offices and institutions existing in Slovakia since the founding of the Czechoslovak Republic in 1918, as well as of the highest governmental institutions of the Slovak Republic from 1939 to 1945, and Slovak central institutions and offices from 1945 until 1989. For the bigger and more important collections there are modern archival aids, inventories and catalogues. Many archival collections from the later period have not been archivally processed so far. Together with conventional archival information systems a computer information system is also being developed. The archive has conservation and restoration laboratories, as well as photo and film laboratories which also serve other archives and historical institutions in Slovakia. The film laboratory records a series of archival documents on photograph and microfilm from the Slovak National Archive and from other archives in Slovakia and abroad, for conservation and study purposes. The Slovak National Archive has its own library and reading room. It is possible to study there from Monday to Thursday, from 8 am to 3:30 pm.

Literature:

Štátny ústredný archív SSR (State Central Archive SSR). Bratislava, Osveta 1993.

Štátny slovenský ústredný archív v Bratislave. Sprievodca po archívnych fondoch, I. oddelenie feudalizmu (State Slovak Central Archive in Bratislava. Guide through the archive collections, I. Department of Feudalism.) Bratislava, SAS 1964.

Štátny slovenský ústredný archív v Bratislave. Sprievodca po archívnych fondoch, II. oddelenie kapitalizmu (State Slovak Central Archive in Bratislava. Guide through the archive collections II. Department of Capitalism.) Bratislava, SAS 1964.

STATE CENTRAL MINING ARCHIVE
Štátny ústredný banský archív
969 00 Banská Štiavnica, Radničné námestie 16
Tel.: /0859/ 217 57, 227 57
Fax: /0859/ 238 06

The State Central Mining Archive in Banská Štiavnica was founded in 1950. The archive collects, processes and makes available documents from mining, metallurgy, geological research and other related branches in Slovakia. From 1958 to 1968, the State Central Mining Archive was only a department of the State Central Slovak Archive. Its basic informational aid was also published under the name of this archive. Among the important collections is that of the Main Chamber Court in Banská Štiavnica (1236) 1524-1918, containing sources for the history of mining; smelting; metallurgy of precious, colorful and ordinary metals; minting, and other processing of copper, iron, etc.; domestic and foreign trade; science and technology; and professional schools. The mining maps also have great importance. Other collections include those of the Mining Chamber in Banská Bystrica (1535-1851); mining directorships, inspectorates and mining offices; the administrations of mining factories and foundries in Slovakia; mining courts in the central and eastern regions of Slovakia; mining administrators and commissions; mutual aid social institutions and fraternal credit unions; chamber estates; and state forest offices. The valuable archival collection of the Mining and Forestry Academy in Banská Štiavnica from 1770 to 1919 is only partly in this archive; the biggest part of the collection is in the County Archive in Sopron, Hungary. An important basic source for the latest history of mining in Slovakia is contained in the collections of mining administration after 1919, that is, the collections of the central mining organizations for directing production; mining police; leisure organizations; mining directorships, factories and offices; as well as personal collections. For the greater part of the archives there are modern archival aids, inventories and catalogues.

Literature:

Štátny slovenský ústredný archív v Bratislave. Sprievodca po archívnych fondoch III. Oddelenie hospodárstva v Banskej Štiavnici (State Slovak Central Archive in Bratislava. Guide to the archive collection III. Department of Economics in Banská Štiavnica.) Bratislava, SAS 1964.

State Regional Archives

STATE REGIONAL ARCHIVE IN BANSKÁ BYSTRICA
Štátny oblastný archív v Banskej Bystrici
974 05 Banská Bystrica, Sládkovičova 1
Tel.: /088/ 619 79, 620 17

The archive was founded in 1954 from the District Archive in Banská Bystrica. It processes and preserves collections of regional importance from the fifteenth to the twentieth century. In 1956 it subsumed the Soil Economy Archive in Radvaň and in Rimavská Sobota. The more important collections include those of: Zvolen County (1254) 1382-1922; Turiec-Zvolen County 1786-1790; Hont County 1576-1922; Malohont District (1595) 1688-1803; Gemer County 1504-1803; Gemer-Malohont County I. (1784) 1786-1790; Gemer-Malohont County II. (1638) 1803-1922; Novohrad County I. (1900-1922); county administration from 1923 to 1928 (Pohronie County I.); county administration from 1940 to 1945 (Pohronie County II.); Hungarian occupational administration from 1938 to 1945; offices of small towns in individual counties; public organizational committees of municipalities 1876-1919; court administration of the Josephine district judiciary; judiciary and courts to 1949 (county, district, regional and designated urban courts and noble courts); financial administration, registers, and other collections. Also historically valuable are archives of noble families, such as the Koháry-Coburg (1241) 1324-1945; the administration of the Esterházy (1282) seventeenth century to 1925; smaller families; forest estates of the Rimamurány-Šalgotarián Society (18th-20th centuries); state forests and estates (18th-20th c.); wood processing factories (19th-20th c.); institutions of land reform (20th c.); ecclesiastical organizations and estates, mostly of the Banská Bystrica Bishopric 1776-1950 and the trustworthy locations of Turiec Convent and the chapter of Banská Bystrica (1259) 1288-1912; and of authorities and organizations of local character. The archive has a reading room and library.

Literature:

Štátny archív v Banskej Bystrici. Sprievodca po archívnych fondoch I.-II. (State archive in Banská Bystrica. Guide to the archive collections I.-II.) Bratislava, SAS 1962, 1969.

STATE REGIONAL ARCHIVE IN BRATISLAVA

Štátny oblastný archív v Bratislave
811 04 Bratislava, Križkova 7
Tel.: / 07/ 496 051, 496 052, 496 053, 496 046
Fax: /07/ 496 046

The archive, founded in 1954, preserves and processes archival documents from the thirteenth century to the present. Among the largest and most interesting collections are Bratislava County, 1396 - 1922; Trenčín County, (1222) 1481-1922; collections of the county administration in 1923-1928 and 1940-1945; of the resort state offices; of the subordinate courts; the families, patrimonies and great estates; church administration; registers, collections of societies and organizations, and personal collections. Other important and extensive collections are those of the Regional National Committee (Krajský národný výbor) Bratislava 1949-1960; the Regional Court in Bratislava 1872-1949, which contains a series of company documents with data about all private firms, joint stock companies, banks, cooperatives, etc.; and the collection of the Office of the Public prosecutor in Bratislava, 1919-1948. The researcher can use the conventional modern archival aids and study in the reading room of the archive. There is also a library.

Literature:

Štátny archív v Bratislave I. Sprievodca po archívnych fondoch (The State Archive of Bratislava I. Guide to the archive collections.) Bratislava, SAS 1959.

Štátny archív v Bratislave III. Sprievodca po archívnych fondoch (The State Archive of Bratislava III. Guide to the archive collections.) Bratislava, SAS 1966.

THE STATE REGIONAL ARCHIVE IN BYTČA

Štátny oblastný archív v Bytči
014 35 Bytča, Kaštieľ (Castle)
Tel.: /0821/ 36 22, 33 11
Fax: /0821/ 36 22

The Archive was founded in 1955 from the former Regional Archive in Žilina. It processes and preserves archival material from 1263 to 1960. Among the most important collections are the archives of Liptov County (1391-1922); Orava County (1584-1922); Turiec County (1486-1922); the County Administration (1923-1928); Podtatranský County; Považie County; and the County Administration (1940-1945); public administration committees (1876-1920);

and small town administrations of the nineteenth and twentieth centuries. From the twentieth century there is the important collection of the Regional National Committee in Žilina (1949-1960); from the nineteenth and twentieth centuries the collections of the district, regional and land register courts; and collections of schools, economic and other institutions, as well as collections of noble families of this region. The archive has a library and reading room.

Literature:

Štátny archív v Bytči. Sprievodca po archívnych fondoch (The State Archive of Bytča. Guide to the archive collections.) Bratislava, SAS 1959.

Štátny archív v Banskej Bystrici, pobočka v Bytči. Sprievodca po archívnych fondoch II. (The State Archive of Banská Bystrica, branch in Bytča. Guide to the archive collections II.) Bratislava, SAS 1965.

THE STATE REGIONAL ARCHIVE IN KOŠICE

Štátny oblastný archív v Košiciach
041 56 Košice, Bačíkova 1
Tel.: / 095/ 224 15, 208 40
Fax: /095/ 208 40

The archive was founded in 1954 from the former Regional Archive in Košice. It processes and preserves archival material from the fifteenth century to the present. Among the most important collections are those of the counties: Abov County (1564-1881); Turňa County (1569-1882); Abov-Turňa County (1785-1922); Košice County (1923-1928); and other counties (1938-1945); as well as the archival collections of the public administration committees, and small town administrations. Also important are the collections of the district, regional and municipal courts, subordinate courts, and land register courts. Others are the archival collection of the Regional National Committee in Košice (1949-1960); the collection of the East Slovakia Regional National Committee in Košice (1960-1989); church registers; collections of economic and other institutions; of secondary schools; and personal collections. The archive has the conventional modern aids. Study is possible in the reading room, and there is also a library available.

Literature:

Štátny archív v Košiciach. Sprievodca po archívnych fondoch I.–II. (The State Archive in Košice. Guide to the archive collections I.–II.) Bratislava, SAS 1963, 1965.(Collections marked with a "K" are part of SRA Košice.)

THE STATE REGIONAL ARCHIVE IN LEVOČA

Štátny oblastný archív v Levoči
054 01 Levoča, námestie Majstra Pavla 60
Tel.: /0966/ 24 86, 24 24
Fax: /0966/ 44 11

This was formerly active as a branch of the State Regional Archive in Košice, and since 1969 has been an independent archive. The archival documents reach from the thirteenth century to the present. Among the most valuable collections are those of Spiš County, which are in fact the predecessors of the present-day archive; as well as those of the privileged regions: the provinces of the Sixteen Spiš Towns (1412-1876); and the County of the Ten Spiš Lancers (1384-1803); of county, district and land register courts; authorities of civil courts; noble families and great estates, such as Andrássy, Csáky, Mariási; directorships of state forests and estates of Solivar (1836-1948); forest offices and inspectorates; and agricultural administration. The archive has a reading room, library, a culture room with modern equipment and a photo laboratory.

Literature:
Sub SRA Košice quoted guides (Collections signified with "L").

THE STATE REGIONAL ARCHIVE IN NITRA

Štátny oblastný archív v Nitre
951 12 Ivanka pri Nitre, Novozámocká 383
Tel.: /087/ 643 84

The archive was founded on July 1, 1969 from the former branch of the State Archive in Bratislava. Its documents reach from the thirteenth century to the present. Basic collections are the county archives of Nitra (1531-1922); Tekov (1290-1923); Komárno (1280-1918); Komárno-Ostrihom/Esztergom (1786-1790); Dolná Nitra (1850-1861); Ráb/Győr-Komárno-Ostrihom (1919-1922); and also the collections of small town administrations; county organizations (1923-1928 and 1938-1945); courts and court administration; church registers; collections of state forest offices; the Regional National Committee in Nitra (1949-1960); ruling families; church organizations; and others. The archives has a reading room and library.

Literature:

Štátny archív v Bratislave, pobočka v Nitre. Sprievodca po archívnych fondoch II. (The State Archive in Bratislava, Nitra branch. Guide to the archive collections II.) Bratislava, SAS 1963.

Štátny archív v Bratislave. Sprievodca po archívnych fondoch III. (The State Archive in Bratislava. Guide to the archive collections III.) Bratislava, SAS 1966. (Collections signified with "N").

THE STATE REGIONAL ARCHIVE IN PREŠOV

Štátny oblastný archív v Prešove
080 06 Prešov - Nižná Šebastová, Slanská 33
Tel: /091/ 764 613
Fax: /091/ 222 31

This were founded in 1954 from the former Regional Archive in Prešov as a branch of the State Archive in Košice. Since July 1, 1969 it has been an independent archive. It processes and preserves archival documents from the fifteenth century to the present. Among the most important collections are those of Šariš County (1400-1922); county administration (1940-1945); public administration committees and small town administrations; courts and court administration from the eighteenth and nineteenth centuries; as well as the Regional Court in Prešov (1921-1934); noble families, including Bornemissza, Csáky, Dessewffy, Szechényi, Stáray, and Zamoyski; schools, institutions and societies and personal collections. The archive has a reading room and library.

Literature:

Štátny archív v Prešove. Sprievodca po archívnych fondoch. (The State Archive in Prešov. Guide to the archive collections.) Bratislava, SAS 1959.

Municipal Archives

THE ARCHIVE OF THE CAPITAL OF THE SLOVAK REPUBLIC BRATISLAVA

Archív hlavného mesta Slovenskej republiky Bratislavy
814 71 Bratislava, Primaciálne nám. 2
Tel: /07/ 333 248, 356 111, 330 848

The origins of the archive date back to the thirteenth century. Today the

Municipal Archive processes written documents from the thirteenth century to the present. Since 1956, it has been included into the State Archives. In addition to valuable collections of documents and books (Public Municipal Books) there are the collections of City Hall; the City Council and representatives; handwritten musical documents; a precious collection of maps and plans; and archival collections of city institutions and factories. The City Scientific Library (Regional Library) and reading room are also part of the archive. Besides conventional modern aids for information and orientation, a computerized archive information system is also being developed.

Literature:

Sprievodca po fondoch a zbierkach Archívu mesta Bratislavy. (Guide to the collections of the Archive of the City of Bratislava.) Praha, AS MV 1955.

Inventár stredovekých listín, listov a iných príbuzných písomností. (Inventory of medieval certificates, letters and other related documents.) Praha, AS 1956.

Inventár listín a listov z rokov 1501-1563. (Inventory of certificates and letters of 1501-1563.) Bratislava, SAS 1966; the volume for the years 1564-1615 and the volume for the years 1616-1859 SAS 1967, rotaprint.

Edition: *Bratislava - fontes*

Kultúrnopolitický kalendár mesta Bratislavy, ročenka (Cultural and political calender of the City of Bratislava, yearbook) rotaprint, published annually.

THE MUNICIPAL ARCHIVE OF KOŠICE

Archív mesta Košíc
040 01 Košice, Kováčska 20/I
Tel.: /095/ 218 25

The history of the archive reaches back to the beginning of the sixteenth century. Since 1951 it has functioned as the modern Municipal Archive. It contains archival material from 1239 to the present. Among the important collections are those of the Free Royal Town of Košice; Košice City Hall; the Municipal Notary; Košice county administration; and the National Committee of the City of Košice. Also in the archive is the oldest document connected with a city coat of arms in Slovakia, from 1369. For those interested, there is a reading room and library.

Literature:

Sprievodca po fondoch a zbierkach Archívu mesta Košíc. (Guide to the collections of the Archive of the City of Košice.) Praha, AS MV 1956.

State District Archives

Important regional archival material is managed by the State District Archives which are active in individual districts of Slovakia. They began to be organized in 1951 and, more intensively, after 1960. The forerunners of the current district archives did not develop in the same manner although the majority of them were based upon city archives. These archives preserve, manage and make available documents of district and local provenance, concerning the written legacy of secondary state and administrative institutions. The biggest and most important collections are those of former district offices, cities and small towns, notaries, schools, guilds and societies. From the later period are collections of district and local national committees and other local offices and institutions. The district archives also produce modern archival aids for the collections. Some branches have published guides to their own collections. Each archive has a reading room.

THE STATE DISTRICT ARCHIVE IN BANSKÁ BYSTRICA
Štátny okresný archív v Banskej Bystrici
974 00 Banská Bystrica, námestie SNP 1
Tel.: /088/ 248 46, 257 57
Fax: /088/ 539 77
Office in Brezno - Tel.: /0876/ 23 13

The period covered by the archival documents is 1255-1973. Important collections are of the towns of Banská Bystrica, Ľubietová and Brezno and the small towns of Slovenská Lupča and Poniky.

THE STATE DISTRICT ARCHIVE IN BARDEJOV
Štátny okresný archív v Bardejove
085 77 Bardejov, Dlhý rad 16
Tel.: /0935/ 53 62

Covering the fourteenth to the twentieth century important collections are of the district and city authorities of the state administration, and Bardejov City Hall (1319-1922).

THE STATE DISTRICT ARCHIVE OF BRATISLAVA - ENVIRONS
Štátny okresný archív Bratislava - vidiek
900 01 Modra, Dolná 140
Tel.: /070492/ 39 26

The fourteenth to the twentieth century is also the period covered by this archive. The most valuable are the archives of the towns Svätý Jur, Modra, and Pezinok; the musical collections of the Piarist monastery in Svätý Jur and Podolínec (1741 to the twentieth century); and collections of district offices, notaries, financial offices, district and city national committees, schools and other district institutions.

Literature:

Štátny okresný archív Bratislava - vidiek. Sprievodca po archívnych fondoch. (The State District Archive of Bratislava - environs. Guide to the archive collections.) Bratislava, AS MV SSR 1980.

THE STATE DISTRICT ARCHIVE OF ČADCA
Štátny okresný archív v Čadci
022 01 Čadca, Palárikova 1150
Tel.: (0924) 213 32, 217 40

This contains archival documents from 1923 to 1972.

THE STATE DISTRICT ARCHIVE OF DOLNÝ KUBÍN
Štátny okresný archív v Dolnom Kubíne
026 01 Dolný Kubín, Matúškova 1654/8
Tel.: /0845/ 34 98, 34 23

This contains archival documents from the seventeenth to the twentieth century. Among them are archival collections of the district and city administrations of Dolný Kubín, Námestovo, Trstená, Tvrdošín and Veličná.

Literature:

Štátne okresné archívy v Dolnom Kubíne, Liptovskom Mikuláši a Martine. Sprievodca po archívnych fondoch. (The State District Archives of Dolný Kubín, Liptovský Mikuláš and Martin. Guide to the archive collections.) Bratislava, AS MV SSR 1980.

THE STATE DISTRICT ARCHIVE OF GALANTA
Štátny okresný archív v Galante
927 00 Šaľa, ulica Petra Pázmáňa 27
Tel.: /0706/ 22 60

Archival documents are from 1340 to the twentieth century. The more important collections are from town Šamorín, and of the district offices and district national commitees of Galanta, Šaľa, Dunajská Streda, Šamorín, Čalovo and Sereď. Many documents are pertinent to the peculiarities of the southern region of Slovakia, and to Slovak- Hungarian relations.

THE STATE DISTRICT ARCHIVE OF HUMENNÉ
Štátny okresný archív v Humennom
066 80 Humenné, Štúrova 1
Tel.: /0933/ 27 70

This contains archival collections from the twentieth century, of the district offices of Humenné, Medzilaborce, and Snina, and collections of the district national committees.

THE STATE DISTRICT ARCHIVE OF KOMÁRNO
Štátny okresný archív Komárno
945 36 Komárno, Župná 15
Tel.: /0819/ 28 87

Archival material is from 1277 - 1972. The more valuable collections: from the town hall, the town national committee and district offices and district national committee Komárno and Hurbanovo. Also here is the privilege of Matúš Čák for Komárno from 1307.

THE STATE DISTRICT ARCHIVE IN KOŠICE
Štátny okresný archív v Košiciach
042 11 Košice, Kováčska 20/II
Tel.: /095/ 246 75

This contains archival documents from the seventeenth to the twentieth century of the collections of the mining cities Nižný Medzev, Vyšný Medzev, Štos, Jasov and the free town of Moldava.

THE STATE DISTRICT ARCHIVE OF LEVICE
Štátny okresný archív v Leviciach
935 23 Rybník 192
Tel.: /0813/ 922 261

Archival documents are from 1406-1970. Archival collections of the towns and small towns Bátovce, Pukanec, Levice, archives of the guilds in Levice and Bátovce.

THE STATE DISTRICT ARCHIVE IN LIPTOVSKÝ MIKULÁŠ
Štátny okresný archív v Liptovskom Mikuláši
031 01 Liptovský Mikuláš, Školská 4
Tel.: /0849/ 233 32

This contains archival documents from the thirteenth to the twentieth centuries. More important collections of the towns and small towns Ružomberok, Liptovský Mikuláš, Hybe, Liptovská Sielnica, Partizánska Ľupča, collections of the district and town administration, schools and cultural institutions, collections of the justice and financial administraton, family archives and personal collections.

Literature:
Sub "The State Disctrict Archive of Dolný Kubín" quoted guide.

THE STATE DISTRICT ARCHIVE OF LUČENEC
Štátny okresný archív v Lučenci
984 01 Lučenec, Kubányiho námestie
Tel.: /0863/ 269 38

Archival material from the nineteenth and twentieth centuries. The more important collections of the secondary school in Lučenec 1836 - 1962.

THE STATE DISTRICT ARCHIVE OF MARTIN
Štátny okresný archív v Martine
036 01 Martin, Bystrička 397
Tel.: /0842/ 341 23

This contains archival material from 1348 - 1970. The more important collections of the towns and small towns Martin, Kláštor pod Znievom, Mošovce, Slovenské Pravno, Turany, collections of the notaries, collections of the district and town administration, schools, guilds, cooperatives.

Literature:

Sub "The State District Archive of Dolný Kubín" quoted guide.

THE STATE DISTRICT ARCHIVE OF MICHALOVCE
Štátny okresný archív v Michalovciach
071 01 Michalovce, ulica Š. Tučeka 4
Tel.: /0946/ 244 27, 244 81

Archival material is from the nineteenth and twentieth centuries, archival collections of the district offices and the distric national commitees.

THE STATE DISTRICT ARCHIVE OF NITRA
Štátny okresný archív v Nitre
949 05 Nitra, Pod Katrušou 1
Tel.: /087/ 416 620

This contains the material from 1609 to 1969. More important collections of the town hall of Nitra, collections of the district and town administration, collections of the political parties and trade unions.

Literature:

Sprievodca po okresných archívoch v Nitre, Prievidzi a Topoľčanoch. (Guide through the district archives in Nitra, Prievidza and Topoľčany.) Bratislava, SAS MV SSR 1975.

THE STATE DISTRICT ARCHIVE OF NOVÉ ZÁMKY
Štátny okresný archív v Nových Zámkoch
940 65 Nové Zámky, Tyršova 1
Tel.: /0817/ 272 39

Archival material from the eighteenth to twentieth centuries. More important collection of the town hall of Nové Zámky 1707-1922.

THE STATE DISTRICT ARCHIVE OF POPRAD
Štátny okresný archív v Poprade
058 44 Poprad, Popradské nábrežie 16
Tel.: /092/ 620 25

Time span of the collections is from 1269 to 1972. Important are the archives of some Spiš cities and little towns (10) and archival documents of the institutions of the state administraton and government, schools and financial administration. Archive of the free town Kežmarok.

THE STATE DISTRICT ARCHIVE OF POVAŽSKÁ BYSTRICA
Štátny okresný archív v Považskej Bystrici
017 01 Považská Bystrica, ulica Slovenských partizánov 1135/55
Tel.: /0822/ 250 60

The archive contains archival material from 1376 - 1971 although archival documents from the nineteenth and twentieth centuries prevail in the collections of the district and local administration.

THE STATE DISTRICT ARCHIVE OF PREŠOV
Štátny okresný archív v Prešove
080 01 Prešov, Slovenská 40
Tel.: /091/ 330 05, 311 84

Time span of the archival material covers 1245 - 20th century. More important collections: Archive of the free royal town Prešov, from 1245, town hall of Sabinov, locality Lipany, Piarist order in Sabinov.

THE STATE DISTRICT ARCHIVE OF PRIEVIDZA

Štátny okresný archív v Prievidzi
972 01 Bojnice, Tehelná 1
Tel.: /0862/ 324 19

This contains the collections from 1383 to 1960. More valuable are the collections: town hall of Prievidza, district office of Prievidza, district and city offices of the national commitees from the twentieth century and other collections.

Literature:

Sub "The State District Archive of Nitra" quoted guide.

THE STATE DISTRICT ARCHIVE OF RIMAVSKÁ SOBOTA

Štátny okresný archív v Rimavskej Sobote
979 80 Rimavská Sobota, Hlavné námestie 2
Tel.Fax: /0866/ 237 75

Time span of the material covers the years 1335 - twentieth century. More interesting are the Turkish documents, royal and sovereign privileges since 1335, town hall of Tisovec 1615 - 1945.

THE STATE DISTRICT ARCHIVE OF ROŽŇAVA

Štátny okresný archív v Rožňave
049 51 Brzotín, Kaštieľ (Castle)
Tel.: /0942/ 821 18, 240 69

Time span of the archival material covers the years 1299 - twentieth century. To the more important collections belong: town hall Jelšava 1299 - 1922, town hall Dobšiná 1326-1920, collections of the district offices, town offices, small towns Plešivec, Štítnik and Revúca, town hall Rožňava.

THE STATE DISTRICT ARCHIVE OF SENICA

Štátny okresný archív v Senici
909 01 Skalica, Kráľovská 16
Tel.: /0801/ 944 567

The archive contains materials from 1389 to the twentieth century and the most important collections are: the archive of the town of Skalica, the archives of small towns and villages, collections of guilds, the archive of the gymnasium in Skalica since 1736, and of the Haban community (descendents of Anabaptists) in Sobotište, collections of farming construction cooperatives, and the personal collection of Daniel G. Lichard.

THE STATE DISTRICT ARCHIVE OF SPIŠSKÁ NOVÁ VES
Štátny okresný archív v Spišskej Novej Vsi
052 80 Spišská Nová Ves, Letná 67
Tel.: /0965/ 243 39
Office in Levoča /0966/ 22 81

The period covered by the material is 1294 to the present. Important collections are of the towns of Spišská Nová Ves, Levoča, Spišské Vlachy, Smolník, village Švedlár, Nálepkovo.

THE STATE DISTRICT ARCHIVE OF STARÁ ĽUBOVŇA
Štátny okresný archív v Starej Ľubovni
064 80 Stará Ľubovňa, námestie Sv. Mikuláša 5
Tel.: /0963/ 219 83

Time span of the collections from 1280 to 1970. More important collections: Free royal town Podolínec, town Hniezdne, with guild articles of brewers, smiths, tailors, shoemakers, privilege of the Polish king Sigmund August from 1559, document of the king Ján Kazimír of 1649 and others.

THE STATE DISTRICT ARCHIVE OF SVIDNÍK
Štátny okresný archív vo Svidníku
089 01 Svidník, Partizánska 625/12
Tel.: /0937/ 223 02

The period covered by the archival material is only twentieth century. Collections are of the district and town administration.

THE STATE DISTRICT ARCHIVE OF TOPOEČANY

Štátny okresný archív v Topoľčanoch
955 01 Topoľčany, Pod Kalváriou 2140
Tel.: /0815/ 221 26

Time span covers 1376 to present, prevail the collections of the district and local administration from the twentieth century. Early important collections of the small town Bánovce nad Bebravou, archive of the village Chynorany.

Literature:
Sub "The State District Archive of Nitra" quoted guide.

THE STATE DISTRICT ARCHIVE OF TREBIŠOV

Štátny okresný archív v Trebišove
075 01 Trebišov, ulica M. R. Štefánika 201
Tel.: /0948/ 35 00

The period covered by the archival material is 1784-1973. The earliest documents are in the collections of the National School of Čičarovce 1784-1953, water regulation cooperative of Trebišov and boot guild of Kráľovský Chlmec.

THE STATE DISTRICT ARCHIVE OF TRENČÍN

Štátny okresný archív v Trenčíne
911 00 Trenčín, Kožušnícka 1
Tel.: /0831/ 523 96

Time span covered by the archival material represent the years 1324-1965. More valuable documents: Privilege of Karol Róbert of 1324, town book of Trenčín of 1476 with the oldest Slovak text in Trenčín, Protocollum auxiliare of 1578 refering to rights and duties of the citizens of the villein villages.

THE STATE DISTRICT ARCHIVE OF TRNAVA

Štátny okresný archív v Trnave
917 38 Trnava, Štefánikova 46
Tel.: /0805/ 221 19, 248 59
Fax: /0805/ 248 59

The period covered by the archival collection is 1238 - 1970. Important archival collections and documents are in the archive of the town of Trnava, documents from 1238 (king Bela IV.), economic privileges of the kings Louis and Sigmund for Trnava, decrees of Mathias Corvinus and other sovereigns, 70,000 letters to Trnava with many Slovak documents of the villages of the district to its capital from the sixteenth century, last wills of the Trnava burghers, official and public books from the end of the fourteenth century and collections of the modern offices of the district and local administration.

Literature:

Štátny okresný archív v Trnave. Sprievodca po fondoch a zbierkach. (The State District Archive of Trnava. Guide through the collections.) Bratislava, AV MV SSR 1978.

THE STATE DISTRICT ARCHIVE OF VEĽKÝ KRTÍŠ

Štátny okresný archív vo Veľkom Krtíši
990 01 Veľký Krtíš, Za parkom 851
Tel.: /0854/ 229 37

Archival material of the nineteenth and twentieth centuries. Archival collections of the district and local administration, courts, financial administration, collections of the schools, societies and unions.

Literature:

Štátny okresný archív vo Veľkom Krtíši. Sprievodca po fondoch a zbierkach. (The State District Archive of Veľký Krtíš. Guide through the collections.) Bratislava, AS MV SSR 1982.

THE STATE DISTRICT ARCHIVE OF VRANOV NAD TOPĽOU

Štátny okresný archív vo Vranove nad Topľou
093 01 Vranov nad Topľou, Námestie Slobody 3
Tel.: /0931/ 236 84

The period covered is only the twentieth century. Archival collections are of the district and local administration.

THE STATE DISTRICT ARCHIVE OF ZVOLEN
Štátny okresný archív vo Zvolene
962 61 Dobrá Niva, Ostrá Lúka, Kaštieľ (Castle)
Tel.: /0855/ 912 34

Archival documents of 1238 to 1973. More important collections include those of the town halls of Zvolen and Krupina, collection of the family Ostrolúcky.

THE STATE DISTRICT ARCHIVE OF ŽIAR NAD HRONOM
Štátny okresný archív v Žiari nad Hronom
976 01 Kremnica, Námestie 1. mája 4/7
Tel.: /0857/ 925 508
Branch Banská Štiavnica, Kammerhofská 15, Tel.: /0859/ 214 05

The basis of the archive is the municipal archive of Kremnica and the district archive of Banská Štiavnica. There are 789 charters from the Middle Ages, the oldest town book "Liber civitatis Statbuch" of 1426 - 1700, old guild documents, oldest fragments of the archive are the notations - from the twelfth and thirteenth centuries. Also valuable is the collection of the towns of Banská Štiavnica and Banská Belá 1430 - 1922 and the town of Nová Baňa.

THE STATE DISTRICT ARCHIVE OF ŽILINA
Štátny okresný archív v Žiline
010 03 Žilina, Predmestská 1
Tel.: /089/ 445 76

The most important is the archival collection of the town hall of Žilina with the privilege of Charles I. to the town of Žilina from 1321 and with the Žilina book of 1378 and the Privilege pro Slavis, a charter from 1381 by which King Louis I of Hungary granted the privilege that Slovaks would enjoy a parity on the city council.

The Archives of Special Importance

THE ARCHIVE OF LITERATURE AND ARTS, MATICA SLOVENSKÁ
Archív literatúry a umenia, Matica slovenská
036 52 Martin, ulica L. Novomeského 32
Tel.: /0842/ 313 71, 314 92, ext. 153

It is connected with the foundation of Matica slovenská 1863 but was created only in 1954. The archive manages the literature manuscripts, musical memorials, pictures and objects. The oldest documents are the glagolitic texts of Hlohovec and the Cyril letters from the end of the thirteenth century, then the manuscripts of the works from middle ages and of modern times of the important Slovak secular and ecclesiastic personalities, writers and scholars, extensive personal collections of the Slovak writers of the nineteenth and twentieth centuries, as well as the valuable items of many important non-Slovak authors (Karel Slavoj Amerling, Björsterne Björnson, Wilhelm Humboldt, František Xaver Šalda, Johann Friedrich Schiller, Lev Nikolajevič Tolstoj, Miguel de Unamuno, Jaroslav Vrchlický, Richard Wagner and others). Important are also musical memorials mostly of the eighteenth - twentieth centuries, photos and other documents. The archive has a reading room with modern aids.

Literature, editions:
Literárny archív (Literary Archive), almanac is published from 1964
Hudobný archív (Music Archive) 1 volume
edition *Documenta Litteraria Slovaca*
edition *Výskum dejín Matice slovenskej* (Research of the history of Matica Slovenská)
edition *Výskum literárneho a hudobného archívnictva* (Research of the literary and music archival science)

THE CENTRAL ARCHIVE
OF THE SLOVAK ACADEMY OF SCIENCES
Ústredný archív Slovenskej akadémie vied
841 05 Bratislava, Dúbravská cesta 9
Tel.: /07/ 378, ext. 20 75, 26 22, 37 56 65

It was founded in 1963 and protects and manages the collections of the documents and documentary material of authorities, working places and offices of the Slovak Academy of Sciences, its legal predecessors of scientific societies, members of the academy and research workers. It is possible to study there by the help of the modern archival aids in the reading room of the archive.

THE ARCHIVE OF COMENIUS UNIVERSITY OF BRATISLAVA

Archív Univerzity Komenského v Bratislave
811 01 Bratislava, Šafárikovo námestie 6
Tel.: /07/ 580 41, ext. 325

The archive was founded in 1965. It preserves and manages the collections from 1919 (since the foundation of the Comenius University).

THE ARCHIVE OF THE SLOVAK TECHNICAL UNIVERSITY

Archív Slovenskej technickej univerzity
812 43 Bratislava, Námestie Slobody 19
Tel.: /07/ 571 20

THE ARCHIVE OF THE SLOVAK NATIONAL MUSEUM

Archív Slovenského národného múzea
814 36 Bratislava, Vajanského nábrežie 2
Tel.: /07/ 336 551
Office in Martin: /0842/ 310 11

THE ARCHIVE OF THE SLOVAK NATIONAL GALLERY

Archív Slovenskej národnej galérie
815 13 Bratislava, Riečna 1
Tel.: /07/ 332 081, 330 707

THE ARCHIVE OF THE MUSEUM
OF THE SLOVAK NATIONAL UPRISING

Archív Múzea Slovenského národného povstania
974 00 Banská Bystrica, Moyzesova 23
Tel.: /088/ 232 59, 257 81

THE ARCHIVE OF SLOVAK RADIO
Archív Slovenského rozhlasu
812 50 Bratislava, Mýtna 1
Tel.: /07/ 406 11, 444 62

THE ARCHIVE OF SLOVAK TELEVISION
Archív Slovenskej televízie
845 45 Bratislava, Mlynská Dolina
Tel.: /07/ 325 500, 324 800

THE ARCHIVE OF THE SLOVAK FILM
Archív Slovenského filmu
833 14 Bratislava - Koliba
Tel.: /07/ 420 51, 430 21

THE CENTRAL ARCHIVE OF GEODESY, CARTOGRAPHY AND LAND REGISTER
Ústredný archív geodézie, kartografie a katastra
827 45 Bratislava, Chlumeckého 4
Tel.: /07/ 234 801, 234 822

THE ARCHIVE OF THE STATE MINT OF KREMNICA
Archív Štátnej mincovne v Kremnici
967 15 Kremnica, Štefánikovo námestie
Tel.: /0857/ 925 441, 925 482

LIBRARIES

Historical and Historiographical Information Sources in Libraries

The task of a historiographer requires that basic information sources be collected, preserved and made accessible by libraries of different types and purposes, with different scopes of collections and types of services. These differences are primarily the result of the role of the library or the character of the establishing institution, without regard to whether they are located in Bratislava or other regions of Slovakia.

Literature of domestic provenance (books and periodicals) from history, related disciplines and other branches is generally available because publishers were required to deposit copies of each of their publications in almost every one of the scholarly libraries. Among libraries exist variations in the extent and depth of literature from each given scholarly branch. These variations are the result of the responsibility of a particular library to acquire foreign literature, deaccession older literature (with the exception of repository libraries), and historical collections that were taken over at founding by gift, transfer or purchase, or confiscation.

The libraries of archives and museums have a different character than public libraries. They have two levels of collections: select reference libraries to provide immediate information for the needs of the particular workplace and materials that are part of the special collection itself or an independent assemblage of historical books.

For this overview, a variety of libraries (scholarly, university, ecclesiastical, archival and museum) have been chosen to indicate connections with a given branch or region. We have tried to introduce those institutions which, because of their peculiarities, will be interesting to scholars. While many of the most significant items have been identified[1] there still could be some interesting

---

[1] HISTORICKÉ knižničné fondy na Slovensku. Martin, MS 1988. Teória a výskum knihovníctva a bibliografie. Výskumy č.40.

items in smaller private or organizational collections[2] but since the holdings of these libraries have not been elaborated they will not be discussed. Collections of recent literature have been clarified by secondary sources.

The description of each library in this overview contains the essential data that especially characterizes it, the system of catalogues and other aids. When administered by another party, we give only the owner's name. Among published works, we mention only the independent inventories of the material and not other works dealing with these collections or larger works in which the collections are mentioned.

Public Libraries

The choice of libraries, especially for the foreign historiographer, is influenced by a number of factors: his or her theme, orientation, language, time at hand, and opportunity for research outside of Bratislava. Of first significance for most researchers are the collections of the Slovak Academy of Sciences and others institutions in Bratislava.

THE SLOVAK ACADEMY OF SCIENCES
1. Central Library
Ústredná knižnica SAV
Klemensova 19, 814 67 Bratislava
Tel.: /07/ 326 321, 321 733

The collection contains the historical collections of the predecessors of the library, above all of the Šafárik Scholarly Society, Slovak Scholarly Society, and Bratislava Medical and Natural History Society, which are not independently preserved but parts of the whole. Orientation is provided by an author catalogue (from 1943) and systematic subject catalogue (from 1952).

The collection of the *Chamber of Commerce and Industry* is specially preserved. Its approximately 8,000 items include reports of the chamber, encyclopaedias, maps, directories, and literature from economics, commerce, justice,

---

[2] HISTORICKÉ knižné fondy na Slovensku. Martin, MS 1991. Teória a výskum knihovníctva a bibliografie. Výskumy č.44.

industry, politics, transport, administration and schools, and 1,240 titles of periodicals (incomplete annuals). Orientation is provided by a subject catalogue and title catalogue of periodicals. This collection was taken over in 1994 by the original owner, the regional office of the Slovak Chamber of Commerce and Industry.

Since 1954, the Central Library of SAV has administered the *Lyceum Library,* the owner of which is the Evangelical Church. This historical collection contains 13,000 items from the Šimko Library, with literature from philosophy, philology, justice, natural sciences, a theological and school library and manuscript collection. Parts of the collections of the Evangelical Gymnasium in Banská Bystrica, the Theological Faculty in Modra, school administrations from throughout Hungary (appoximately 10,000 items), and of duplicates were added. The Lyceum library has approximately 90,000 items and more than 1,200 manuscripts. Among them are thirteen codices from the Middle Ages. In the collection are forty-four incunabulae[3] and around 2,000 prints from the sixteenth century.[4] In addition to the publications mentioned there are also partial thematic inventories (Habaner imprints, Comeniana, Anabaptist manuscripts, and so on). The original catalogues of the library have not been preserved as a whole, which is why the collection is being recatalogued and an author and systematic subject catalogue are being developed. The collection is available for use on the premises by scholars.

2. The Basic Information Center of the Institute of Historical Studies of the Slovak Academy of Sciences
Základné informačné stredisko Historického ústavu SAV
Klemensova 19, 813 64 Bratislava
Tel.: /07/ 326 321

The monograph collection contains over 43,000 items of history, related disciplines and connected branches. In addition to these, the institution also has a rich collection of offprints, dissertations, photocopies, pictures, film, and scholarly papers (over two million). Orientation in the collection is through the author catalogue. Extensive bibliographic work since 1957 has been added to by the bibliographic data base registering historiographical literature since 1990.

---

[3] KOTVAN, Imrich: Prvotlače Lyceálnej knižnice v Bratislave. Bratislava, UK 1957.
[4] ČAPLOVIČ, Ján: Tlače vydané na Slovensku do roku 1700 v bývalej Lyceálnej knižnici. Bratislava, ÚK SAV 1963.

THE UNIVERSITY LIBRARY
Univerzitná knižnica
Michalská 1, 814 17 Bratislava
Tel.: /07/ 331 151-4

At its foundation in 1919, the library took over the collection of the Elizabeth University Library, which was made up of three units:
- *The Public Municipal Library:* ca. 23,000 items, chiefly from philosophy, justice and history;
- *The Royal Law Academy Library:* ca. 28,000 items, containing imprints from the sixteenth to the twentieth century, from justice, history and linguistics;
- *The Old Library:* The Library of the Jesuit Gymnasium in Bratislava, and part of the collection of the Library of Trnava University, ca. 7,000 items from theology, history, philosophy and other disciplines.

The library also bought or received as gifts other historical libraries or their parts. From these we should mention the Rizner Library (more than 2,000 Slovak books); the Jozef Bellai Library (more than 7,000 items); the Sclauch Library (ca. 8,000 items of Hungarica); as well as a quantity of smaller collections from Slovak figures (such as the Comenius scholar Ján Kvačala, the brothers Ján and Samo Chalupka, Daniel Wagner the natural scientist, and Jozef Gašparík the book printer). The collection of *Judaica* deserves special attention, containing more than 1,200 items, mostly of Bratislava Hebraic and Hebraic-German imprints. Another significant collection is the *Štúr Library,* containing around 1,300 items from philosophy, history, linguistics, pedagogy, geography, theology, natural sciences, folk and popular literature as well as belles lettres–a catalogue of which has been published[5]. There is also the *Baša-gič Library,* which contains a precious collection of Islamic manuscripts and books from theology, philosophy, history and belles lettres. The purchased addition has over 500 volumes in Arabic, Turkish and Persian, and around 600 manuscripts. Two catalogues have been printed[6], in addition to a card catalogue and two inventories.

The library also owns the former collections of noblemen, for example a part of the Lobkovic Library (more than 5,000 items of Bohemica of different branches from the sixteenth to the twentieth century); and the Erdödy Library

---

[5] FERIENČÍKOVÁ, Anna: Knižnica Slovanského ústavu v Bratislave. Bratislava, UK 1972.

[6] PETRÁČEK, Karel - BLAŠKOVIČ, Jozef - VESELÝ, Rudolf: Arabische, türkische und persische Handschriften der Universitätsbibliothek in Bratislava. Bratislava, UK 1961; MOLNÁR, Ján: Orientálne tlače z knižnice Bega Bašagiča v Univerzitnej knižnici v Bratislave. Bratislava, UK 1980.

(more than 6,000 items from the sixteenth to the nineteenth century, from philosophy, literature, theology and belles lettres).

In its collection the University Library has over 1,000 manuscripts (the oldest from the thirteenth century)[7], and more than 500 incunabulae from branches of the social and natural sciences.[8]

The above mentioned collections as well as other collections of Slovakiana and foreign literature are made available to the readers through these catalogues:

Readers' Catalogues (books since 1953)
- Author Catalogues
  card catalogue of books
  computer catalogue of books (books since 1992)
  catalogue of periodicals
- Subject Catalogues
  systematic catalogue of books
  subject catalogue of books
  foreign dissertation catalogue
  defended candidate and doctoral dissertation work from the Slovak Republic
- Special Catalogues
  serial monograph catalogue
  Slovak publishers' collections catalogue

Books published before 1953 are only available for study on the premises.

Bibliographic information services are available, including book searches. A bibliographic reading room makes available basic works of Slovak national bibliography, foreign national bibliographies, biographical dictionaries, information manuals, inventories and books of quotations.

THE SLOVAK PEDAGOGIC LIBRARY
OF THE INSTITUTION OF INFORMATION, AND PROGNOSTICS
OF EDUCATION, YOUTH AND SPORT
Slovenská pedagogická knižnica
Ústavu informácií a prognóz školstva, mládeže a telovýchovy
Klariská 5, 842 44 Bratislava
Tel.: /07/ 330 308, 330 307

---

[7] KOTVAN, Imrich: Rukopisy Univerzitnej knižnice v Bratislave. Bratislava, UK 1970.

[8] KOTVAN, Imrich: Inkunábuly Univerzitnej knižnice v Bratislave. Bratislava, UK 1960.

In this library there is a special collection of *annual school reports* (more than 5,000 items). This collection contains material from the nineteenth and twentieth centuries, stressing the second half of the nineteenth and the first half of the twentieth century, from the region of Slovakia and the Austro-Hungarian Empire. Orientation in the collection is through an acquisition inventory and catalogues (author, and subject according to the type of school).

In addition to this collection, the library owns valuable collections which have been specially processed, including works from the 16th to the 19th centuries, concentrating on the 18th and 19th centuries. In more than 5,700 items, textbooks and literature from philosophy, history and justice prevail. Further, we find literary scholarship, bibliographies, dictionaries, pedagogy, linguistics, topography, natural sciences, military science, medicine, belles lettres and so on. Information on the collection can be obtained through the acquisition inventory and author and subject catalogue. Both collections are available for study on the premises.

THE CENTRAL LIBRARY OF THE FACULTY OF PHILOSOPHY OF COMENIUS UNIVERSITY
Ústredná knižnica Filozofickej fakulty Univerzity Komenského
Gondova 2, 818 01 Bratislava
Tel.: /07/ 304 111

One of the sections of the Central Library is the *Library of the History Department,* whose size (ca. 50,000 items) is among the largest ones. Its foundation in 1921 continued the collection of the previous Hungarian history seminary. The library built its collection with purchases and gifts of individuals (for example, Josef Fiedler, Gizela Wertnerová, Milan Hodža) as well as confiscations. The special collection of history and historiographical literature is accessible through an author catalogue and also, since 1990, a subject catalogue. The library collection was designed for and serves the needs of teachers and students. In addition to this collection, literature from other branches can be found in in the Central Library or departmental libraries.

Outside Bratislava, the mecca of research is Matica slovenská in Martin. Of other scholarly libraries, mention should be made of those in eastern Slovakia, including Prešov and Košice, and Banská Bystrica in central Slovakia.

MATICA SLOVENSKÁ – THE SLOVAK NATIONAL LIBRARY
Matica slovenská - Slovenská národná knižnica
Novomeského 32, 036 52 Martin
Tel.: /0842/ 313 71

This is the central acquisition, conservation and processing location for Slovakiana and other documents. The library is the owner and administrator of historical book collections from monasteries, schools, societies, individuals, nobelmen and so on. First mention should be made of the *Slovakiana Conservation Collection,* which is of national importance. Its peculiarity is the fact that it is not completed but is constantly added to. Its precious collection is predestined to be one of historical importance.

Among the rich historical collections are those of monastic libraries (ca. 650,000 items), including as Franciscan (Bratislava and Hlohovec), Piarist (Podolinec, Prievidza, Svätý Jur), Bratislava Jesuit and Capuchin, as well as Premonstrate of Jasov. Of the *school libraries,* special mention should be made of the Banská Bystrica College of Theology (ca. 7,000 items) and seminary library of the Spiš Chapter (ca. 33,000 items). The *libraries of societies* include those of the Malohont Society (40,000 items), Alliance Francaise (7,000 items) and Bratislava Typographer's Society (2,600 items). Among *nobelmen's libraries* are the Zay library (20,000 items), Oponický library (13,000), and the body of the Lontovský library (3,000). The library of Anton Augustín Baník (100, 000 items), Jozef Škultéty (5,000), Alice Masaryková (2,500), as well as smaller ones such as Milan Rastislav Štefánik's and Theo H. Florin's (each 300 items), are some of the *personal libraries.* A particular group is formed of specially preserved collections, including ca. 600 incunabulae[9] and prints from the sixteenth century.[10] Information on the collection is available through these catalogues:

(A) Readers' catalogues
Author's catalogue of books: information on books since 1800, the catalogue in development since 1927
Systematic catalogue of books since 1977
Subject catalogue of books since 1954
Subject catalogue of textbooks since 1977

---

[9] KOTVAN, Imrich - FRIMMOVÁ, Eva: Inkunábuly Slovenskej národnej knižnice v Martine. Martin, MS 1988.
[10] TLAČE 16. storočia vo fondoch Slovenskej národnej knižnice MS. Martin, MS 1993.

Catalogues of old imprints since 1800 (author, title, systematic, topographical, chronological, typographical, and artist)
Catalogues of special documents (phonograph records, postcards, book plates, microfilms)
(B) Service catalogues
General author catalogue since 1927
Systematic catalogue from 1800 to 1927
Systematic catalogue since 1977
Repository catalogue

Data on Slovak national production from a retrospective and continuous point of view are made available through the **National Bibliographical Institution** of the Slovak National Library, Matica slovenská. All works of Slovak national bibliography as well as important foreign bibliographies and other aids are available in the reading rooms of Matica slovenská.

THE STATE SCHOLARLY LIBRARY OF PREŠOV
Štátna vedecká knižnica Prešov
Hlavná 99, 081 37 Prešov
Tel.: /091/ 241 75

The library administers historic collections of the College and Diocese Libraries. The *College Library* is formed of the library of the Evangelical College, which was developed from the seventeenth century till 1918. It contains almost 50,000 items, including works from all sciences, and periodicals, semi-periodicals, manuscripts and around 1,000 imprints from the sixteenth century. From the book collections of benefactors as a closed unit, are the Ján Szirmay library (more than 15,000 items) and the Karol Binder library (1,500 items), which contains a valuable regional collection on Prešov and Šariš. The basic aid for orientation is the author card catalogue. Older systematic catalogues were preserved from the Binder collection and the library of the Evangelical College. A partial inventory has been published.[11]

The *Diocesan Library* was founded at the beginning of the nineteenth century and was developed till 1945. Among the roughly 25,000 items, half are theological literature, thirty percent literary scholarship, and the rest from other disciplines. It contains some incunabulae, and the works of some of the Ruthe-

---

[11] KOLODZIEJSKÝ, Ladislav: Katalóg slovacikálnych kníh do roku 1918 kolegiálnej knižnice v Prešove. Martin, MS 1969.

nien and/or Ukrainian figures who were active in eastern Slovakia. The catalogues of the librarians from the nineteenth century were preserved, of which the most valuable is Lacko's catalogue, *Diarium*.

THE STATE SCHOLARLY LIBRARY OF KOŠICE
Štátna vedecká knižnica Košice
Hlavná 10, 042 30 Košice
Tel.: /095/ 622 27 89, 622 27 80

The library took over most of the collection of the library of the Academy of Justice, which was founded in the seventeenth century and active until 1922. The collection contains imprints from the sixteenth century (more than 400), from the seventeenth century (more than 1200), and almost 3000 imprints from the eighteenth century. In the collection of roughly 30,000 items theological literature is richly represented, with other branches of the social sciences, with emphasis on justice and history. Texts from the sixteenth century are catalogued thematically in twenty-three groups. Separate groups include incunabulae and antique Hungariana designated Régi magyar könyvtár. In 1914 the author and subject catalogue was published, and from 1914 to 1917 it was added to with notebooks of annual acquisitions.

THE STATE SCHOLARLY LIBRARY OF BANSKÁ BYSTRICA
Štátna vedecká knižnica Banská Bystrica
Lazovná 9, 975 58 Banská Bystrica
Tel.: /088/ 548 41

The library today owns only a part of its original historical collection, parts of which were distributed to other institutions (museums and archives) in the 1950s. The historical collection of almost 1,000 volumes contains part of the collection of the Banská Bystrica Evangelical Gymnasium, First Girls Gymnasium (mostly textbooks and belles lettres), and a gift of the town of Lučenec, which contains texts from almost all disciplines. The library complements these historical collections with individually acquired items, with orientation towards Banská Bystrica imprints. The collection concentrates on literature from 1690 to 1919. The inventory of the historical collection is in manuscript (compiled by Terézia Uherková).

Libraries in Archives

Basic archival and historical texts (books and periodicals) are expert guides of different extent. Books of a given period are in archives in smaller files, ranging from dozens of volumes to 10, 000. They can be peculiar collections or large, independent libraries. We would like to stress some of the different varieties.

In Bratislava it is necessary to mention two:

THE SLOVAK NATIONAL ARCHIVE
Slovenský národný archív
Drotárska 42, 817 01 Bratislava
Tel.: /07/ 311 321, 311 300, 311 362

In this archive we can find the larger part of the *Bratislava Chapter Library* (the smaller is in the parish house by the St. Martin's Cathedral). The collection, whose development can be traced from the thirteenth century, contains more than 3,000 items, including, in seventeen thematic groups, more than 140 manuscripts, seventy-eight incunabula, and more than 600 imprints from the sixtennth century. In the collections are liturgical books, commentaries on evangelia, manuals for priests, polemical tracts mostly from the period of the Counter-Reformation, theological literature, and material from geography, poetics, rhetoric, economics, medicine, history and justice, as well as annuals, dictionaries, and so on.

Information on the collection is available from the card catalogue and inventory books. A catalogue of incunabula was published independently.[12]

THE ARCHIVE OF THE CAPITAL
OF THE SLOVAK REPUBLIC BRATISLAVA
Archív hlavného mesta Slovenskej Republiky Bratislavy
Radničná 1, 815 91 Bratislava
Tel.: /07/ 356 464, 333 248

One department of this archive is the *Regional Library,* which has today more than 90,000 items. In its development, it went through many organizational

---

[12] KOTVAN, Imrich: Inkunábuly kapitulnej knižnice v Bratislave. Bratislava, UK 1959.

changes, but it has retained its character as a scholarly library. The most precious part of the collection is made up of more than fifty incunabula and 2,000 antique imprints to 1800, as well as a quite complete collection of items relating to Bratislava (*Posoniensia*).

Since 1965, the library has had the right to an obligatory copy of every newspaper and magazine produced in Bratislava. In this way the development of a regional bibliography started, which became the basis of the *Cultural, Political and Historical Calendar of the City of Bratislava,* published till 1986. In addition, a number of bibliographies connected with the town were created. Part of the regional bibliography is the dictionary of personalities connected with the town and sister cities of Bratislava.

Detailed information on the collection is available through acquisition inventories (on the same system since 1928) and catalogues. Since 1945 the new catalogue has been developed, adding to the old catalogue information on literature published till 1945. A catalogue of incunabulae has been published independently.[13]

From the regional archives we choose Levoča and Kremnica.

THE STATE REGIONAL ARCHIVE OF LEVOČA
Štátny oblastný archív Levoča
Námestie Majstra Pavla 60, 054 01 Levoča
Tel.: /0966/ 2486, 2424

The book collection of the archive reflects its development. The library was founded by fusion of the libraries of three archives. It is characterized by an orientation on the Spiš region. The library acquired not only parts of nobelmen's libraries, but also that of the Spiš History Society, of the Pedagogical School, professors' library of the Gymnasium, and other institutions and libraries of Spiš inhabitants. The library has a collection of about 40,000 items, of which more than half have been processed and are accessible. The collection is divided into thirteen groups: history, justice, economics, geography and travel books, natural sciences, linguistics, mathematics and geometry, schools and pedagogy, philosophy, military science, religion and so on. The collection processed so far contains dozens of books from the sixteenth and seventeenth centuries, and more

---

[13] KOTVAN, Imrich: Katalóg prvotlačí Vedeckej knižnice mesta Bratislavy. Bratislava, UK 1956.

than 300 from the eighteenth century. Most are from the nineteenth century. The most important part contains literature on Spiš (*Scepunsensia*), with more than 1,100 items. Orientation to the collections is through author and subject catalogues.

THE STATE DISTRICT ARCHIVE OF ŽIAR NAD HRONOM
Štátny okresný archív Žiar nad Hronom
Námestie 1. mája 4/7, 976 01 Kremnica
Tel.: /0857/ 925 508

The study library was built together with the city archive. It also contains historical book collections. In eddition to estate purchases of partial collections already in the eighteenth century, the *Franciscan library,* which contains around 7,000 items from the fourteenth to twentieth century, is an important part. In the collection are precious manuscript codices, incunabula, Slovakiana, etc. More detailed information is available through the two original catalogues (1859 and 1889) and newer card inventory. A further part of the collection is the *library from the Roman Catholic parish,* which is ordered chronologically. It contains 1,500 volumes, from the fifteenth to the twentieth century: not only liturgical literature, but books from older Slovak historiography and linguistics. There are also twenty-six medieval codices and incunabula.

Orientation is from the card catalogue. An inventory of the valuable collection has been published.[14]

Libraries in Museums

Libraries in the bigger museums contain collections for study with basic historical museological literature, books and periodicals. Besides these, they collect historical book collections of varying size and completeness. According to statistical reports of the Slovak National Museum, about 1,000 volumes each are in Kežmarok, Košice and Banská Bystrica.

The book collections of the following museums deserve closer attention.

---

[14] KOTVAN, Imrich: Inkunábuly knižníc mesta Kremnice. Martin, MS 1959.

THE ORAVA MUSEUM OF PAVOL ORSZÁGH HVIEZDOSLAV – ČAPLOVIČ LIBRARY

Oravské múzeum Pavla Országha Hviezdoslava - Čaplovičova knižnica
Hviezdoslavovo námestie 7, 026 01 Dolný Kubín
Tel.: /0845/ 2056

The Čaplovič Library is an independent department of the museum. A valuable historical collection (ca. 20,000 items) was given in 1839 to the Orava County by Vavrinec Čaplovič, one of the important book collectors of the nineteenth century. The collection was expanded by the founder till his death, whereupon other librarians continued his work. Today the collection has 84,000 items and is organized into twelve groups: dictionaries, bibliographies, history, geography, sociology, theology, law, linguistics, belles lettres, mathematics, natural sciences, art and review. A separate group contains the most valuable books (R) and manuscripts from the fifteenth to the nineteenth century (C).

A seven-volume inventory, eight-volume list of acquisitions, and author card catalogue provide information on the collection. Two catalogues have been published.[15]

PODTATRANSKÉ MUSEUM

Vajanského 72/4, 058 01 Poprad
Tel.: /092/ 322 75

The historical book collection consists largely of the library of the Hungarian Carpathian Society and part of the former Tatra Museum, as well as fragments from the collections of the region's inhabitants. The collection contains more than 10,000 items, among which texts of natural science, ethnography and history, and maps and travel books prevail. Most of the books are from the nineteenth century, some from the seventeenth and eighteenth centuries, and some imprints and manuscripts are from the sixteenth century.

The list of acquisitions provides a guide to the collection. Author and systematic catalogues are being developed.

---

[15] KOTVAN, Imrich: Inkunábuly Čaplovičovej knižnice v Dolnom Kubíne. Bratislava, UK 1960.; SMETANA, Ján - TELGÁRSKY, Jozef: Katalóg tlačí 16. storočia v Dolnom Kubíne. Martin, MS 1981.

THE SLOVAK MINING MUSEUM
Slovenské banské múzeum
Kammerhofská 2, 069 00 Banská Štiavnica
Tel.: /0589/ 215 41-2, 215 44

A part of the collection is the *Lyceum Library,* which is the property of the Evangelical Church. This library was assembled mostly from the gifts of individuals and the scholarly and cultural institutions of Hungary. It comprises roughly 20,000 items from theology, philosophy, linguistics, the natural sciences and history, as well as belles lettres. Of interest is the collection of journals and annual reports of the secondary schools of Hungary. The library was divided into sections for professors and students.

Information on the collection is provided by incomplete inventories. The real situation of the collection will be apparent after revision and reprocessing.

THE TRENČÍN MUSEUM
Trenčianske múzeum
Mierová 46, 911 01 Trenčín
Tel.: /0831/ 355 89, 344 31 - 3

The museum owns parts of historical libraries. The most distinctive collection is the *Library of the Natural Science Society of Trenčín County* (more than 2,000 volumes, currently being processed). Also being catalogued is the *Zamarovský library* (ca. 4,000 items), which contains literature from the natural and social sciences, and travel books of the eighteenth century. Most important is the law literature. A small collection from the library of the Trenčín Evangelical Seniorate contains Protestant theological literature from the seventeenth to the twentieth century. In addition to these, the museum has made valuable acquisitions from heirs of figures active in the region (J. Holák, M. Bibza).

THE WEST SLOVAKIA MUSEUM
Západoslovenské múzeum
Múzejné námestie 3, 918 09 Trnava
Tel.: /0805/ 255 25, 255 26

The basis of the historical collection contains part of the Archbishop's Gymnasium library in Trnava and part of the library of the Trnava Jesuit monastery.

More than 46,000 items are organized chronologically from the sixteenth to the twentieth century, while items of Trnava interest (*Tyrnaviensia*) and Slovakiana are separate, as well as maps and undated volumes. The collection contains imprints from all branches of science, technology and the arts. The state of processing is not satisfactory, two efforts to catalogue having been interrupted. From the processed portion, an author catalogue is available. Several inventories give more detailed information about the collection.[16]

Important among historical collections are those in castles. Of larger ones we should mention Červený Kameň, Antol (part of the Coburg library), and above all two nearly complete libraries in Betliar and Topoľčianky.

THE CHATEAU AT BETLIAR

Kaštieľ v Betliari
Kaštieľska 6, 049 21 Betliar
Tel.: /0942/ 831 18, 831 95

The historical library is part of the house's inventory, and contains more than 14,000 items from the fifteenth to the twentieth century. Among them are texts of history, philosophy, law, theology, the natural sciences and medicine, as well as encyclopaedias and belles lettres. The collection is not specially organized. Part of the library is made up of manuscripts of the eighteenth and nineteenth century, and annual reports of Hungarian, Slovak, and some Czech and German gymnasia (1850-1950), which form a special collection.

The collection is introduced by acquisition inventories, and for the 3,000 processed items there is an author and title card catalogue.

THE CHATAEU AT TOPOEČIANKY

Kaštieľ v Topoľčiankach
951 93 Topoľčianky, Zámok
Tel.: /0814/ 811 11

---

[16] RADVÁNI, Hadrián: Inkunábuly a tlače 16. storočia vo fondoch Západoslovenského múzea v Trnave. Trnava, Západoslovenské múzeum 1984; RADVÁNI, Hadrián - MINAROVÝCH, Jozef: Súpis kníh územných a rečových slovacík (okrem trnavských tlačí a vydaní). Trnava, Západoslovenské múzeum 1983; MINAROVÝCH, Jozef - HRUŠOVSKÁ, Viera - RADVÁNI, Hadrián: Súpis kníh XVII. storočia (okrem územných a rečových slovacík). Trnava, Západoslovenské múzeum 1984.

The historical library is located in its original rooms. It has 14,000 items, which are thematically arranged: encyclopaedias, theology, philosophy, history, pedagogy, geography, economics, the natural sciences, law, medicine, classical literature, poetry, art, periodicals and miscellany. In addition, the library contains manuscripts, letters and pictures. According to inventories, it includes texts from the fifteenth to the twentieth century.

Information on the collection is available from a two-volume catalogue and an alphabaet card catalogue from 1913, which are not very precise.

Besides the above mentioned historical libraries, large collections are also owned by the Literary and Musical Museum in Banská Bystrica and the Literary and Historical Museum of Janko Kráľ in Liptovský Mikuláš.

Ecclesiastical Libraries

In this section we will introduce two large and interesting libraries directly under ecclesiastical administration. Other libraries owned by churches but under the administration of other institutions are mentioned under the appropriate organizations (libraries and museums).

THE DIOCESAN LIBRARY IN NITRA
Diecézna knižnica v Nitre
Pribinovo námestie 14, 949 01 Nitra
Tel.: /087/ 419 003

Till 1990, the Library was administered by the District Library in Nitra. The collection of the library has more than 65,000 items from the fifteenth to the twentieth centuries, concerning mostly theological literature. Roughly a third is lay literature from history, philosophy, law, pedagogy, linguistics, the natural sciences, medicine, agriculture and art, with periodicals. The orientation aid is the acquisition inventory and a card catalogue. Precious parts of the collection are incunabula, an inventory of which has been published,[17] and imprints from the sixteenth century (more than 1,200 items).

---

[17] KOTVAN, Imrich: Inkunábuly v Nitre. Nitra, Okresné múzeum 1963.

THE LYCEUM LIBRARY IN KEŽMAROK
Lyceálna knižnica v Kežmarku
Hviezdoslavova 2, 060 01 Kežmarok
Tel.: /0969/ 2242, 2618

The library is owned by the Evangelical Church in Kežmarok. The basis of the library was learning and teaching aids for pupils and teachers. At first it was developed from the gifts of professors and pupils; later the libraries of Evangelical schools and societies were added; and in the nineteenth and twentieth centuries, the collection was supplemented by purchase. The collection has 150,000 items, which include books, manuscripts and journals.

The Book Collection: This contains fifty-three incunabula, 3,000 imprints from the sixteenth century, around 7,000 items of Slovakiana, and other literature. The oldest texts deal with philosophy, history, law and theology, to which the natural sciences, medicine, geography, textbooks and belles lettres were added in the sixteenth century. In the later period, the collection was enriched above all by the broad scale of natural scientific literature, sociology, pedagogy, economics, biography and agriculture.

The Manuscript Collection: This has more than 2,600 items, which include documents having to do with the activities of Evangelical schools, the history of the Evangelical Church in Slovakia, literary work of the teachers and pupils of the Lyceum, activities of Kežmarok societies, and a variety of compendia.

The Periodical Collection: This contains 1,200 titles of journals, with exceptionally valuable collections of annual reports from Hungary, Bohemia and Austria, as well as a rich collection of Spiš regional newspapers and journals. The collection can be accessed through an alphabetical card catalogue, with the manuscript collection through an independent card catalogue. The rich collection of the library appears in several inventories from the end of the nineteenth century. An inventory of incunabula has been published separately.[18]

---

[18] KOTVAN, Imrich: Inkunábuly Lyceálnej knižnice v Kežmarku. Bratislava, UK 1959.

MUSEUMS

In this article I employ the definition of the museum from the statutes of the International Council of Museums (ICOM):

"A Museum is a non-profit making, permanent institution in the service of society and of its development, and open to the public which acquires, conserves, researches, communicates and exhibits, for purposes of study, education and enjoyment, material evidence of people and their environment. The above definition of a museum shall be applied without any limitation arising from the nature of the governing body, the territorial character, the functional structure or the orientation of the collections of the institution concerned. "

I must stress that this definition from ICOM concerns institutions open to the public. Therefore, the history of noble and private collecting or the collections of learned societies and schools, which have a rich tradition in Slovakia but which are not open to the public will not be considered. Only those museums which directly or indirectly serves historiography or the dissemination of historical knowledge are included and therefore specialized natural history museums and collections are not treated, even if they have recently attracted the attention of historians as a source of knowledge about the environment and the economic activity of man.

In the nineteenth century, Slovakia was a region of collecting interest for the great museums of the capitals of the monarchy: Vienna, Budapest and, from the end of the nineteenth century, especially in the field of ethnography, Prague. Even after the foundation of museums in Slovakia in the 1860s and 1870s, the ebb of precious material continued not only through purchases by foreign antiquarians, but also to the big museums, mostly in Budapest, where most of the gifts and bequests by noble families and collectors were aimed. These central museums were in the vanguard of the time, including specialization, financing and prestige. Even now, the National Museum in Budapest has the finest collection of Gothic art from Slovak territory.

The social atmosphere in Hungary in the second half of the nineteenth century was filtered through history. Hungary searched in history for recourse against Vienna; the declining aristocracy and nobility found in the past justifications against the new social classes; and the bourgeoisie searched for its self-confidence in the rich history of medieval towns.

Among large museums continuously active to the present, the museum in Bratislava was founded in 1868 and that in Košice in 1872, and up till the First World War another score were established. Museums established regional homeland societies, and a frequent inspiration in Slovakia was the well known German institutions of the Heimatmuseum. Sometimes the foundation of the museum collection was material brought together for municipal and county exhibitions about the past and present of the region. In some cases (Kremnica, Zlaté Moravce, Trnava and Šahy) the core was from items stored in the municipal archives: flags, stamps and documents. Only in two cases (Oravský Podzámok and Krásna Hôrka) were the museums founded by the opening of older collections of a noble family.

The typical regional museum in Slovakia, up to the first half of the twentieth century, not only had objects of material culture but a specialized library open to the public and also archival documents. Libraries varied in scale, from 1,107 volumes in Banská Bystrica up to 23,145 volumes in Košice in 1908. Collections of archival documents were also rich, the museum at Bardejov maintaining 5,612 charters from the fourteenth to the sixteenth century, and that in Košice 4,000. Collections of material culture, works of art, libraries and many archival documents made the museum a center of regional research, a function it performs to the present. Regional historical societies, normally located in towns, also published annuals (Košice, Spiš, Trenčín and Komárno). They published contributions on local history, selection of documents from local archives and extracts of documents from central archives important for local historians.

The museums only occasionally had a professional specialized staff and were usually administered by teachers at the gymnasium, amateur historians and natural historians, archaeologists and ethnographers. Specialized guidance, instructions and a certain amount of financial support from the government was given through the National Inspectorate of Museums in Budapest.

Richer and larger museums tried to adjust to the models their staff knew from travel and literature. At the opening of the exhibition in Košice, it was stated that the museum was organized in the manner "not only used in many museums of Vienna, Munich, and Nuremberg but also Italy".

Many museums ceased to exist after some years. Before World War I, only eighteen continued their regular activity. Annually, these were visited by approximately 60,000 people.

Museums in Hungary, as in the case of culture and education as a whole, were not only tools of knowledge but also of state politics. Objects expressing the idea of a united Magyar political nation and the struggle for independence of Hungary from the Habsburgs, were emphasized: archaeological finds pertaining to "the possession of the homeland" by the Magyars, and documents from the revolt of estates in the seventeenth and eighteenth centuries and from the revolution of 1848-1849. In collecting items, museums concentrated on the histories of noble families and towns, completely ignoring their peasant, mostly Slovak environment. Even at the turn of the century, after the influence of Scandinavian museums in Europe made ethnographic research and documentation the fashion, almost nothing changed. The exception was the Slovak-oriented museum in Martin.

The first museum in Turčiansky Svätý Martin (present-day Martin) was created as a function of the Slovak cultural, scientific and educational institution, the *Matica slovenská*, founded in 1863. Besides works of art, archaeological finds, coins, stamps and so on, from the beginning the museum also collected ethnographic material and records of the Slovak folk way of life. This was the logical result not only of the structure of Slovak society but also the prevailing orientation of its politics. The exhibition of the museum was opened in 1870, but already by 1875, government officials had abolished the Matica slovenská and confiscated the library and museum collection.

In Martin in 1893 the *Slovak Museum Society* was founded as an institution of the Slovak people. In modest conditions it had to carry out the same tasks as the Hungarian National Museum in Budapest, founded in 1802, and the National Museum in Prague, founded in 1818. The president of the society was Andrej Kmeť, a priest, amateur archaeologist, historian, ethnographer and very active botanist, who is considered to be the father of Slovak museology. He is also the namesake of the prize for outstanding museum professional work in Slovakia.

By 1918 the museum in Martin had its own building, more than 21,000 items and 70,000 manuscripts and books. *Zborník Muzeálnej slovenskej spoločnosti* (The Annals of the Slovak Museum Society) was at that time the only scholarly publication in Slovak. The Museum Society, as one of only a few Slovak associations accepted by the government, transcended the common role of a museum.

The dismantling of the Hungarian Empire and foundation of Czechoslovakia in 1918 was a landmark in the development of Slovak museums. Direct military damage in museums was small, but the departing Hungarian administration in museums took with them parts of collections, sometimes very precious ones. From Košice they took 80% of the more valuable objects, among them four Gothic wing altars. From the mint in Kremnica, in operation since 1324, they took the numismatic collection, and also from Banská Štiavnica they removed valuable items. The activity of many museums was paralyzed by political changes in the leadership of towns and in the state administration. With the abolition of traditional counties, some of the museums lost their superstructure and their protection. Gradually, nearly all pre-War museums resumed functioning, and until 1938, six museums have been founded.

The museum in Martin, labelled as unpatriotic during Hungarian rule, became the *Slovak National Museum*. Within its framework the Slovak National Archive was also founded, and in 1932 the Slovak National Gallery was installed in a magnificent new building. In the mid-thirties the museum in Martin also tried to install a sizable exhibition of Slovak history. It was professionally and methodologically a very difficult project, because here for the first time was to be portrayed the continuous history of the land from earliest times to the present. Nothing similar had existed till that time, even in "written history". The project required discussion about the history of Slovakia, and the history of the state in relation to the national group and society. It had to resolve the problem with which Slovak historiography had already been struggling some dozen years earlier: How to free the history of Slovakia from absorption in Hungarian and later Czecho-Slovak history? By the time of the Second World War, only part of the exhibition had been installed.

In addition to the museum in Martin, which took on the role of a national museum, in 1924 interested parties started the *Homeland Museum* (Vlastivedné múzeum) in Bratislava. It had in its program museum methods for documenting the culture and history of all Slovakia. In Bratislava, the new, rapidly growing capital of Slovakia, a *Museum of Agriculture* (Zemedelské múzeum) and *Museum of Forestry* (Lesnícke múzeum) were founded. With the support of the preeminent agrarian party, they built a mighty building on the Danube banks, where the Homeland Museum also gained quarters. The Agriculture and Forestry Museums were of technical character, but they also had strong historical divisions. A similar specialized museum for mining was founded in Banská Štiavnica.

The Second World War brought changes in the work and goals of museums, depending on whether they were, between 1939 and 1945 on the territory of the independent Slovak Republic or that occupied by Hungary. The Homeland, Agricultural and Forestry Museums in Bratislava, connected with the previous Czechoslovakia, were merged into one institution, the *Slovak Museum*. However, this didn't solve the existing quarrel with the museum in Martin over primacy; on the contrary, it sharpened it. A newly-founded interest organization, the Union of Slovak Museums, tried to demarcate their roles, so that the museum in Martin was that of the "whole nation," and the museum in Bratislava that of the "whole state". This development draws attention to a crucial problem of Slovak history and politics, the relation between citizen, nation (ethnicity) and state, which could no longer be taken for granted.

In 1944 both institutions were caught up in the mill of war. The Bratislava museum was heavily damaged by air bombardment, and the museum in Martin was damaged some weeks later by German artillery trying to suppress the Slovak National Uprising.

In the first post-war years, after repairing the damage, the museums continued their work without very significant changes. Rapid and radical change began only after February 1948, when the Communist Party began to rule.

By Act No. 12 in 1948, the Slovak Museum in Bratislava and Slovak National Museum in Martin were nationalized and gradually thereafter all other museums. Until then, all had belonged to towns, societies or the church. Museum societies gradually declined and in 1960 even the Slovak Museum Society, one of the pillars of Slovak tradition, was abolished. Up till 1990, museums and their employees had no special organization that could be a partner or opponent of the sole owner of museums, the state.

From 1948 to 1989, the museums underwent great changes, the most significant of which were:

1. growth in size and numbers;
2. biased, centralized ideological orientation;
3. strengthening as centers of regional historical research;
4. growth of specialized museums; and
5. concentration of collecting and research activities on objects of material culture.

In 1948, forty-eight museums were active, and by 1970 their number had grown to eighty, with sixty-eight branches. The number of visitors in 1947 was 92,196, and in the seventies it had reach 3.5 million (Slovakia having a population of five million). In 1945, the museums had forty-five permanent staff, and in 1971 they already had 1,143, among whom were 272 with university education. In addition, the collection and exhibition space multiplied. Several modern museum buildings were built, but primarily monasteries, castles and historical buildings were reconstructed for museum needs. Sometimes the reconstruction was extensive, for example the restoration of Bratislava Castle, which had stood as a ruin for more than 150 years after a fire. In 1961 the act on museums and galleries was passed by the Slovak National Council, and the nationalization of museums was completed. The law stressed the function of museums in the imposition of ruling ideology and state politics, but fortunately it also stressed the scientific function of museums, by which to acertain extent they were preserved from total degradation as tools of propaganda.

Museum were under political pressure also before 1918, between the wars, and during the Second World War, above all through financing and the participation of representatives of political parties and the state in museum societies.

After 1948, the museums were openly placed in the role of propagaters of the official ideology and concept of history, with emphasis on the revolutionary traditions, the workers' movement, and above all the Communist Party. Understanding of the purpose of museum exhibition was shifted from education to indoctrination. Before, the visitor was assumed to possess the basic school knowledge of history, which was then enlivened, supplemented and enriched by aesthetic experience. According to the new understanding, the museum was a place for the visitor to learn history in its new pseudo-Marxist form. The fulfillment of this task became the basic criterion for judging the work of museums by party and state organs.

The tendency of the regime for simple, stereotyped, and easily centrally-controlled schemes led to the strict adjustment of museums to the territorial organization of the state. First among these were museums whose activities spread nationally, controlled directly from the center by the ministry of culture or other central organs. The second group consisted of regional museums, controlled on this level (after 1960 each of the regions having approximately 1.5 million inhabitants). Then there were the museums of districts, each area comprising about 150,000 people. In some districts there were more museums than in others, usually having been founded earlier. A typical district homeland museum employed ten to thirty people, among whom were two to three natural historians, and four to five historians, archaeologists or ethnographers. Regional museums had as many as 100 employees, among whom twenty to thirty would be university educated.

The museums were fully dependent on state funding, relinquishing all income and receiving money from the state administration through the given region or district, or through the ministry for central museums. At the same time, they were also subject to the party organs of the given area. Permanent exhibitions and the larger temporary exhibitions were approved through the regional or district ideological commissions, or in the case of central museums, directly from the commission of the Central Committee of the Communist Party. Party and state organs often used museums as a political service in different jubilees, elections and political campaigns. Exhibitions of revolutionary traditions, which from the mid-seventies all homeland museums were obliged to install, served as the historical stamp of political power.

The strictly zoned division of museums supported their function as regional centres of research. Regional and stronger district museums published proceedings, annuals, and monographs on cities, towns and villages. Together with exhibition catalogues and inventories of museums on Slovak territory and abroad, these are an important part of historical literature.

The nationalization of museums, their collections, buildings and employees created the conditions for changes in museums' goals, collecting regions, and even the collections themselves. In 1961 the Slovak National Museum was joined with its old rival, the Slovak Museum in Bratislava, and specialized as a museum of ethnography. The museum in Bratislava took the traditional name of Slovak National Museum, as well as taking part of the collection in Martin. By Act No. 24 in 1949, the Slovak National Gallery was established in Bratislava, where the majority of the works of art in the Slovak Museum in Martin were transferred. Gradually a network of regional galleries was created, to which the museums of the given region had to hand over their works of art. But because these museums needed such objects for their exhibitions, and because the boundaries between universal museums and museums of art was ambiguous, after some time many of them again created extensive collections, mostly of small and applied graphic art, other applied art, naive art, and so on.

An important feature of post-war development was specialization of museums. The agricultural museum in Nitra and the forestry museum in Zvolen were reopened, and the collection of the *Mining Museum* in Banská Štiavnica was broadened. Already by 1947, the *Technical Museum* in Košice was founded. The older museums had to hand over part of their collections to the specialized museums. In addition to many literary historical museums, the *Museum of Schools and Teaching,* the *Museum of Physical Culture* and the *Museum of Coins and Medals* were established.

An interesting attempt–possible only in a political system controlling the entire economy and whole social life–was Governmental Decree No. 200 from 1981, allowing the network of specialized museums to be broadened. The decree also ordered all economic organizations, state institutions, societies and so on to collect and document the material objects of their activity, and in the same way documents were collected in the state archival network. Industrial firms, agricultural cooperatives and athletic clubs could choose either to establish their own museum or "memorial chamber," or subsequent to an agreement with some museum, they could collect and store in it products, models, typical tools, insignia, flags, plans and photographic and audio documentation. The first possibility enabled the establishment of the *Museum of Trade* in Bratislava and the *Museum of the Glass Industry* in Lednické Rovne. The second helped broaden the collections in the history of paper-making in Ružomberok, of fruit cultivation and brewing in Topoľčany, and so on. After 1989, this decree was forgotten.

Special groups created museums from the beginning, concentrating on promoting state ideology and its view of history, for example the *Lenin Museum* in

Bratislava, the *Museum of the Communist Press,* memorial exhibitions on the sites of important moments in the history of the Communist Party (in Ľubochňa, Prešov and Košice). Usually these were not complete museums with original collections. An exception is the museum established on the site of the battle of 1944 in the Dukla Pass in the Carpathians where, besides the traditional museum with an exhibition, there is a reconstruction of the battlefield. In the *Museum of the Slovak National Uprising* in Banská Bystrica, objects from the anti-fascist resistance and its culmination in the 1944 uprising are collected.

A peculiar phenomenon on the margin of museum activity was the establishment of several hundred "memorial chambers" and "halls of revolutionary traditions" in schools, factories, cooperative farms, barracks and administration buildings. Usually these were only improvised, though in some cases the local cultural employees used the money and space for the establishment of a small museum of the village or factory, with a good collection of original historical items.

Even in the continuing specialization, the homeland museum always prevailed, in an effort at the complex documentation of nature, history, ethnography and culture in a given region. From sixty public museums controlled at the end of the eighties by the Central Administration of Museums and Galleries, we can identify forty-two of this type. In the eighties they had ceased to collect archival material, documents and manuscripts. Governmental order No. 29 from 1954 made official the so-called unified state archival collection at the head of the central archive and regional and district archives. Archival collections of museums were gradually moved to this network, and only a few received the right to establish a so-called "special archive". In a similar way was established the hierarchically constructed network of libraries, to which came many book collections of the museums.

The "clearing" of many museums of archival documents, libraries and works of art, diverted their attention to material evidence of history, culture and way of life. On the other hand, the divide between museums and the historians working in the Academy of Sciences, archives and universities was deepened.

For the themes of interest in Slovak historiography before 1948 (that is, above all, the building of the nation, the national revival, and the defence of the language, culture and national identity), largely only written documentation was available. Similarly, the focus on the Slovak version of Marxism in historiography after 1948, "the history of the People," and "revolutionary traditions," did not lead historians to museum collections. Historians were not interested in how "the People," or the working class, lived, but mostly in their political actions: strikes, uprisings, demonstrations, the development of organizing.

For this, only written material existed, and it was concentrated in archives rather than museums. Copies and reproductions of archival materials, as well as written documents, leaflets and photographs, were the core of exhibitions of later history. Three-dimensional material was only illustrated.

Such an understanding of history shifted museums to a secondary role, to a siding. Often they were understood as educational centers, which presented the public with the results and conceptions of "true" historians in a specific way. A museum historian, if he wanted scholarly advancement and recognition, had to go not to his collections but to the archive. On the other hand, this under-valuation of museums created a certain amount of free space for them. Beyond the pale of ideological direction, but also outside of the interest of most of the historical world, museum workers could collect and process and from time to time publish artifacts and themes from the applied arts, numismatics, faleristics, vexicology, heraldry, iconography, military science, historical dress, ways of life, eating, crafts, transport, trade, catering, different non-political societies, and so on: that is, the themes in which "serious historiography" had little interest. To a certain extent, two parallel histories existed. The academic variety, dealing with the macrocosmic, didn't deal at all with the results of museum micro-history. This was most clearly expressed in the concise work of official histor-iography, The History of Slovakia, published by the History Institute of the Slovak Academy of Sciences in six volumes, 1986-1992.

The conflict between what the museum workers collected and the grey, official, textual exhibitions was great. That is why as its first action after the changes of 1989, the conference of museum workers from throughout Slovakia accepted the idea to "open the storerooms". In a short time, the ideologically motivated exhibitions without real historical value were removed, and even a few museums so oriented were closed. In temporary exhibitions, museums presented objects which before they could display only rarely or not at all: that is, sacred objects, artifacts of "bourgeois" or "nationalistic" organizations and "non-persons". The public was surprised by the rich contents of the storerooms, and the number and quality of the objects which finally were able to be displayed for their value, beauty and communicative ability, without the necessity for immersing them in the stream of ideological circumstances. The paradox is that the majority of these previously concealed objects were purchased, other-wise acquired or at any rate restored during the period when the opportunities for their display was extremely limited. In addition, some new museums were established. The Jewish Museum abolished during the war was replaced by a new *Museum of Jewish Culture* in Bratislava, continuing its tradition.

The years 1990-1991 were for Slovaks museum workers ones of a certain euphoria and great hopes. Fifty-one new permanent exhibitions were established, 1,182 temporary displays were organized, and in 1990, museums welcomed an unbelievable 3,892,204 visitors. A year later it was one million fewer. The crisis of the difficult restructuring of the economy and of the whole post-communist society reached the entire sphere of culture. Inflation gutted museum incomes by a third. Some museums by the restructuring of the state and economy lost their founders and financers. Regions were abolished, districts took over new functions, and some ministries that had supported successful museums were wound down. Large industrial concerns which had financed collecting activities of museums disintegrated. This is why the Ministry of Culture had to temporarily take under its wings not only national but regional institutions. Museums are having to find new sources of income in the unfavorable environment of a multi-year economic crisis.

The restitution of real estate seized after 1948 from cities, the church and individuals has been harshly felt. Of the nineteen museums involved, eight believe their existence threatened. These must return to their original owners buildings frequently and expensively reconstructed for exhibition and storage in late years. Many museums will lose the most attractive historical buildings, which they counted on using as sources of income from tourism, lease or catering in the new market economy.

Three organizations founded after 1989 struggle to overcome these problems: the Union of Museums in Slovakia and the Council of Galleries in Slovakia, together as the Union of Institutions, and the refounded Slovak Museum Society, serving as the interest group of museum workers. The concerns of museums' very existence has pushed to the background the transformation of the work of museums, and their placement in the mainstream of Slovak historiography.

I have spoken about a certain parallelism between the work of historians in museums and so-called academic historiography. It does not seem that the situation has changed. Slovak historiography after a half century of leadership under two dictatorships has been thrown unprepared into the free competition of ideas. In the years after the "Velvet Revolution," it has been devoured by the historical discussion of the subduing of totalitarianism, the support of national emancipation, and the building of a new state. More intensively than at any time before, it has been directed towards political and state history, and towards the history of institutions about which it could not speak before, such as the church. As for museum historiography, the loosening of ideological pressures has meant a greater orientation towards the original museum perception of history: research of ways of life as they are portrayed in material objects, pictures, recordings and other evidence. In this sense, museum historiography is more modern and complex than its parellel. However, it does not have the strength or authority to influence the mainstream of the Slovak perception of the past.

In 1991, from the sixty-one museums and their twenty-two branches from which it had received information, the Museological Information Center in Bratislava recorded a total of 6,472,587 scientifically inventoried objects and documents on the development of nature, man and society. Another 568,997 pieces have yet to be processed. The history of Slovak museums is not so long and rich as to hold out the same possibility as in other museums of the discovery of cultural treasures of epochal importance in a box in the cellar. Even so, the more than seven million known artifacts is a rich research base. Its scholarly and de-ideologicized processing and integration in the interpretation of historical events might not change substantially but it certainly could make more accurate and human our picture of Slovakia.

The most important museums and museum organizations*

THE SLOVAK NATIONAL MUSEUM, BRATISLAVA
Slovenské národné múzeum
814 36 Bratislava, Vajanského nábrežie 2
Tel.: /07/ 333 986, 330 479
Fax: /07/ 335 471

The Slovak National Museum (SNM) includes:
The Museum of Archaelogy SNM
The Museum of History SNM
The Museum of Jewish Culture in Slovakia
The Music Museum SNM
The Natural History Museum SNM
The Ethnography Museum, Martin
The Museum of the Slovak National Council, Myjava

---

* The new publication, available in Slovak, German and English, gives basic information concerning addresses, concentrations and opening hours of museums:
SLOVAKIA. MUSEUMS AND GALLERIES GUIDE-BOOK. Edited by Ilja Okáli and Gabriela Podušelová. Bratislava, Slovak National Museum 1994.

The main regional museums

THE CENTRAL SLOVAKIA MUSEUM, BANSKÁ BYSTRICA
Stredoslovenské múzeum
975 90 Banská Bystrica, Námestie SNP 4
Tel.: /088/ 249 38
Fax: /088/ 542 92

THE EAST SLOVAKIA MUSEUM, KOŠICE
Východoslovenské múzeum
041 36 Košice, Hviezdoslavova 3
Tel.: /095/ 62 203 09
Fax: /095/ 62 286 96

THE WEST SLOVAKIA MUSEUM, TRNAVA
Západoslovenské múzeum
918 08 Trnava, Múzejné námestie 3
Tel.: /0805/ 255 25, 255 26
Fax: /0805/ 275 85

THE MUNICIPAL MUSEUM, BRATISLAVA
Mestské múzeum Bratislava
815 18 Bratislava, Primaciálne námestie 3
Tel.: /07/ 334 742
Fax: /07/ 334 631

The main specialized museums and galleries

THE SLOVAK NATIONAL GALLERY, BRATISLAVA
Slovenská národná galéria
815 13 Bratislava, Riečna 1
Tel.: /07/ 330 746, 332 081
Fax: /07/ 333 971

THE MUSEUM OF THE SLOVAK NATIONAL UPRISING, BANSKÁ BYSTRICA

Múzeum Slovenského národného povstania
975 59 Banská Bystrica, Kapitulská 23
Tel.: /088/ 232 59, 257 81
Fax: /088/ 237 16

THE SLOVAK MINING MUSEUM, BANSKÁ ŠTIAVNICA

Slovenské banské múzeum
969 42 Banská Štiavnica, Kammerhofská 2
Tel.: /0859/ 215 41, 215 52
Fax: /0859/ 227 64

THE SLOVAK AGRICULTURAL MUSEUM, NITRA

Slovenské poľnohospodárske múzeum
950 50 Nitra, Dlhá ulica 9
Tel.: /087/ 366 47

THE SLOVAK TECHNOLOGY MUSEUM, KOŠICE

Slovenské technické múzeum
043 82 Košice, Hlavná ulica 88
Tel.: /095/ 240 35, 240 36
Fax: /095/ 259 65

Information Centers and Organizations

THE MUSEUM INFORMATION CENTER

Muzeologické informačné centrum
814 36 Bratislava, Vajanského nábrežie 2
Tel. Fax: /07/ 335 471

THE SLOVAK MUSEUMS UNION

Zväz slovenských múzeí
974 00 Banská Bystrica, Kapitulská 23
Tel.: /088/ 232 59
Fax: /088/ 237 16

THE SLOVAK MUSEUM SOCIETY
Muzeálna slovenská spoločnosť
Sekretariát. Etnografické múzeum SNM
036 80 Martin, Malá Hora
Tel.: /0842/ 310 11
Fax: /0842/ 324 57

THE HERITAGE INSTITUTE
Pamiatkový ústav
813 14 Bratislava, Cesta na Červený most 6
Tel.: /07/ 374 444
Fax: /07/ 375 844

LIST OF ABBREVIATIONS USED

AS MV	Archívna správa Ministerstva vnútra
ČSAV	Československá akadémie věd
ČSČH	Československý časopis historický
HČ	Historický časopis
HŠt	Historické štúdie
HÚ	Historický ústav
MS	Matica slovenská
SAP	Slovak Academic Press
SAS	Slovenská archívna správa
SAV	Slovenská akadémia vied
SAVU	Slovenská akadémia vied a umení
Sb FFUK	Sborník Filozofickej fakulty Univerzity Komenského
SHS	Studia historica Slovaca
SlArch	Slovenská archeológia
SlArchiv	Slovenská archivistika
SlŠt	Slovanské štúdie
SNM	Slovenské národné múzeum
SNP	Slovenské národné povstanie
SPN	Slovenské pedagogické nakladateľstvo
SV	Stredoslovenské vydavateľstvo
SVKL	Slovenské vydavateľstvo krásnej literatúry
SVPL	Slovenské vydavateľstvo politickej literatúry
UK	Univerzita Komenského
ÚČSSD	Ústav československých a světových dějin
VPL	Vydavateľstvo politickej literatúry
VV	Východoslovenské vydavateľstvo
Zb FFUK	Zborník Filozofickej fakulty Univerzity Komenského
Zb SNM	Zborník Slovenského národného múzea
Zb ÚML UK	Zborník Ústavu marxizmu-leninizmu Univerzity Komenského

STUDIA HISTORICA SLOVACA XX

A Guide to Historiography in Slovakia

Zostavovatelia: Elena Mannová a David Paul Daniel

Rozsah: 212 strán
Miesto a rok vydania: Bratislava 1995
Vydavateľ: Historický ústav SAV
Vytlačila: Polygrafia vedeckej literatúry a časopisov SAV

ISBN 80–967150–8–9